*Dante's*

# The Divine Comedy

AF623455

MODERN CRITICAL INTERPRETATIONS

*Dante's*

# The Divine Comedy

Edited and with an Introduction by

**Harold Bloom**

Viva Books

New Delhi | Mumbai | Chennai | Kolkata | Bengaluru | Hyderabad | Kochi | Guwahati

Copyright © Chelsea House Publishers, a subsidiary of Haights Cross Communications
Introduction © Harold Bloom

**First Indian Edition 2007**
**Reprinted 2011**

**VIVA BOOKS PRIVATE LIMITED**

- 4737/23 Ansari Road, Daryaganj, New Delhi 110 002
E-mail: vivadelhi@vivagroupindia.net, Tel. 42242200
- 76, Service Industries, Shirvane, Sector 1, Nerul, Navi Mumbai 400 706
E-mail: vivamumbai@vivagroupindia.net, Tel. 27721273, 27721274
- Jamals Fazal Chambers, 26 Greams Road, Chennai 600 006
E-mail: vivachennai@vivagroupindia.net, Tel. 28290304, 28294241
- B-103, Jindal Towers, 21/1A/3 Darga Road, Kolkata 700 017
E-mail: vivakolkata@vivagroupindia.net, Tel. 22836381, 22816713
- 7, Sovereign Park Apartments, 56-58, K. R. Road, Basavanagudi, Bengaluru 560 004
E-mail: vivabangalore@vivagroupindia.net, Tel. 26607409, 26607410
- 101-102 Mughal Marc Aptt., 3-4-637 to 641, Narayanguda, Hyderabad 500 029
E-mail: vivahyderabad@vivagroupindia.net, Tel. 27564481, 27564482
- First Floor, Beevi Towers, SRM Road, Kaloor, Kochi 682 018, Kerala
E-mail: vivakochi@vivagroupindia.net, Tel: 0484-2403055, 2403056
- 232, GNB Road, Beside UCO Bank, Silpukhuri, Guwahati 781 003
E-mail: vivaguwahati@vivagroupindia.net, Tel: 0361-2666386

*Published by arrangement with:*

Facts on File, Inc.
132 West 31st Street
New York NY 10001
USA

All rights reserved. No part of this book may be reproduced or transmitted in any form or by any means now known or to be invented, electronic or mechanical, including photocopying, recording or by any information storage or retrieval system without written permission from the publisher.

*This edition is for sale in the Indian subcontinent only. Not for export elsewhere.*

ISBN : 978-81-309-1884-6

Published by Vinod Vasishtha for Viva Books Private Limited, 4737/23, Ansari Road, Daryaganj New Delhi - 110 002. Printed and bound by Anand Sons, Delhi - 110 092.

# Contents

Editor's Note / vii

Introduction / 1
HAROLD BLOOM

Dante / 11
ERNST ROBERT CURTIUS

Justification / 21
CHARLES S. SINGLETON

The Presentation / 33
ERICH AUERBACH

The Vistas in Retrospect / 57
CHARLES S. SINGLETON

The Prologue Scene / 77
JOHN FRECCERO

The Imageless Vision and Dante's *Paradiso* / 103
MARGUERITE MILLS CHIARENZA

Bestial Sign and Bread of Angels: *Inferno* 32 and 33 / 121
JOHN FRECCERO

The Language of Faith: Messengers and Idols / 135
GIUSEPPE MAZZOTTA

Casella's Song / 151
TEODOLINDA BAROLINI

Chronology / 159

Contributors / 161

Bibliography / 163

Acknowledgments / 165

Index / 167

# Editor's Note

This book brings together a representative selection of the best criticism available in English on Dante's *Commedia*. The essays are arranged in the chronological order of their original publication. I am grateful to Cathy Caruth for her erudition and judgment in helping me to edit this volume.

My introduction follows the approach to Dante of Ernst Robert Curtius, particularly on the difficult question of Dante's originality. Curtius himself begins the chronological sequence of criticism, with his powerful insistence that Dante saw himself as an apocalyptic figure or prophet, with expectations that the prophecy would be fulfilled in his own lifetime. Charles S. Singleton comes after Curtius, expounding two crucially different modes of justice and justification in the *Commedia*.

Erich Auerbach, rightly renowned as the major modern critic of mimesis, presents the poem in its true originality, which inheres in Dante's visions of persons and personality. A second essay by Singleton brilliantly attempts to recover vistas within the poem that we tend to lose when we study it only as a great poetic structure.

The fine Dante critic of my own generation, John Freccero, gives us a superb reading of the ways in which "for Dante, the distance between protagonist and author is at its maximum at the beginning of the story and is gradually closed by the dialectic of poetic process until pilgrim and poet coincide at the ending of the poem." Marguerite Mills Chiarenza achieves a supporting insight in her essay, which centers upon her realization that "in the *Paradiso* it is the poet who struggles while the pilgrim is safe."

Freccero returns with his strong essay upon Ugolino, with its fierce warning: "Just as Ugolino misreads his own dream and then acts out his misreading, so the critics continue to trope the text itself." Giuseppe Mazzotta, working in Freccero's spirit, also emphasizes the quandaries of troping the text while expounding Dante's crucial tropes of "messengers and idols." In this book's final essay, Teodolinda Barolini analyzes Casella's song, in

*Purgatorio* 2, as "the textual emblem of . . . misdirected newcomers' enthusiasms" as the souls arrive freshly in Purgatory. Since Barolini raises issues of "textuality and truth" in the context of Dante's relation to his precursors, she too, like the editor, is of the school of Freccero, who has taught all of us to see how strong the agon is between Dante and every crucial poet before him.

# Introduction

I

Dante, by common consent, stands with the supreme Western masters of literary representation: the Yahwist, Homer, Chaucer, Shakespeare, Cervantes, Milton, Tolstoy, Proust. Our ideas as to how reality can be represented by literary language depend, to a considerable extent, on this ninefold. Perhaps it can also be said that these writers have formed a large part of our experience of what is called reality. Certain aspects of reality might not be nearly so visible, had we not read these nine masters of mimesis. Setting the Yahwist and Homer aside as being both ancient and hypothetical, only Shakespeare, again by common consent, is judged to be Dante's rival as a great Original in representation. But Shakespearean representation has naturalized us in its domain. Dante is now an immensely difficult poet partly because we are so much at home with Shakespeare.

Erich Auerbach, who with Charles S. Singleton and John Freccero makes up a celestial trinity of Dante interpreters, gave us the definitive opening description of Dante's ways of representing reality:

> Dante in the *Comedy* transcended tragic death by identifying man's ultimate fate with the earthly unity of his personality, and . . . the very plan of the work made it possible, and indeed confronted him with the obligation, to represent earthly reality exactly as he saw it. Thus it became necessary that the characters in Dante's other world, in their situation and attitude, should represent the sum of themselves; that they should disclose, in a single act, the character and fate that had filled out their lives. . . .
>
> . . . from classical theory Dante took over only one principle, the *sibi constare*, or consistency, of his persons; all other tenets had lost their literal meaning for him . . . Dante's vision is a tragedy according to Aristotle's definition. In any event it is far more a tragedy than an epic, for the descriptive, epic elements

> in the poem are not autonomous, but serve other purposes, and the time, for Dante as well as his characters, is not the epic time in which destiny gradually unfolds, but the final time in which it is fulfilled.

If time is the final time, past all unfolding, then reality indeed can be represented in a single act that is at once character and fate. Dante's personages can reveal themselves totally in what they say and do, but they cannot change *because* of what Dante has them say and do. Chaucer, who owed Dante more than he would acknowledge, nevertheless departed from Dante in this, which is precisely where Chaucer most influenced Shakespeare. The Pardoner listens to himself speaking, listens to his own tale, and is darkly made doom-eager through just that listening. This mode of representation expands in Shakespeare to a point that no writer since has reached so consistently. Hamlet may be the most metamorphic of Shakespeare's people (or it may be Cleopatra, or Falstaff, or who you will), but as such he merely sets the mode. Nearly everyone of consequence in Shakespeare helps inaugurate a mimetic style we all now take too much for granted. They, like us, are strengthened or victimized, reach an apotheosis or are destroyed, by themselves reacting to what they say and do. It may be that we have learned to affect ourselves so strongly, in part because involuntarily we imitate Shakespeare's characters. We never imitate Dante's creatures because we do not live in finalities; we know that we are not fulfilled.

A literary text can represent a fulfilled reality only if it can persuade itself, and momentarily persuade us, that one text can fulfill another. Dante, as Auerbach demonstrated, relied upon the great Christian trope of *figura*, whose basis was the insistence that the Christian New Testament had fulfilled what it called "the Old Testament," itself a phrase deeply offensive to normative Jews who continue to trust in the Covenant as set forth in the Hebrew Bible. But the Hebrew Bible indeed must be the Old Testament, if Christianity is to retain its power. What must the New Testament be, if Dante's poem is to develop and maintain its force?

Auerbach, quoting the Church Father Tertullian's comments upon the renaming of Oshea, son of Nun, by Moses as Jehoshua (Joshua, Jesus), speaks of Joshua as "a figure of things to come." The definition of this figure of prophecy or *figura* by Auerbach is now classic: "*Figura* is something real and historical which announces something else that is real and historical." Equally classic is Auerbach's formulation of "figural interpretation":

> Figural interpretation establishes a connection between two events or persons, the first of which signifies not only itself but also the second, while the second encompasses or fulfills the

> first. The first two poles of the figure are separate in time, but both, being real events or figures, are within time, within the stream of historical life. Only the understanding of the two persons or events is a spiritual act, but this spiritual act deals with concrete events whether past, present, or future, and not with concepts or abstractions; these are quite secondary, since promise and fulfillment are real historical events, which have either happened in the incarnation of the word, or will happen in the second coming.

What happens when figural interpretation is transferred from sacred to secular literature? When Dante takes the historical Virgil and reads him as a *figura* of which Dante's character, Virgil, is the fulfillment, are we seeing the same pattern enacted as when Tertullian reads Joshua as the *figura* of which Jesus Christ was the fulfillment? Auerbach's answer is "yes," but this is a dialectical affirmative: "Thus Virgil in the *Divine Comedy* is the historical Virgil himself, but then again he is not; for the historical Virgil is only a *figura* of the fulfilled truth that the poem reveals, and this fulfillment is more real, more significant than the *figura*." Auerbach, writing on *figura* back in 1944, thought back to his book on Dante as poet of the secular world (1929), from which I quoted earlier, and insisted that he had acquired "a solid historical grounding" for his view of fifteen years before.

I am not certain that the earlier Auerbach is not to be preferred to the later. In secularizing *figura*, Auerbach dangerously idealized the relationship between literary texts. Appropriating the historical Virgil is not an idealizing gesture, as John Freccero shows in his superb essay, "Manfred's Wounds and the Poetics of the *Purgatorio*." Poetic fathers die hard, and Dante understood that he had made the historical Virgil the *figura*, and his own Virgil the fulfillment, partly in order to suggest that he himself was the poet Virgil's true fulfillment. Great poets are pragmatists when they deal with precursors; witness Blake's caricature of Milton as the hero of his poem "Milton," or James Merrill's loving and witty portrayal of Stevens and Auden in "The Changing Light at Sandover." Dante's Virgil is no more the historical Virgil than Blake's Milton is the historical Milton. If texts fulfill one another, it is always through some self-serving caricature of the earlier text by the later.

## II

Charles S. Singleton, carefully reminding us that "Beatrice is not Christ," expounds Dante's use of the principle of analogy which likens the advent of Beatrice to the advent of Christ:

> Thus it is that the figure of a rising sun by which Beatrice comes at last to stand upon the triumphal chariot is the most revealing image which the poet might have found not only to affirm the analogy of her advent to Christ's in the present tense, but to stress, in so doing, the very basis upon which that analogy rests: the advent of light.

Whitman, certainly a poet antithetical to Dante, opposed himself to the rising sun as a greater rising sun:

> Dazzling and tremendous how quick the sun-rise would kill me,
> If I could not now and always send sun-rise out of me.
>
> We also ascend dazzling and tremendous as the sun,
> We found our own O my soul in the calm and cool of the
> daybreak.

This is not analogy but a subversive mode akin to Nietzsche's, and learned from Emerson. The figure of the Whitmanian sun here is not an advent of Christ ("a great defeat" Emerson called that advent) but is "now and always," a perpetual dawning ("we demand victory," as Emerson said for his Americans, prophesying Whitman). The figure of Beatrice, to Whitman, might as well have been the figure of Christ. Can we, with Singleton, accept her as an analogy, or is she now the principal embarrassment of Dante's poem? As a fiction she retains her force, but does not Dante present her as more than a fiction? If Dante wrote, as Singleton says, the allegory of the theologians rather than the allegory of the poets, how are we to recapture Dante's sense of Beatrice if we do not accept the analogy that likens her advent to Christ's?

Singleton's answer is that Beatrice is the representation of Wisdom in a Christian sense, or the light of Grace. This answer, though given in the allegorical language of the theologians rather than that of the poets, remains a poetic answer because its analogical matrix is light rather than Grace. Dante persuades us not by his theology but by his occult mastery of the trope of light, in which he surpasses even the blind Milton among the poets:

> There is a light up there which makes the Creator visible to the creature, who finds his peace only in seeing Him.
>
> (*Paradiso* 30.100–102)

This, as Singleton says, is the Light of Glory rather than the Light of Grace, which is Beatrice's, or the Natural Light, which is Virgil's. Dante's peculiar gift is to find perpetually valid analogies for all three lights. Since his poem's fiction of duration is not temporal, but final, all three modes of light must be portrayed by him as though they were beyond change. And yet an unchanging fiction cannot give pleasure, as Dante clearly knew. What does he give us that more than compensates for his poem's apparent refusal of temporal anguish?

Auerbach, in his essay on St. Francis of Assisi in the *Commedia*, turned to *figura* again as his answer. To the medieval reader, according to Auerbach, the representations of forerunning and after-following repetitions were as familiar as the trope of "historical development" is (or was, to those who believe that Foucault forever exposed the trope). To us, now, "forerunning and after-following repetitions" suggest, not *figura* and its fulfillment, but the Freudian death-drive as the "fulfillment" of the compulsion-to-repeat. The repetition-compulsion perhaps is the final Western *figura*, prophesying our urge to drive beyond the pleasure principle. That is to say, for us the only text that can fulfill earlier texts, rather than correct or negate them, is what might be called "the text of death," which is totally opposed to what Dante sought to write.

## III

What saves Dante from the idealizing lameness that necessarily haunts the allegorizing of the theologians? The earlier Auerbach was on the track of the answer when he meditated upon Dante's originality in the representation of persons. As seer, Dante identified character and fate, *ethos* and *daemon*, and what he saw in his contemporaries he transferred precisely to the three final worlds of *Inferno*, *Purgatorio*, and *Paradiso*. Dante's friends and enemies alike are presented, without ambiguity or ambivalence, as being consistent with themselves, beyond change, their eternal destinies overdetermined by their fixed characters.

There are endless surprises in his poem for Dante himself, as for us, but there are no accidents. Farinata standing upright in his tomb, as if of Hell he had a great disdain, is heroic because he is massively consistent with himself: in his own tomb, he can be nothing but what he is. His marvelous disdain of Hell represents a kind of necessity, what Wallace Stevens called the inescapable necessity of being that inescapable animal, oneself. Such a necessity is presented by Dante as being the judgment of Heaven upon us.

In Shakespeare, there are always accidents, and character can be as metamorphic as personality. Hamlet yields himself up to accident, at the last, perhaps because he has all but exhausted the possibilities for change that even his protean character possesses. This is our mode of representation, inherited by us from Shakespeare, and we no longer are able to see how original it originally was. Shakespeare therefore seems "natural" to us, even though we live in the age of Freud, who suspected darkly that there were no accidents, once we were past infancy. Dante no longer can be naturalized in our imaginations. His originality has not been lost for us, and yet his difficulty or strangeness for us is probably not caused by his authentic originality.

The allegory of the theologians simply is not an available mode for us, despite the labors of Auerbach and Singleton. Freccero has replaced them as the most relevant of Dante critics because he has returned Dante to what may be the truest, because least idealizing, allegory of the poets, which is the agon of poet against poet, the struggle for imaginative priority between forerunner and latecomer. Despite a marvelous parody by Borges, theologians are not primarily agonists. Dante understood that poets were. The light of glory, the light of grace, the light of nature are not competing lights, and yet all tropes for them necessarily compete, and always with other tropes.

Singleton, rejecting the allegory of the poets, said that it would reduce Dante's Virgil to a mere personification of Reason:

> For if this is the allegory of poets, then what Virgil does, like what Orpheus does, is a fiction devised to convey a hidden meaning which it ought to convey all the time, since only by conveying that other meaning is what he does justified at all. Instead, if this action is allegory as theologians take it, then this action must always have a literal sense which is historical and no fiction; and thus Virgil's deeds as part of the whole action may, in their turn, be as words signifying other things, but they do not have to do this all the time, because, being historical, those deeds exist simply in their own right.

But what if Virgil, as allegory of the poets, were to be read not as Reason, the light of nature, but as the trope of that light, reflecting among much else the lustres of the tears of universal nature? To say farewell to Virgil is to take leave not of Reason, but of the pathos of a certain natural light, perhaps of Wordsworth's "light of common day." Dante abandons Virgil not so as to substitute grace for reason, but so as to find his own image of voice, his own trope for all three lights. In the oldest and most authentic allegory of the poets, Virgil represents not reason but poetic fatherhood, the Scene of Instruction that Dante must transcend if he is to complete his journey to Beatrice.

IV

The figure of Beatrice, in my own experience as a reader, is now the most difficult of all Dante's tropes, because sublimation no longer seems to be a human possibility. What is lost, perhaps permanently, is the tradition that moves between Dante and Yeats, in which sublimated desire for a woman can be regarded as an enlargement of existence. One respected feminist critic has gone so far as to call Beatrice a "dumb broad," since she supposedly contemplates the One without understanding Him. What James Thurber grimly celebrated as the War between Men and Women has claimed many recent literary casualties, but none perhaps so unmerited as Dante's Beatrice. Dante, like tradition, thought that God's Wisdom, who daily played before His feet, was a woman, even as Nietzsche, with a gesture beyond irony, considered Truth to be a woman, presumably a deathly one. We possess art in order not to perish from the truth, Nietzsche insisted, which must mean that the aesthetic is a way of not being destroyed by a woman. Dante hardly would have agreed.

Beatrice is now so difficult to apprehend precisely because she participates both in the allegory of the poets and in the allegory of the philosophers. Her advent follows Dante's poetic maturation, or the vanishing of the precursor, Virgil. In the allegory of the poets, Beatrice is the Muse, whose function is to help the poet remember. Since remembering, in poetry, is the major mode of cognition, Beatrice is Dante's power of invention, the essence of his art. That means she is somehow the highest of the Muses, and yet far above them also, since in Dante's version of the allegory of the poets, Beatrice has "a place in the objective process of salvation," as Ernst Robert Curtius phrased it. Curtius rightly emphasized the extent of Dante's audacity:

> Guido Guinizelli (d. 1276) had made the exaltation of the beloved to an angel of paradise a topos of Italian lyric. To choose as guide in a poetic vision of the otherworld a loved woman who has been thus exalted is still within the bounds of Christian philosophy and faith. But Dante goes much further than this. He gives Beatrice a place in the objective process of salvation. Her function is thought of as not only for himself but also for all believers. Thus, on his own authority, he introduces into the

> Christian revelation an element which disrupts the doctrine of the church. This is either heresy—or myth.

It is now customary to speak of Dante as *the* Catholic poet, even as Milton is called *the* Protestant poet. Perhaps someday Kafka will be named as *the* Jewish writer, though his distance from normative Judaism was infinite. Dante and Milton were not less idiosyncratic, each in his own time, than Kafka was in ours, and the figure of Beatrice would be heresy and not myth if Dante had not been so strong a poet that the Church of later centuries has been happy to claim him. Curtius centered upon Dante's vision of himself as a prophet, even insisting that Dante expected the prophecy's fulfillment in the immediate future, during his own lifetime. Since Dante died at the age of fifty-six, a quarter-century away from the "perfect" age of eighty-one set forth in his *Convivio*, the literal force of the prophecy presumably was voided. But the prophecy, still hidden from us, matters nevertheless, as Curtius again maintains:

> Even if we could interpret his prophecy, that would give it no meaning for us. What Dante hid, Dante scholarship need not now unriddle. But it must take seriously the fact that Dante believed that he had an apocalyptic mission. This must be taken into consideration in interpreting him. Hence the question of Beatrice is not mere idle curiosity. Dante's system is built up in the first two cantos of the *Inferno*, it supports the entire *Commedia*. Beatrice can be seen only within it. The Lady Nine has become a cosmic power which emanates from two superior powers. A hierarchy of celestial powers which intervene in the process of history—this concept is manifestly related to Gnosticism: as an intellectual construction, a schema of intellectual contemplation, if perhaps not in origin. Such constructions can and must be pointed out. We do not know what Dante meant by Lucia. The only proper procedure for the commentator, then, is to admit that we do not know and to say that neither the ophthalmological explanation nor the allegorical interpretations are satisfactory. Exegesis is also bound to give its full weight to all the passages at the end of the *Purgatorio* and in the *Paradiso* which are opposed to the identification of Beatrice with the daughter of the banker Portinari. Beatrice is a myth created by Dante.

Very little significant criticism of Dante has followed this suggestion of Curtius, and a distorted emphasis upon Dante's supposed orthodoxy has been the result. Curtius certainly does not mean that Dante was a Gnostic, but he does remind us that Dante's Beatrice is the central figure in a purely personal gnosis. Dante indeed was a ruthless visionary, passionate and willful, whose poem triumphantly expresses his own unique personality. The *Commedia*, though one would hardly know this from most of its critics (Freccero is the sublime exception), is an immense trope of pathos or power, the power of the individual who was Dante. The pathos of that personality is most felt, perhaps, in the great and final parting of Beatrice from her poet, in the middle of Canto 31 of the *Paradiso*, at the moment when her place as guide is transferred to the aged St. Bernard:

> Already my glance had taken in the whole general form of Paradise but had not yet dwelt on any part of it, and I turned with new-kindled eagerness to question my Lady of things on which my mind was in suspense. One thing I intended, and another encountered me: I thought to see Beatrice, and I saw an old man, clothed like that glorious company. His eyes and his cheeks were suffused with a gracious gladness, and his aspect was of such kindness as befits a tender father. And "Where is she?" I said in haste; and he replied: "To end thy longing Beatrice sent me from my place; and if thou look up into the third circle from the highest tier thou shalt see her again, in the throne her merits have assigned to her."
>
> Without answering, I lifted up my eyes and saw her where she made for herself a crown, reflecting from her the eternal beams. From the highest region where it thunders no mortal eye is so far, were it lost in the depth of the sea, as was my sight there from Beatrice; but to me it made no difference, for her image came down to me undimmed by aught between.
>
> "O Lady in whom my hope has its strength and who didst bear for my salvation to leave thy footprints in Hell, of all the things that I have seen I acknowledge the grace and the virtue to be from thy power and from thy goodness. It is thou who hast drawn me from bondage into liberty by all those ways, by every means for it that was in thy power. Preserve in me thy great bounty, so that my spirit, which thou hast made whole, may be loosed from the body well-pleasing to thee." I prayed thus; and she, so far off as she seemed, smiled and looked at me, then turned again to the eternal fount.

It is difficult to comment upon the remorseless strength of this, upon its apparent sublimation of a mythmaking drive that here accepts a restraint which is more than rhetorical. Freud in his own great *summa*, the essay of 1937, "Analysis Terminable and Interminable," lamented his inability to cure those who could not accept the cure:

> A man will not be subject to a father-substitute or owe him anything and he therefore refuses to accept his cure from the physician.

Dante too would not owe any man anything, not even if the man were Virgil, his poetic father. The cure had been accepted by Dante from his physician, Beatrice. In smiling and looking at him, as they part, she confirms the cure.

# Dante

*Ernst Robert Curtius*

## MYTH AND PROPHECY

We have seen that Dante claims an epistemological function for his poetry and thus places himself in opposition to Scholastic philosophy. We reached this conclusion simply by analyzing a passage in the epistle to Can Grande. Our conclusion is confirmed by Gilson's study of Dante's relation to philosophy. That study finally rid us of the mistaken idea that Dante was a Thomist. In the canon of the blessed intellectuals in the Heaven of the Sun we found an independent and autocratic treatment of the tradition. But even this is far outdone by the singular "apparatus of salvation" of the *Commedia*. Dante's guides on his journey through the otherworld are successively Virgil, Beatrice, and St. Bernard. On this Gilson well says: "L'ordonnance générale du poème requiert que la charité s'ajoute à la foi, et la couronne, comme la foi s'ajoute à la raison et l'illumine." He appears, then, to agree with the currently accepted view which sees reason incarnated in Virgil, faith in Beatrice, and love in Bernard. For Gilson these are "des faits massivement évidents."

The most "massive" of these facts is certainly the function of Beatrice —if Beatrice was a Florentine woman who died in 1290 at the age of twenty-five. That a poet should have a religious awakening and be purified through his beloved is a psychological experience which can occur in a thousand gradations. It is reflected in Goethe's *Marienbader Elegie* and in the conclusion of *Faust*. Guido Guinizelli (d. 1276) had made the exaltation of

---

From *European Literature of the Latin Middle Ages*. © 1953 by the Bollingen Foundation. Princeton University Press, 1973.

the beloved to an angel of paradise a topos of Italian lyric. To choose as guide in a poetic vision of the otherworld a loved woman who has been thus exalted is still within the bounds of Christian philosophy and faith. But Dante goes much further than this. He gives Beatrice a place in the objective process of salvation. Her function is thought of as not only for himself but also for all believers. Thus, on his own authority, he introduces into the Christian revelation an element which disrupts the doctrine of the church. This is either heresy—or myth.

The most eminent Dante scholars and specialists in Florentine history are agreed that Dante's Beatrice was the daughter of the banker Folco Portinari. But the earliest commentaries know nothing of this. Graziuolo de' Bambaglioli, state secretary of Bologna, in his commentary (1324) on *Inferno*, 2.70:

I' son Beatrice che ti faccio andare

says only "ipsa domina erat anima generose domine Beatrice condam domini . . ." ("this lady was the soul of the noble lady Beatrice, daughter of the late . . ."). Then a blank. The author, then, could learn nothing of Beatrice's father. Iacopo della Lana (1328) has nothing to say about Beatrice. The author of the *Ottimo commento* (ca. 1334) asked Dante about Beatrice on several occasions, but learned nothing. The anonymous author of the glosses (before 1337) knows no more. Boccaccio is the first to make the identification, and this was in the commentary which he wrote in 1373–74: In October 1373 he had been called to Florence to lecture publicly on the *Commedia*. The information, then, appears for the first time more than eighty years after the hypothetical death of Beatrice. Boccaccio claims to have learned it from a "trustworthy person" who was closely related to Beatrice. Searching for this trustworthy lady, Zingarelli came upon Boccaccio's stepmother, Margherita dei Mardoli. Her mother, Monna Lippa (d. 1340), was the daughter of a cousin of Folco Portinari's and hence second cousin to Beatrice. Did Boccaccio know the old lady? It could only have been in the year before her death; Boccaccio *is supposed* to have lived in his father's house during 1339. On that occasion he *could*—Zingarelli surmises—have secured the information. How remarkable that he kept this interesting piece of biography to himself for thirty-five years thereafter! How remarkable that the commentators mentioned above could learn nothing! To be sure, Pietro di Dante also gives the information, but not until the third redaction of his commentary, which is contemporary with Boccaccio's *Vita* and can have been derived from it. The identification of Dante's Beatrice with the daughter of Folco Portinari, who died in 1289, is, then, first maintained fifty years after Dante's death and is unknown to Dante's contemporaries, as well as to the four commentators who wrote between 1324 and 1337. This is very remarkable and justifies us in doubting Boccaccio's information. But above all—if Boccaccio's step-grandmother had been able to identify Dante's Beatrice with the daughter of Folco Portinari in 1339, she would have talked about it to other people too in the course of her long life. It would have been known in Florence. Dante's contemporaries recognized that he was a great poet. The *Commedia* was circulated in numerous copies, versified abridgments were made of it, several commentaries were written on it in the first two decades after Dante's death. Interest in Dante, then, was widespread—and yet no one was able to produce any information about Beatrice.

But Boccaccio's testimony is also suspect for another reason. His exposition of Dante involved him in a polemic. An opponent whose name has not survived reproached him with having bared the mysteries of poetry to the uninitiate. Boccaccio justified himself in four sonnets (nos. 122–25 in A. F. Massèra's critical edition [Bologna, 1914]). In the last sonnet he boasts that he has merely led the ungrateful vulgar astray:

> Io ò messo in galea senza biscotto
> L' ingrato vulgo, et senza alcun piloto
> Lasciato l' ò in mar a lui non noto,
> Benchè sen creda esser maestro et dotto.

> [I put the ungrateful vulgar in a ship without biscuit, and left them without any pilot on a sea that they know not, although they think themselves masters and men of learning.]

Are Boccaccio's allegations supported by documents? Zingarelli remarks on Boccaccio's testimony that the documents confirm it to the extent that documents can do so. They frequently mention Folco Portinari. In his will, drawn up in 1288, six daughters are remembered; among them Madonna Bice appears as the wife of Simone de' Bardi. That is all. We know the date neither of the birth nor death of Beatrice Portinari. What current Dante literature is able to say on the subject is drawn entirely from the *Vita nuova*, hence from a conscious mystification. If one attempts to grasp its intellectual content, one feels that one has been transported into a maze. The entire little book is devoted to demonstrating a set of theses. The most important of these, strange as it may seem to us, is the following: "The number three is the root of the number nine, because it gives nine of itself without any other number, as we manifestly see that three times three makes nine. Consequently, if the three is by itself the maker of the nine, and likewise the maker of miracles is by Himself three, namely Father, Son, and Holy Ghost, which are three and one, so was this lady accompanied by the number nine, to make it understood that she was a nine, that is, a miracle, whose root is solely the wondrous Trinity. Perhaps some more subtle person would see a more subtle reason for this; but this is the reason which I see for it and the one which pleases me best." And how is it proven that Beatrice was a nine? First proof: Dante wrote a poem on the sixty most beautiful ladies in Florence (which unfortunately he does not give us). And "it befell in wondrous wise that my lady's name would not suffer itself to stand in any place but in the ninth." The second proof is more complicated. It requires the assistance of the Arabic and Syrian eras and of astrology: "I say that according to the use of Arabia her most noble soul departed hence in the first hour of the ninth day of the month; and according to the use of Syria she departed in the ninth month of the year, because the first month there is Tismin, which for us is October. And according to our use she departed in that year of our era (that is, in the year of the Lord) in which the perfect number was nine times made full in that century in which she was placed in this world; and she was of the Christians of the thirteenth century. Why this number was so nearly allied to her, this might be the reason thereof: Since according to Ptolemy and according to Christian truth, the heavens which move are nine, and according to the common astrological opinion the said heavens work here below according to their position in respect to one another, therefore that number was allied to her, to make it understood that at her conception all the nine moving heavens stood in the most perfect relation to one another." Beatrice must, then, have died in 1290 if the contention that she was a nine is true. Dante scholars regard this date as an historical fact—which is questionable. The only thing of which we can be sure is that the nine is a "soteriological numerical riddle." Here Dante is within a widespread antique and medieval tradition. The nine of the *Vita nuova* is to be regarded in the same way as the 515 of the *Commedia* (*Purgatorio* 33.43 [all further references to this text will be abbreviated as *Purg.*]). Dante scholarship appears to pay no attention to this. Barbi falls back upon the position that certain questions are not of importance for an understanding of what "counts most" in Dante's work (which is "the miracle of poetry and ideality"); hence it is better not to discuss them at all. There is a great deal to be said for such restraint. It is indicated as a means of self-defense against the dilettante solvers of riddles. And the deciphering of these hieroglyphics is irrelevant to an appreciation and comprehension of Dante's poetry. But the fact that, beginning with the

*Vita nuova,* Dante interspersed his works with references to an esoteric meaning, is to be accept-d. The numerical and alphabetical mysticism remains. This is philologically established—not least for Beatrice, who was a nine. To overlook it is impossible. This must be objected to all those who insist upon the insufficiently attested historical Beatrice—including Robert Davidsohn who, for his part, holds it "inadmissible to doubt that she lived and no less so to doubt that she was the daughter of the banker Folco Portinari." He did not succeed in entirely convincing Barbi, who in 1931 stated that, though he inclined toward the identification, he regarded the problem as a matter of mere curiosity; for the study of Dante it was enough to know that Beatrice was a real person. We must, then, distinguish two theses which affirm the historical Beatrice: identification (a) with Beatrice Portinari; (b) with an unknown Florentine woman. On the basis of the tradition I believe that the first thesis must be eliminated.

There is no doubt that some of the *Rime* are dedicated to a real Beatrice, for example "Lo doloroso amor" (Contini, no. 21), where Beatrice is named in line 14. Presumably also the canzone "E' m' incresce di me" (Contini, no. 20). But here Beatrice has characteristics which do not accord with the legendary style of the *Vita nuova,* for which reason the poem is not included in it. The exclusion of this canzone from the *Vita nuova,* then, together with *Lo doloroso amor,* demonstrates two things: Dante paid homage to a Florentine woman, whom he called Beatrice; later he stylized her into the myth of the Lady Nine. We know that Dante performed this process of stylizing a "real" woman into a myth, symbol, or allegory once again when he transformed the *donna gentile* of the *Vita nuova* into the Lady Philosophy of the *Convivio.* Furthermore there are a number of women in the *Commedia* who are obviously to be taken allegorically—for example Lucia, Lia (*Purg.* 27.101), Matelda (*Purg.* 28.37 ff.).

At the beginning of the *Commedia* Beatrice is addressed by Virgil: "O lady of virtue, through whom alone the race of man excels all that is within the heaven which has the smallest circles" (*Inferno* 2.76 ff. [all further references to this text will be abbreviated as *Inf.*])—namely, the heaven of the Moon. Through Beatrice alone, mankind surpasses everything earthly. Whatever this may mean: Beatrice has a metaphysical dignity for all men—Beatrice alone. She is addressed by Lucia as "true praise of God" (*Inf.* 2.103). Neither of these things can be said of the soul of a dead Florentine woman. Beatrice is sent by Lucia, Lucia by a *donna gentile* of heaven whose throne is yet higher (usually identified with Mary, but not named). Why the Syracusan martyr Lucia? She is supposed to be of special efficacy against eye trouble, and Dante had sometimes strained his eyes by overstudy (*Convivio* 3.9.15 [all further references to this text will be abbreviated as *Conv.*]), "presumably he therefore had a special devotion to St. Lucia"—thus Rossi, after many others. But Dante says: "Lucia, nimica di ciascun crudele" (*Inf.* 2.100). Now this obviously has nothing to do with eye trouble. So Lucia is interpreted as "illuminating grace" (first by Buti at the end of the fourteenth century) or as the personification of hope, etc. But if Beatrice is more than and different from the immortalized woman of Florence, if Lucia is more than and different from an almost unknown saint of the Breviary, if both intervene in the action at the bidding of a higher who remains unnamed—then the three heavenly ladies must be understood as parts of a supernatural dispensation. Pietrobono attempts this: The liberation of mankind from the she-wolf requires a process of redemption in which the "tre donne benedette" act together as did the three persons of the Trinity in the "first" redemption. The explanation is unsatisfactory in this form. But it is in the right direction: Beatrice can be understood only as a function within a theological system. To this system belong the three beasts which block Dante's road and which have always been interpreted as three vices. These beasts draw the Veltro after them, and later the "Cinquecento cinque e dieci." With this the theological system becomes a prophetic system. No amount of ingenuity has yet succeeded in unraveling it. But it is there. No one should deny it. It was Dante's central message. It concerns a prophecy whose fulfilment he expected in the immediate future. When he died at fifty-six, his certainty was presumably still unshaken. Had he reached the "perfect" age of eighty-one (*Conv.* 4.24.6), he would perhaps have been obliged to admit the collapse of his historical construction. But he could not retract his work. His imperious spirit believed that it could command even the future. A future, however, which could envisage only fourteenth-century Italy.

Even if we could interpret his prophecy, that would give it no meaning for us. What Dante hid, Dante scholarship need not now unriddle. But it must take seriously the fact that Dante believed that he had an apocalyptic mission. This must be taken into consideration in interpreting him. Hence the question of Beatrice is not mere idle curiosity. Dante's system is built up in the first two cantos of the *Inferno*, it supports the entire *Commedia*. Beatrice can be seen only within it. The Lady Nine has become a cosmic power which emanates from two superior powers. A hierarchy of celestial powers which intervene in the process of history—this concept is manifestly related to Gnosticism: as an intellectual construction, a schema of intellectual contemplation, if perhaps not in origin. Such constructions can and must be pointed out. We do not know what Dante meant by Lucia. The only proper procedure for the commentator, then, is to admit that we do not know and to say that neither the ophthalmological explanation nor the allegorical interpretations are satisfactory. Exegesis is also bound to leave their full weight to all the passages at the end of the *Purgatorio* and in the *Paradiso* which are opposed to the identification of Beatrice with the daughter of the banker Portinari. Beatrice is a myth created by Dante.

The transformation of experience into myth was Dante's basic attitude in the *Rime* and in the *Vita nuova*; an attitude given as an elemental phenomenon of his personality; materialized in creations which are consummated in a series of discrete experiments. They burst out from Dante—"prorumpunt ad summa summe canenda." These outbursts often have something ruthless about them. Ruthlessness is itself the theme in the "stone" canzoni. In the *Vita nuova* it assumes the character of mystification. In *De vulgari eloquentia* it narrows a spiral of demands on language and poetry to the limit of the possible. In the *Commedia* it challenges—and conquers!—the universe: the entire historical cosmos (foreshadowed in the catchword Orosius), the entire astral cosmos, the entire cosmos of salvation. The mediatrix of this "metacosmos" is the beatifying female power—"luce e gloria della gente umana" (*Purg.* 33.115). This Beatrice is not the recovered love of youth. She is the highest salvation in the form of a woman—an emanation of God. For no other reason can she appear without blasphemy in a triumph in which Christ himself has a place.

## Dante and the Middle Ages

Those who wish to see Dante's place in the transition from the Middle Ages to the Renaissance from the point of view of universal history may be referred to the medallion, cast as it were in bronze, which we owe to Alfred Weber. Our considerations must remain within the more modest framework of literary history.

On October 20, 1828, Goethe said to Eckermann: "Dante appears great to us, but he had a culture of centuries behind him." Carlyle heard in Dante the voice of "ten silent centuries." What Goethe and Carlyle saw, we can designate precisely in historical terms: It is the cultural cosmos of the Latin Middle Ages, and of Antiquity seen through the eyes of the Middle Ages. The clash between Dante's philosophically transformed imperial idea, which rises high above any Ghibellinism, and the new, capitalistic, highly organized city-state of Florence, is the fountainhead of

Dante's political passion. From this conflict springs his consciousness of a world-historical mission, which he clothed in the form of a prophecy concealed in symbols. The prophecy could not but apply to both Church and state: To Dante as to the entire Middle Ages both universal powers were ordained by God. But they were corrupt and required reform. The Church must renounce power and the thirst for power. It must become a church of the spirit. The thirteenth-century mendicant orders had failed in their work of reform, were themselves degenerate. Another, one more powerful, would and must come: the hound ("veltro"). He would drive the she-wolf back into hell. Dante puts this prophecy into Virgil's mouth at the beginning of the *Inferno* (1.101). At the end of the *Purgatorio* (33.37 ff.) it is resumed by Beatrice. Theologico-political prophecy is a feature which constantly recurs in the twelfth- and thirteenth-century picture. But in Dante it is given an intellectual substructure, and the power of his poetic vision, the passion of his denunciation, the unbroken articulation and concatenation of the one hundred cantos raise it to a fortissimo. It is a leaven which Dante casts into the tradition of the medieval West. The leaven penetrates the coagulated mass to its most remote regions and organizes it into a realm of new forms. It is the projection of Dante's personality on "the book and school of the ages" (George)—on the total literary tradition. Dante's mind and soul, his architectonic thinking and his glowing heart, the tension of his will, which demanded stupendous efforts of itself, which stubbornly forced itself to express the inexpressible—these are the powers which conjured "ten silent centuries" into form. A single man, a solitary man, sets himself face to face with an entire millennium and transforms that historical world. Love, order, salvation are the foci of his inner vision—spheres of light in which immense tensions are collected. They dart together, circle one another, become constellations, figures. They must be expanded into shapes, choirs, chains of spirits, laws, prophecies. The whole plenitude of his inner vision must be applied to the whole extent of the world, to all the depths and heights of the world above. The most immense frame of references is required. From every point of his mythically and prophetically amplified experience connections run to every point of the given matter. They are forged and riveted in material as hard as diamonds. A structure of language and thought is created—comprehensive, with many layers of meaning, and as inalterable as the cosmos. Its medium is terza rima: a metrical form which combines the principle of continuous progressive concatenation with ineluctable discipline. Goal and accomplishment of the whole: perfect superposition of Dante's within upon the cosmic without, and mutual interpenetration of the two; congruence of soul and world.

The world drama of the Latin Middle Ages is played for the last time in the *Commedia*—but transposed into a modern language, reflected in a soul which ranks with Michelangelo's and Shakespeare's. The Middle Ages is thereby transcended—but also, of course, the periodization of a short-sighted science of history. Its periods will be long forgotten when Dante is still admired.

Before Dante scholarship lies the great task of methodically studying Dante's relation to the Latin Middle Ages, which has here been made apparent.

# Justification

*Charles S. Singleton*

Justification can be defined as "movement towards justice." This may well seem over simple and too vague to have much meaning, but it is a definition which St. Thomas and contemporary theology found satisfactory: "justificatio est motus ad justitiam." Such bare terms call, of course, for further definition. What are we to take "justice" to mean in such a formula? And what, moreover, shall we understand "movement" to be?

The answer to the latter question is readily found in theological doctrine following the triumph of Aristotle with the schoolmen of the thirteenth century. "Movement," in this instance, must mean "alteration" (*alteratio*) taking place in a given subject or "matter"; movement will mean change in the "matter" with respect to an end. That is to say, obviously, that justification is to be conceived on the pattern of the Aristotelian conception of *generatio*, which, we now know, is "motus ad formam." This being so, one must think of such a process in terms of the two elements involved, matter and form. Movement to form is thus change on the part of the matter to the end that it may receive the form. By such a change a given matter is "made ready," is "disposed," to receive. The whole movement ends when form is received by the matter which has been prepared for it. One thus conceives a process which has extension in time and manifests two successive moments or phases. The first is the moment of *preparation*, the second the moment of *completion*, at the end, when form is attained.

But if justification as movement be so conceived in this recognizable

From *Dante Studies 2: Journey to Beatrice.* © 1958 by the Estate of Charles S. Singleton. Harvard University Press, 1958.

and simple outline of event, what meaning can the two terms "matter" and "form" have in such a conception? Surely the form in this case, i.e., that which is the end of the movement, will be justice itself. But justice in what sense? And as for the "matter" which will thus undergo change in preparation to receive justice, what will that be?

Such concepts, at first sight, are no doubt quite strange to us. We need some fuller statement which can clarify the meaning of these elements of a process. And for this we may once more turn to St. Thomas's view on this point as one representative of the doctrine which came to prevail following the Aristotelian revival. For one thing, we shall see, and with no surprise, to be sure, how closely Thomas is following Aristotle, not only in taking *generatio* to be the mold in which the whole notion of justification is cast, but in the very conception of justice which is thought to lie at the end, as the form. Or, perhaps, in order that this may be the clearer, we might first recall a definition which Aristotle himself, in the *Nicomachean Ethics*, gives of justice. It is the definition to which St. Thomas will be seen to refer:

> Metaphorically and in virtue of a certain resemblance there is a justice, not indeed between a man and himself, but between certain parts of him; yet not every kind of justice but that of master and servant or that of husband and wife. For these are the ratios in which the part of the soul that has a rational principle stands to the irrational part; and it is with a view to these parts that people also think a man can be unjust to himself, viz. because these parts are liable to suffer something contrary to their respective desires; there is therefore thought to be a mutual justice between them as between ruler and ruled.

Justice, then, as Aristotle would understand it here, is justice within, justice as the inner rule of the rational part of the soul over the other parts. Justice is that same right order in the soul of which Plato wrote in the *Republic.* It is a matter of a man's inner disposition, of reason's rule over those faculties which are properly subject to reason—the passions, the sensitive appetite.

In turning, now, to St. Thomas's definition of justice in this sense, we shall hardly avoid being struck by one thing: Thomas extends Aristotle's definition in a notable way, carrying it quite beyond anything Aristotle or Plato intended. To be sure, for Thomas, justice remains a matter of order in the inner man, but for him that order is, first of all, one which is due subjection to God and to God's will. This, as St. Thomas means it, brings a Christian requirement into the matter of justice not dreamt of by the Philosopher. Of course, students of Aquinas will at once recognize here a common manner of thought with him. Aristotle, in this case, a given definition in Aristotle, is used as far as it can carry our understanding of the matter in question. Whereupon, if it is then evident to the Christian theologian, by the revealed truth of Christian doctrine, that the point to which Aristotle can bring us is not the whole truth, and if the revealed truth can carry us further, then we proceed further with that. Only St. Thomas, typically, will not make explicit mention of the point at which we pass beyond Aristotle, will make no specific acknowledgment of any limitation or shortcoming on the part of his Philosopher. Thomas seems simply to assume that his Christian reader will know and understand where that point is, without his calling attention to it. A clear instance is the definition, modelled on Aristotle, which Thomas gives of justice in the sense concerning us here:

> Justification taken passively implies a movement towards justice, as heating implies a movement towards heat. But since justice, by its nature, implies a certain rectitude of order, it may be taken in two ways:—First, inasmuch as it implies a right order in man's act, and thus justice is placed among the virtues. . . . Secondly, justice is so called inasmuch as it implies a certain rectitude of order in the interior disposition of a man, in so far as what is highest in man is subject to God, and the inferior powers of the soul are subject to the superior, i.e., to the reason; and this disposition the Philosopher calls *justice metaphorically speaking* (Ethics, 5.2). Now this justice may be in man in two ways:—First, by simple generation, which is from privation to form; and thus justification may belong even to such as are not in sin, when they receive this justice from God, as Adam is said to have received original justice. Secondly, this justice may be brought about in man by a movement from one contrary to the other, and thus justification implies a transmutation from the state of injustice to the aforesaid state of justice. And it is thus we are now speaking of the justification of the ungodly, according to the Apostle (Rom. 4:5): "But to him that worketh not, yet believeth in Him that justifieth the ungodly," etc. And because movement is named after its term *whereto* rather than from its term *whence*, the transmutation whereby anyone is changed by the remission of sins from the state of ungodliness to the state of justice, takes its name from its term whereto, and is called *justification of the ungodly.*

When we shall have seen finally, and as clearly as may be, that the whole "movement" of Dante's *Comedy*, conceived in allegory as a journey, is itself a "movement toward justice," then we shall recognize the close relevance to the poem of such a conception of justice and justification as St. Thomas here offers us. If justice means right order in the soul and right order before God, then we shall see that such is indeed Dante's conception in the poem; such is, in fact, the "end" of his journey. It may be that we shall be helped to see this in clearer outline if we recall an image which is given in certain verses of the *Purgatorio*, when the journey reaches the first terrace, where pride is purged. There, as so often elsewhere, "we" are addressed, readers who are proud Christians in need of the sternest warning respecting this our gravest sin:

O superbi cristian, miseri lassi,
  che, della vista della mente infermi,
  fidanza avete ne' retrosi passi,
non v'accorgete voi che noi siam vermi
  nati a formar l'angelica farfalla,
  che vola alla giustizia sanza schermi?
Di che l'animo vostro in alto galla,
  poi siete quasi entomata in difetto,
  sì come vermo in cui formazion falla?

[O proud Christians, woeful wretches, who sick in the mind's vision, place trust in backward steps, do you not see that we are worms born to form the angelic butterfly which flies to justice without shields? How is it that your spirit soars so high, when you are as imperfect insects, like the larva lacking its full formation?]

(*Purgatorio* 10.121–29)

What the verses and their metaphor declare of pride and its effect is evident enough. Pride stops us short of full formation. By pride we are arrested at a first and imperfect stage of growth. We are as butterflies to be, but remaining in pride, at the larva stage, we shall never become the winged creatures we were created to become. But it is the notion of justice and of movement to justice as to a goal which interests us especially here. For if we do attain to our full formation, then justice is the end to which we fly, a justice "sanza schermi," which must mean a justice before God. And it is through such an image as this that we may profitably look at the entire *itinerarium* to God as the *Comedy* presents it, asking ourselves where it is along the way that the first phase of this movement ends and the second begins: in short, within the metaphor, where does Dante pass from larva stage to butterfly? The answer is easy. This surely is when Dante passes from Virgil to Beatrice; and it is clear, looking through the image, that if Dante had not passed on to Beatrice, he would never have had his "wings." With her he flies upward to justice, becoming "angelic," even as Glaucus became like a sea-god.

But there must be a goal of justice short of that final justice at the end of the *Paradiso*, before God. Another justice is, in fact, reached before that. It lies precisely at the point where the journey attains to Beatrice, and is therefore at the summit of the mountain of Purgatory. One may view this justice, to be sure, as the beginning of movement toward that other higher and perfect justice before God. But it is this first justice as goal which most concerns us in the present study, together with the whole process or movement through which that goal is reached. For when justification is conceived as a movement toward justice, a movement which a poet may represent as a journey, then the kind of justice which lies at the top of the mountain is that justice which is the end goal of justification. Indeed, the attentive reader of the poem must have some sense of this from the outset, for the mountain which he is given to see in the first canto is surely, in some sense, the very mountain of Purgatory which is later climbed; and, on that moral landscape of the first canto, the mountain seen must be none other than the "mountain of justice" of which Scripture speaks, meaning a mountain having justice at its summit, a mountain to be ascended. In that first prologue scene, the sun is shining upon that summit. Must this not be the "sun of justice" (*sol iustitiae*) also known to us from Scripture? And then later the reader will see, when he reaches the summit with Dante, that Beatrice comes there in the figure of a rising sun; and there too he is reminded, where she comes in triumph, that the Sun had no finer chariot than hers.

But such meanings come clear only through perspectives yet to be examined. Enough at the moment if we note the limits of our present concern with the outline of this journey. At the summit of the mountain lies a kind of justice which is a goal for Dante, the wayfarer.

That we should think of justification as completed when the summit is reached is something which the very definition by St. Thomas can strongly suggest to us. One notes how in the context of justification, Thomas has remembered Adam and the justice that he, in his creation, received from God. This indeed is an element of the statement by Thomas which makes his whole formulation of special interest for present purposes. Eden, that very place wherein Adam received justice, is precisely what lies, in Dante's conception, at the top of this mountain. There, in Eden, Adam received justice by "simple generation," as Thomas puts it. For Adam was without sin. This being so, one might think that Adam's receiving justice (as a form is received) would not be viewed in the pattern of *generatio*. But Thomas does so view it, for Thomas can regard Adam as being, in a first moment, without the form which is justice, as being (without sin) ready or disposed to receive that form, and then, in a second moment, as receiving justice. And we know that two such successive moments suffice as the essential elements to make this a case of "generation," even if it is *simple* generation.

Adam lost this gift of justice when he lost Eden. And men, after Adam, are no longer placed here, at this summit, at birth. Men are born in a fallen condition. No longer is justice given to a man by simple generation because no man, after Adam, is without sin, either Adam's or his own. But the question must be put: may not a man, some men, regain Eden and the justice that was originally given to man there? May not regeneration replace the simple generation which would have continued to be in Eden, had the first man not fallen in sin? May we not regain justice through a journey back to Eden?

Dante's journey in the poem is such a regeneration, and whatever the specific answers to the questions must prove to be in strict theology (and these we shall see), his journey to Beatrice at the summit is in fact a return to Eden and, in some sense, to justice.

Regeneration, however, is not a matter as simple as that original generation in which Adam received justice, when he was without sin. Regeneration is complex. It is a matter of a man rising out of his sinful nature and out of his own burden of actual sin, to attain to justice. Sin and the consequences of sin in the soul must first be put off, before justice (which is the form, in this instance) may be received in the soul. And, since *generatio* is defined as movement, this must mean of course that the matter which is made ready to receive the form is the soul, or, as we shall see, the will, more exactly, since justice specifically means right order in the will. Such, in any event, is the matter to be disposed; and, as St. Thomas has indicated, we must keep our eyes on two terms or points of reference in viewing the process. There is the term "whence" and there is the term "whereto." Clearly, in this instance, the "whence" is the condition of sin (which a poet can figure as a dark wood), and the "whereto" is a condition of justice (which a poet can place at the summit of a mountain). And between the two terms, the two contraries, lies process, which is alteration. Therefore a movement "away from" is at the same time an "approach to."

The process might be named with respect to either term, but, even as Thomas says, we must consider the end in these matters and give a name to the movement according to its goal, the "whereto." Thus, since justice is that goal, this movement will properly be termed justification; and in this more complex kind of generation, it will be known specifically as the "justification of the ungodly" (*iustificatio impii*).

The journey to Eden and to Beatrice is such an event, and when we have understood it, we may mark off its phases. Movement with Virgil as guide is movement as preparation. This is the first phase, extending from the beginning in the dark wood of sin all the way to the summit of the mountain. In this first phase, a matter is disposed to receive the form, a soul is made ready for justice. And the aspect of movement "whence," as indicated by St. Thomas, is made plain enough in the climb up the mountain. The wayfarer is led through one terrace of Purgatory after another, and as he moves, a burden of sin and the consequence of sin is put off. *Impedimenta* to the reception of the form, as St. Thomas would say, are removed; and all the while there are varying statements in metaphor of what those obstacles are: they are "stains," "knots," "blemishes," left in the soul or the will through sinful acts. And the seven letters "P" inscribed upon Dante's forehead are the visible sign of those *impedimenta*. These are marks which must be erased in the long hard climb. And so they are, one on each of the terraces of Purgatory. All have been removed (*remotio* is Thomas's term) when Dante comes finally to stand upon the topmost level, at the summit: at which point exactly, Virgil turns to him and speaks the words which announce that the goal "as far as Virgil can discern" has now been reached. And as he reads Virgil's words, the reader who has in mind the conception of justice and of justification which we were concerned to note in Aristotle and in St. Thomas will recognize that those words declare an attainment in terms which clearly mean "justice." This is justice *metaphorice dicta*, justice in the interior disposition of a man, justice which is right order in the will:

> Comme la scala tutta sotto noi
> fu corsa, e fummo in su 'l grado superno,
> in me ficcò Virgilio li occhi suoi,
> e disse: "Il temporal foco e l'etterno
> veduto hai, figlio, e se' venuto in parte
> dov'io per me più oltre non discerno.
> Tratto t'ho qui con ingegno e con arte.
> Lo tuo piacere omai prendi per duce,
> fuor se' de l'erte vie, fuor se' de l'arte.

Vedi lo sol che in fronte ti riluce;
vedi l'erbetta, i fiori e li arbuscelli,
che qui la terra sol da sè produce.
Mentre che vegnan lieti li occhi belli
che lacrimando a te venir mi fenno,
seder ti puoi e puoi andar tra elli.
Non aspettar mio dir più nè mio cenno:
libero, dritto e sano è tuo arbitrio,
e fallo fora non fare a suo senno;
per ch'io te sovra te corono e mitrio."

[When all the stair was put beneath us, and we stood on the topmost step, Virgil fixed his eyes on me and said: "You have seen the temporal and the eternal fire, my son, and you are come to a point beyond which I discern no further. I have brought you here with intelligence and skill. Take henceforth your pleasure for your guide. You are out of the steep and the narrow ways. See the sun that shines on your brow; see the tender grass, the flowers, and shrubs, which the earth here produces of itself alone. Until the fair eyes come rejoicing which with their tears sent me to you, you may sit and you may go among these things. Await no further word nor sign from me. Your will is free, straight and whole, and it would be wrong not to follow its discernment; wherefore I crown and miter you over yourself."]

(*Purgatorio* 27.124–42)

Now, with an eye on the Philosopher's definition of justice above, and again on St. Thomas's extension of that definition, it is important to take note of one thing here: this justice to which Virgil has led, and which he thus announces, is justice only as far as Aristotle goes in his definition. If Dante's will is now free and straight and whole again, and if it would now be wrong not to follow its "senno," this must mean that the rule of reason over the lower parts of the soul, of which Aristotle and Plato spoke, has now been attained. Indeed, Plato's great metaphor of the *Republic* emerges in Virgil's last words: "I crown and miter you over yourself." Right order in the soul brings to mind right order in the state. Reason and right will now rule in the soul; and in the state, by suggestion, there would now rule that one universal monarch through whom alone, as Dante believed, the world would come to justice in all its parts.

This is justice as far as Virgil can discern. Virgil's limit here is thus precisely the limit of ancient pagan wisdom itself, the wisdom of the "philosophers." Beyond this limit is Beatrice, beyond is justice as St. Thomas's definition would have it extended beyond Aristotle, in Christian terms unknown to a Virgil or a Plato or to "the Philosopher." The poet's deliberate design is here most evident. Virgil may guide only as far as the natural light extends, that light which is the only light that was given to him in life, or to those who now dwell with him in Limbo.

Clearly this whole pattern of event is one which we may profitably refer back to those two master patterns of three lights and three conversions already examined. By the light of those we may see that this whole movement or journey to justice, to which we rightly assign the name *iustificatio impii*, must be thought to extend through the area of the first light and over into the area of the second, or, on the other pattern, to reach through the area of the first conversion and over into that of the second conversion. Such a measurement of justification on those two broad paradigms serves to show us exactly how the two phases of the process of justification are to be distinguished. Those two phases are, as we know, 1) preparation to receive a form and 2) reception of the form. Now, the whole area of Virgil's guidance is the area of preparation; and such an area, on the pattern of three lights and three conversions, is precisely that of the first light in the one scheme and the first conversion in the other. We come to see that all three notions, "preparation," "natural light," "first conversion," are exactly co-extensive. Movement under the first light extends only as far as Virgil can discern; the first conversion which is preparation for the second conversion extends also just so far. And Virgil's words dismissing Dante from further guidance by him announce that preparation is completed. Preparation, one might ask, for what? Virgil's words themselves give the answer, for he not only declares an attainment, he makes a promise. Beatrice is expected, Beatrice will come at any moment. Dante has now been made ready for her. She is the very goal to which Virgil has brought him. Yet when she comes finally into view, Virgil will no longer be there by Dante's side. Beatrice as the goal to which Virgil has led is quite beyond Virgil. Here, actually, the pattern of meaning reaches beyond our perspective of the moment and enters another, soon to be examined. But on the pattern of justification itself, the meaning is clear if measured by the two master patterns. To pass from Virgil to Beatrice must mean to pass from the first natural light to the second, which is supernatural. It means to pass over out of a first conversion into a second, wherein the soul attains to that meritorious justice which is given with sanctifying grace and the infused virtues.

On such a test, we see the truth of what was noted at the outset: that we may understand a part of this journey to God only if we see that part within the pattern of the whole. Thus, justification finds its proper and enlightening measure within the whole pattern of the three lights and three conversions, as a part thereof. And by that measure we can understand what the phase of preparation is, as well as what the end moment of completion must be. Perhaps quite the most important thing of all in this is that we see how Beatrice is thus both an end or goal in one pattern of event, and at the same time a beginning of another, within the broader pattern. Where journey with Beatrice begins, there journey to Beatrice ends. It seems a simple truth. Yet where journey to Beatrice ends is precisely where a whole line of event ends the proper name of which in established theology is *iustificatio impii.*

Perhaps enough has already been said of the first conversion with Virgil under the natural light to provide a sufficient view of that phase as "preparation to receive," a first phase in the whole event of justification. But we ought here to face a matter of terminology which can at first cause some perplexity. It would appear, as noted, that Virgil leads his charge to a kind of justice, which is right order in the will, and which implies the dominion of the will over the faculties which are properly subject to it. We must therefore speak of an actual attainment to justice with Virgil. But then, again as noted, Beatrice herself is the further goal, beyond Virgil, and to attain to her means also to attain to justice. Thus, if justification, in its simplest definition, is a "movement to justice," it would appear that Dante has staged a journey to two kinds of justice, both situated at the summit of Purgatory. We might call the first, to which Virgil leads, "justice according to the Philosophers," and we might rightly call the second, which is given with Beatrice, "justice according to the Apostle." But the important point we shall not forget is this: the justice to which Virgil leads is a preparation for the justice which is given with Beatrice, because the first conversion leads to the second, even as the first light leads to the second. The first justice is therefore *ordered to* the second. This being so, it would seem important to take note of a name which the second justice, given with Beatrice, may bear, a name, indeed, which can be one of Beatrice's names when she is seen as the completion and end of justification according to St. Paul. That name is "justifying grace" (*gratia justificans*), which is only to say that Beatrice, as the completion towards which justification of the ungodly has moved, is Sanctifying Grace.

"Justifying grace": what we gain by realizing that such a name fits Beatrice at this point is important, as we are soon to see. For, however much Beatrice's advent may be seen as a justice given from above and beyond human limits, it will not do to lose sight of such justice as the *grace* which it is when so given. Such justice is gratuitous and it sanctifies. This not only serves to keep a proper focus upon the essential features, in terms of the theology involved; it further makes visible a pattern which we have yet to consider in its greater extensions of meaning—a pattern, that is, which consists essentially and simply of a first moment when justice is attained (as with Virgil), followed by a second moment when grace is given (as with Beatrice). In this conception, Virgil's justice is the preparation for grace. And once more we may refer this to the Aristotelian scheme of *generatio*, now so familiar, which provides precisely for two such moments: 1) a preparation for the form, and 2) reception of the form.

# The Presentation

*Erich Auerbach*

We find in the *Comedy* an image of the earthly world in all its diversity, transposed into the world of ultimate destiny and perfect order. And now that we have spoken [elsewhere] in the most general terms of its content and structure we shall try to show how they are reflected in the particular scenes and images.

Dante journeys through the Other World and there, in the stations which mark their ultimate destiny, he encounters the souls of men he has known or with whose lives he is familiar. Even one who knows nothing of the *Comedy* can, by reflecting on the situation, easily imagine the emotion aroused by those meetings and the natural occasion they offer for the most authentic, most powerful, and most human expression. The encounters do not take place in this life, where men are always met with in a state of contingency that manifests only a part of their essence, and where the very intensity of life in the most vital moments makes self-awareness difficult and renders a true encounter almost impossible. Nor do they take place in a hereafter where what is most personal in the personality is effaced by the shadows of death and nothing remains but a feeble, veiled, or indifferent recollection of life. No, the souls of Dante's other world are not dead men, they are the truly living; though the concrete data of their lives and the atmosphere of their personalities are drawn from their former existences on earth, they manifest them here with a completeness, a concentration, an actuality, which they seldom achieved during their term on earth and assuredly never revealed to anyone else. And so it is that Dante finds them;

---

From *Dante: Poet of the Secular World.* © 1961 by the University of Chicago Press.

surprise, astonishment, joy, or horror grips both parties to the meeting, for the dweller in the Other World as he is shown there is also deeply moved by an encounter with one of the living; the mere fact of seeing and recognizing one another reaches into the deepest foundations of human feeling and creates images of unparalleled poetic force and richness.

Thus the meetings between souls in the *Comedy* offer a number of scenes which, though they derive the elements of their expression from the memory of earthly encounters, far surpass any possible earthly encounter by the degree of emotion that accompanies them and the wealth of situations they disclose. They are most moving where Dante was bound to the other by earthly ties, either of actual life together or of inner, spiritual influence. The passion which, either from diffidence or from lack of occasion to speak, tends in temporal existence to hide, bursts forth here, all in one piece, as though moved by the awareness that this is its one and only opportunity to express itself.

In Dante's extreme need in the face of impending ruin, the helper sent by divine grace appears before him: and it is Virgil! But even before he has recognized him, Dante's distress impels him to throw the whole of himself into his cry of supplication; and when the master of his art and precursor of his thinking makes himself known, Dante's love and admiration spring forth naturally and uncontrollably, and in his situation the constitutive words, which provide the essential picture both of the other and of himself, seem quite self-evident, words full of pathos, yet genuinely rooted in the specific occasion. And when in the triumphal procession in the Earthly Paradise Beatrice appears; when Dante, in need of help, turns to Virgil to say: "Less than a dram of blood is left in me that trembleth not" and no longer finds the "dolcissimo padre" at his side; and when the name of Dante rings out like a call at the Last Judgment, the well-prepared emotion, grounded in his past and present fate, legitimated no less by reason than by the heart, the emotion which is true readiness to know and acknowledge himself, grips us scarcely less than it does him, so that the reader too might well say in Dante's words: "men che dramma di sangue m'è rimaso che non tremi."

In these two special cases the emotion strikes only the one partner to the meeting, Dante: for the two others, Virgil and Beatrice, know in advance whom they are to encounter, they have received their mission from above and are from another sphere. But everywhere else the encounter grips both participants in it with equal force. To the same category—the meeting with a former mentor or model—belongs the scene with Brunetto Latini, which remains engraved in the memory of every reader of the

*Inferno.* From the raised dike on which he is advancing Dante is unable to recognize the Sodomites peering up at him through the darkness from the burning desert, until one of them plucks him by the skirt and calls: "What a wonder!" "And I, when he stretched out his arm to me, fixed my eyes on his baked aspect, so that the scorching of his visage hindered not my mind from knowing him; and bending my face to his, I answered: 'Siete voi qui, ser Brunetto?' ['Are you here, Ser Brunetto?'] And he: 'O figluol mio . . .' ['O my son . . .']." And yet that picture, which introduces and justifies Brunetto's significant words, seems only a sketch, a foretaste of a later image which fully develops the feeling implicit in the theme here suggested, namely, the meeting between Statius and Virgil. There for the first time Dante develops all the wealth of possibilities offered by the subject and locale of the *Comedy* and employs them in connection with the same theme, the encounter between a spiritual father and his pupil. Those two men were not contemporaries; they did not know one another; twelve centuries had passed since they lived; Virgil dwelt in Limbo with the pagans; Statius, according to Dante's fiction a secret Christian, made atonement in Purgatory. At the very hour when Virgil is leading his pupil Dante through Purgatory, Statius attains the end of his term of purification; he feels free and ready to ascend to heaven; an earthquake announces the redemption of a soul; he begins his ascent; the two pilgrims are joined by the still unrecognized third, who does not know whom he has before him. He informs them of his life and poetic work and concludes with the praise of Virgil: the *Aeneid* was his nurse, without it he could have accomplished nothing; to have lived when Virgil lived, he would gladly have awaited his liberation for another year in Purgatory. At those words Virgil turns to Dante and beckons him to be silent: but the power of the will has its limits . . . "I did but smile, like one who makes a sign; at that the shade was silent and looked me in the eyes. . . . And he said: 'So may your great toil achieve its end, why did your face but now display to me a flash of laughter?' Now I am caught on either side; one makes me keep silence, the other conjures me to speak; therefore I sigh and am understood by my master, and he said to me, 'Have no fear of speaking. . . .' Therefore I: 'Perhaps you marvel, O ancient spirit, at the laugh I gave, but I desire that even greater wonder seize you. He who guides my eyes on high, is Virgil. . . .' Already he was stooping to embrace my Teacher's feet; but he said: 'Brother, do not so, for you are a shade and a shade you see.' And he, rising: 'Now can you comprehend the measure of the love that warms me toward you, when I forget our nothingness, and treat shades as a solid thing.' "

Less grandiose of gesture, but permeated with the sweet memory of the old life together are the meetings between friends. Among the emaciated gluttons in Purgatory (canto 23), Dante meets Forese Donati, the friend of his youth with whom he had carried on a sparklingly irreverent controversy in sonnets: "from the hollow of the head a shade turned its eyes to me and fixedly did gaze; then cried aloud. . . . Never had I recognized him by the face, but in his voice was revealed to me that which was blotted out in his countenance. This spark rekindled within me all my knowledge of the changed features, and I recognized the face of Forese [E ravvisai la faccia di Forese!]." The power implicit in such a meeting—in such a place—becomes evident when we note how this last line is the culmination of an inner movement built up step by step, while the ensuing dialogue follows from the contrast between Forese's sunken features and his radiant, exuberant youth. Dante had known Charles Martel of Anjou, the young king of Hungary, in Florence in 1294; the king was then in his early twenties and died soon thereafter. Now he meets him in the heavenly sphere of Venus, swathed in beatitude like a silkworm in its cocoon and thus unrecognizable: he greets Dante with the most beautiful verses of Dante's youth, so disclosing his identity as well as his love for Dante, and the memory of his youthful admiration and devotion shines forth amid the beatitude of the third sphere. Dante does not meet Guido Cavalcanti, for during part of 1300 Guido was still alive, but finds his father among the heretics lying in red-hot sarcophagi. Cavalcanti sits up to see whether his son is not there too, for it seems to the older man that Guido's mind was profound enough to enable him, just as well as his friend Dante, to enter the underworld in his lifetime; but at a word from which he gathers that his son is now no longer among the living, he sinks back lamenting, an image of paternal pride and haughty Epicureanism, for this too is implied in his insistence on "altezza d'ingegno [on the height of genius]," his praise of the sweet light of the sun, and his indifference to Guido's ultimate fate, about which he does not even inquire. The scene is an interruption of Dante's meeting with the Ghibelline leader Farinata degli Uberti, one of the finest among the long series of meetings with his compatriots. In Dante's hereafter, common birthplace and language provide a bond of love and joy, and in the *Comedy* the motif of the compatriot encountered far from home, which may strike us as sentimental, is varied and raised to sublime heights. Engaged in conversation, Virgil and Dante pass by the tombs of the heretics, and Farinata recognizes Dante as a Florentine by his manner of speech; suddenly Dante is terrified by a voice issuing from one of the tombs: "O Tosco che per la città del foco vivo ten vai così parlando onesto

[O Tuscan! who through the city of fire goest alive, speaking thus decorously]." The sentence itself is a magnificent example of lofty speech; consummately modelled down to the very last syllable, it frames a complex thought in the simplest and most direct words; if we say it over a few times, it will bring home to us all the intensity of the great Farinata's emotion and the power beneath which his words conceal their richness; but what Farinata himself means by the "parlare onesto [decorous speech]" is the beautiful Florentine dialect, and so we learn from this passage that Dante speaks Tuscan in discoursing with Virgil, just as Virgil as a Mantuan —as is shown by another, very similar passage—employs the Lombard Italian of the year 1300. In another connection we shall have more to say of this passage, which also contains an adjuration by the common homeland. In regard to our present theme, the encounter with a countryman, we have another Mantuan at our disposal: that is Sordello, the Provençal poet from Mantua, who at nightfall in Ante-Purgatory, solitary and aloof as a resting lion, scarcely wishes to answer Virgil's question until the word Mantua makes him start up: "O Mantovano, io son Sordello de la tua terra—e l'un l'altro abbracciava [O Mantuan, I am Sordello of your city.—And one embraced the other]." There is no better example of the power of the setting which makes such meetings possible; for without the introduction and the occasion it so naturally offers, the ensuing apostrophe to Italy and the Emperor would be mere rhetoric, while, placed as it is, it becomes, with all the strict clarity of its thinking, a cry uttered in a real situation; Dante and the listener, the one creating, the other receiving, are equally prepared to savor the passion that now bursts forth, and yet it is not a product of artifice, but with all its artfulness wholly natural, because it corresponds to the natural movement of human feeling.

With that we conclude our list of encounters, for to exhaust them we should have to copy out a large part of the poem, and we hope we have made it sufficiently clear what they communicate: namely, the state of agitation in which the souls are met, partly because of the place itself and partly because of the presence of a living man in it. Not all are glad of the meeting, for in the lower circles of Hell there are some who would have preferred to remain unrecognized; and not all those who are glad are glad in the same way; the passionate longing of the lower spirits for news of the world, their eagerness to know whether they are remembered on earth, are diminished in Purgatory, mingled with other, more Christian motives for rejoicing; while in Paradise the source of the soul's rejoicing is the love they are able to bestow on the favored guest. But all who are gathered in the Other World, men of all times and countries, with all their wisdom and folly, good and evil, love and hatred of the world, the whole epitome of history—all of them find in the living Dante, who comes to them, an occasion and a need to state what they are and to explain in clear and tangible terms how they came to their ultimate destination.

It is not always easy for them to say what they wish to. Particularly in the *Inferno*, but also in the *Purgatorio*, there seems to be a barrier between their need to communicate and its satisfaction—and that barrier, created by their situation of punishment or atonement, makes their communication all the more poignant when it does break forth. Those men with their terribly disfigured or tormented bodies, some in eternal motion, others in painful immobility, have scarcely strength or time to speak. Yet they wish to speak and must speak; they express themselves painfully and laboriously, and it is their torment and effort that give their words and gestures such compelling power. Wrapped in flames, the elder Montefeltro approaches the two pilgrims; slowly and painfully his words make their way through the roaring flame, and full of fear that his listeners may lose patience, he beseeches them to remain and speak with their countryman; until at length the question toward which he is aiming, and which has filled his heart all the while, bursts forth like an explosion of his whole physical and spiritual being: "'Dimmi se i Romagnuoli han pace or guerra' ['Tell me if the Romagnuols have peace or war']." We have designedly chosen this example precisely because the sentence that crowns the scene is not in itself so significant, for what is more natural than that a dead man, who once played an important part in the destinies of his native place, should ask what is going on there now? But the particular qualities of the setting where the question is asked and here in particular the barrier the speaker must surmount in order to utter it, charge the question itself with all the questioner's yearning and feverish curiosity.

Thus far we have tried to show that the souls encountered in the Other World are of necessity ready and willing to reveal their innermost reality and that the power of their utterance is sometimes further enhanced by the difficulties that stand in its way. But we have not yet considered their "innermost reality" as such, nor have we inquired where Dante derived its constitutive elements. A very general answer suggests itself without difficulty: he took them from his own experience as he remembered it; and in selecting and blending his memories, he employed a definite method of synopsis or abstraction. Thus all the figures of his great poem are derived from Dante's own inner being: that much is obvious and requires no further discussion; the material with which he worked was an almost superhuman fund of experience and a divinatory gift which enabled him to fathom all varieties and degrees of human feeling. Far more difficult is the question of selection, for in each case he had to choose from among a superabundance of traits and interpretations, and the true reality distilled by such selection hinges on the authority Dante invokes. For what he represents is not the whole epic breadth of life, but a single moment of reality; and that single moment, moreover, encompasses a man's ultimate fate as determined by Providence. Thus when Dante has his figures appear in this or that part of the Other World, he not only purports to represent their true essence, but also to know God's judgment upon them or rather to have beheld it in a vision: an absurd and presumptuous falsehood unless the vision is the evident truth; unless it accords with the reader's profoundest convictions and at the same time rises above them, synthesizing disparities and creatively revealing a common element on which the synthesis is based.

All that enters into the synopsis or abstraction by which, as we have said, Dante solved his problem of selection. He does not relate the whole life, he does not spread out the whole soul and analyze it in all its parts; he omits many things. In one of his titles, Rabelais calls himself an "abstracteur de quinte essence [an abstractor of quintessence]"; a modern painter is quoted as saying that painting is omission; Dante seems to proceed somewhat in that way. But our comparisons are taken from more recent times: did any poet work in a similar way before Dante? Apparently not; when the ancient and medieval poets wished to set forth a character's whole personality, they drew the essence from the whole epic breadth of his life; when they gave only an excerpt of the life, it meant that they had no thought of portraying the whole man; in considering a lover, a jealous man, a glutton, or a nuisance, they did not concern themselves in the least with anything else he might be other than loving, jealous, gluttonous, or importunate. Even the classical tragedy, which may be said to "omit" a good deal and yet to aim at the whole of the man, requires an event which unfolds in time; on the basis of this event, the tragic poet decides what is to be included and what omitted, and it is through the event that the hero replies, more and more clearly and in the end definitively, to the question put to him by his destiny, to the question of who he really is. But Dante records no events; he has only a moment in which everything must be revealed; a very special moment, to be sure, for it is eternity. And he gives us something which the Greek tragedy scorned, namely, the individual, concrete qualities of man: through language, tone, gesture, bearing, he penetrates to the essence. The reader of a Greek tragedy, it is true, can form a concrete picture of Prometheus or Antigone or Hippolytus, and the Greek spectator could do so in still higher degree; but the portrayal left far more room for the viewer's imagination than in Dante's poem, where every accent and every gesture are exactly defined.

In this connection it would be interesting to observe how unity of body and soul had become more intense and taken on new meaning since the individual human body, through Christian dogma, had come to partake of eternity. But that would take us too far afield. Instead let us see what it is that Dante omits. This is made clear by our comparison with earlier poets: he omits temporal events. In the hereafter there is no more temporal happening: history is at an end, replaced by memory. Nothing new will ever again happen to the souls except on the Day of Judgment, which will merely bring about an intensification of their present state. They have cast off their *status viatoris* [their wayfarer's state] and entered into the *status recipientis pro meritis* [the state of those rewarded according to merit], and with nonessential reservations that is also true of the souls in Purgatory. No longer is there any hope or fear of change, there is no uncertain future to give the souls consciousness of the dimension of time. Nothing happens to them any longer, or rather, what happens to them will keep happening forever. But that situation without time or history is the fruit of their history on earth, and in thinking and speaking of themselves, they are constrained to see both in one. Among their innumerable experiences, their memory necessarily chooses those which were decisive, and that is the very essence of their memory; for God by His judgment has shown them what was decisive. Thus history with its vicissitudes has been taken from them and what remains is a memory which infallibly strikes the essential. In addition the souls have retained their individual form; however, it is not their changing historical form, influenced by the changing historical situation, but a definitive, true and authentic form, which God's judgment has disclosed and, as it were, fixated for all eternity. In the *Inferno*, to be sure, certain figures, the suicides for instance, have suffered significant changes, and others like the thieves incur continuous change; but in those cases it must be assumed that metamorphosis is their eternal form and represents—if I may use a hazardous expression—the concrete sum of their earthly existence. And with slight modifications all that is equally applicable to the souls in Purgatory; to them too, a decisive and ultimate fate has been meted out, and they too must relate it to the memory of their life on earth; their form, to be sure, is not final, and yet it is, in so far as it symbolizes the sum of their former being, and in so far as it will change only at a time and in a way that have already been determined. True, they do not yet know when that will happen; they still possess hope and expectation, and in this respect the Mountain of Purgatory retains some of the historical character of the *status viatoris*; but their uncertainty is very slight compared to the uncertainty of earthly life; there is no earthly experience in Purgatory, but only the memory of such experience.

And so temporal events are eliminated, only memory is preserved, and it is only by way of memory that reality enters into the Other World, and yet, in the last analysis, memory, from which all chance and every contingent relation to a temporal situation on earth is removed, captures the essence not only with greater intellectual precision but also more concretely and completely than do temporal events with their uncertainty and ambiguity. In the hereafter, men have self-knowledge, for it has been conferred upon them by God's judgment. And self-knowledge, even the fragmentary, ambiguous self-knowledge which we mortals possess on earth, is made possible only by memory. To be sure, the potential simultaneity of all events in memory is always actualized in a definite image; but the image itself is shaped by a consciousness whose whole experience has contributed to the shaping; the moment of the event, by contrast, is obscure; though others may understand us at this moment, we cannot understand ourselves. Thus in making his characters' self-portrayal flow from their memory, Dante brings out their innermost experience; they recollect, and the object or substance of their recollection is given them by their ultimate fate, which shows them its full concordance with their essence. Consequently they cannot help remembering the essential, and whatever the particular image which memory may conjure up from their days on earth, it must always be exhaustive and decisive in respect of their essence; even those who would gladly conceal their innermost being are compelled to speak by their encounter with the living man, and the expression they find must be the sharpest and most personal expression, for they know themselves and the meaning of their lives and in their supreme actuality have remained identical with themselves.

Thus the poem consists of a long series of self-portraits, which are so clear and complete that concerning those men, who have long been dead and who lived under such very different conditions from ourselves or who perhaps never lived at all, we know something which often remains hidden from us in our thoughts about ourselves or those with whom we are in daily contact: namely, the simple meaning which dominates and orders their whole existence. The meaning that Dante gives us is for the most part very simple, often stated in a short sentence; but even when it is so simple as to seem almost threadbare, a well-nigh superhuman penetration was required to find it, and it gains its richness from the abundance of events which surround it and from which it is distilled; only a small part of the man's experience is expressed, but that small part is the essential, what is omitted is present in it by implication. When the elder Montefeltro says: " 'Io fui uom d'arme, e poi fui cordigliero' ['I was a man of arms and then became a Cordelier']," Dante has put his finger on the essential character of that hard, crafty man with his secret but insufficient yearning for purity; and when of all the episodes of his life only a single one is related, the story of how he could not resist the temptation to exercise his often tested guile one last time, that one event not only determines his ultimate fate but also characterizes the man, and all the rest of his life that remains unexpressed—the struggles, the hardships, the intrigues, and the days of vain repentance—is implicit in the characterization.

No imitation of present events can be more real and penetrating than memory in Dante's Other World. Let us consider the theme of the frail young woman whose husband has her secretly murdered in a desert place; let us attempt a dramatic or epic treatment of the theme, enriched with all the motives and atmospheric details which it admits of; and then read the last two tercets of the Ante-Purgatory, in which Pia de' Tolomei, last among those who have met a violent death, raises her voice:

"Deh, quando tu sarai tornato al mondo,
E risposato de la lunga via,"
Seguitò il terzo spirito al secondo,
"Ricorditi di me che son la Pia:
Siena mi fè; disfecemi Maremma;
Salsi colui che innanellata pria
Disposando m'avea con la sua gemma."

["Pray, when you shall return to the world, and are rested
from your long journey," followed the third spirit
after the second.
"Remember me, who am La Pia: Siena made me, Ma-
remma unmade me: 'tis known to him who, first
plighting troth, had wedded me with his gem."]

Here no motivation or detail is given; Dante's contemporaries may well have filled out the allusion, but we ourselves have no definite information about Pia de' Tolomei. Yet nothing seems lacking; she is entirely real and distinct. Her memory is wholly concentrated on the hour of her death, which sealed her final fate; in that memory and in her supplication to remember her on earth, the whole of her being unfolds; and the one line that is not concerned with herself, her sweet and tender words to Dante—"e riposato de la lunga via"—tells us all we need to know of this woman in order to perceive her life in its full actuality.

This quintessence of character, arrived at by self-recollection in the predestined place of ultimate destiny, seldom has its source in what moderns would call the "atmosphere" or "milieu." Almost always memory is directed toward a definite act or event, and it is from this act or event that the character's aura arises. The act, the event, the vice or virtue, the pragmatic historical situation—in short, a decisive concrete fact—suffices to manifest the man connected with it in all his sensuous reality; there are no everyday naturalistic particulars. When one of the souls being scourged in hell, who wished at first to hide, merely says: " 'Io fui colui che la Ghisolabella condussi a far la voglia del Marchese' ['It was I who led the fair Ghisola to do the Marquis's will']," he has no need to recount the details of his former life; in such a place these words suffice. Herein Dante proceeds in the manner of legend or myth, whose poetic characters or concrete figures are always based on tangible data. His method differs not only from that of the later naturalistic poets, who present the character in his social relations, habits, and environment before letting him act, but also from that of the ancient poets, who treated the legends and myths in a tragic or epic manner; for the ancient poets had nothing essential to invent, the characters and fates were there, known to every reader or member of the audience. Dante, however, created his own myths; though the persons and destinies he treated may have been known to many contemporaries, they were in large part subject to varying interpretation and thus unformed before Dante took them up. In his use of known but not yet mythically shaped persons, Dante shows most resemblance to the old Attic comedy, to the plays of Aristophanes, who also liked to lift earthly characters into another realm, where they revealed themselves. Vico saw a connection between the title of Dante's poem and ancient comedy, though he found no basis for supposing the association to be anything more than playful wit. Be that as it may, the presence of contemporaries and critique of the times exhaust the resemblance, for Aristophanes does not mold his figures into a definitive mythical or ideal type, as Dante does in his poem. Dante's naturalism is something new: the directness with which he lifts one among the multitude of his contemporaries into the Other World, there to interpret his essential reality, as though he were as famous as a mythical, or at least historically established figure whose significance is known to all—that directness seems to have been unknown before him. It will be worth our while to illustrate the point by an example. An ancient, for example, might associate the "vanity of glory" with the image of Achilles, who in the underworld owns to Odysseus that he would rather be the last of slaves than a king over the dead; and we too, if we wish to illustrate that idea by an image, might think of a great ruler who by a contemplative life in his last years or by posthumous insight, had become aware of the nothingness of glory. Dante treats the matter differently. In the *Comedy* it is not Caesar who speaks of the emptiness of earthly glory; for Dante, Caesar's glory was not vain, but significant in the context of providential history. Actually, Dante required historical or mythical figures only when dealing with the great situations of political or religious history; for the concrete illustration of a mere ethical or empirical theme he had no need of them. And whom does he take as an example by which to illustrate the "vanity of glory?" The illuminator Oderisi of Gubbio, a contemporary (d. 1299) concerning whom nothing has come down to us but a note by Vasari, who even then knew very little about him. But even supposing him to have been the foremost in his art in Dante's time, what minuscule glory by which to illustrate so grandiose a theme! How many of Dante's contemporaries must have been ignorant of his very existence!—and yet Dante was confident that he would have readers in future centuries and wrote for them. But he required no brilliant example who would strike the reader by the contrast between his present state and the position, known to all, which he once occupied on earth; for him it was enough that Oderisi was known in his field and attached importance to his fame. The scene takes place among the proud, in the eleventh canto of the *Purgatorio*; as they move along ever so slowly, bowed almost to the ground beneath their heavy burdens, Dante speaks with one of them:

Ascoltando chinai in giù la faccia;  
Ed un di lor, non questi che parlava,  
Si torse sotto il peso che l'impaccia,  
E videmi e conobbemi e chiamava,  
Tenendo li occhi con fatica fisi  
A me che tutto chin con loro andava.  
"O!" diss'io lui: "Non se' tu Oderisi,  
L'onor d'Agobbio e l'onor di quell' arte  
Che 'alluminare' chiamata è in Parisi?"  
"Frate," diss' elli, "più ridon le carte  
Che pennelleggia Franco bolognese:  
L'onor è tutto or suo, e mio in parte.  
Ben non sare'io stato si cortese,  
Mentre ch'io vissi, per lo gran disio

De l'eccellenza ove mio core intese.
Di tal superbia qui si paga il fio."

[Listening I bent down my face; and one of them, not he who was speaking, twisted himself beneath the weight which encumbers him;
and saw me and knew me and was calling out keeping his eyes with difficulty fixed upon me, who all bent was going with them.
"Oh," said I to him, "are you not Oderisi, the honor of Gubbio, and the honor of that art which in Paris is called 'illuminating'?"
"Brother," said he, "more pleasing are the leaves which Franco Bolognese paints; the honor now is all his and mine in part.
Truly I should not have been so courteous while I lived, because of the great desire of excellence on which my heart was bent.
For such pride here the fine is paid."]

After the poignant picture of recognition ("e videmi e conobbemi e chiamava") Dante greets him with words of praise, for he knows the other's weakness; but there is a faint note of condescension and irony in Dante's words; ah, Gubbio's pride! One also seems to discern the shadow of a smile in Dante's pointedly circumspect way of referring to Oderisi's art. But how moving is the penitent's answer! "Brother," says he, "more pleasing are the leaves which Franco Bolognese paints." He is still preoccupied with the rival, whose superiority, though he never acknowledged it, tormented him in his lifetime, and a part of his penance consists in acknowledging it now; these are the first words he utters, and then begins the well-known speech about fame, in which Cimabue and Giotto and the poets of the "stil nuovo" are mentioned. Here, then, a grandiose theme is illustrated by a man of small scope, whose immoderate lust for glory is grounded not in any great designs for domination and power but in the narrowness of his vision, whose "desire of excellence" was limited to a mere handicraft, though a beautiful one; the man was widely known, it is true, but his personality had not yet crystallized in the consciousness of the public, and it was Dante who first fashioned a complete image of him as an ideal and typical representative of a vice and of the atonement by which this same vice is transcended. In that sense Dante is almost always the creator and first shaper of his figures. Cacciaguida declares, to be sure, that only souls known to fame, "che son di fama note," are presented to Dante in the Other World, because men would lend no credence to unknown examples. That may have been true for contemporary readers; yet even though Dante's contemporaries knew more than we do about the persons treated and though certain opinions about these figures may have been relatively widespread, it was Dante who, by identifying the reality of these men with their ultimate fate, first gave the opinions concerning them form and permanence. And for us, to whom very many of the dramatis personae are unknown, or who at best may have gleaned a fact or two about them from some historical document, Cacciaguida's words are no longer in any sense applicable; for us most of Dante's examples are no longer famous. And yet we do believe in them. One need only think of Francesca Malatesta da Rimini. In Dante's day her story may have been well known, today it is quite forgotten and nothing remains of it but the second half of the fifth canto of Dante's *Inferno*. But these lines have made her into a high poetic figure of historical, almost mythical stature.

Yet intermingled with the forgotten contemporaries of Dante, we also find the great figures of history and legend. Heroes and kings, saints and popes, princes, statesmen, generals, whose profiles even then had long been clearly engraved in the collective mind, appear in the place of their ultimate destiny and reveal their being. Dante always adheres to the tradition concerning them; but even there, as Gundolf has clearly shown in connection with his Caesar, Dante is the creator of the figure. Just as in dealing with the persons he himself had known or of whom he had heard by word of mouth, he conjured up the sum of their gesture and fate from the contingent particulars of their lives, so here he distilled a real and evident figure from the records—so poor in sensuous images—of the medieval historians. He did not in every case establish them in the European mind: his image was often corrected at a later day through more accurate knowledge of the ancient spirit, though that too was first made possible by Dante. Dante's Homer with sword in hand has been replaced by the Naples bust. But he was the first modern writer to lend them form: even though the ancient characters of the *Comedy* have been changed in passing through the medium of medieval reinterpretation, even though they have been transposed into a world order that is not always appropriate to their actuality, nevertheless, with Dante for the first time, that ordering, reinterpreting spirit of the Middle Ages provides something more than systematic edification. With Dante a new and imponderable element—compounded of poetry, experience, and vision—was gained for all time: but that should not make us forget that the force which guided him in his achievement sprang directly from the universalism of the rational doctrine he was striving to demonstrate by embodying it in a divine vision. The question: how does God see the earthly world?—and its answer: with all its particularities ordered with a view to the eternal goal—are the foundation of this profoundly passionate poem, and in its fifteen thousand lines there is not a scene or a magical chord which did not draw life from that rational foundation. Caesar stands before us unforgettable with his Suetonian "occhi grifagni" [his piercing eyes]; Odysseus comes palpably to life; and Cato, however strangely interpreted, is a figure full of reality. But in each case what their eternal attitude shows is the concordance of their crucial traits with the providential course of the world, in which they acted thus and so and not otherwise; for all their radiant beauty they embody a rigorous doctrine. What a figure is Dante's Odysseus! He is one of the few whose memory does not begin directly with the act that sealed his fate, the betrayal of Troy, mother of Rome; Dante may not address him, for the Greek would not reply; it is Virgil, the ancient poet who had sung of Greek heroes, who beseeches him to relate the end of his life. And cloaked in flames, Odysseus relates his last journey; how he found no peace at home, how his desire for knowledge and adventure drove him forth once more; how finally, old and tired, having already pressed forward as far as the Pillars of Hercules, he once again summons his companions to a bold undertaking:

"O frati," dissi "che per cento milia
  Perigli siete giunti a l'occidente
  A questa tanto picciola vigilia
De'nostri sensi, ch'è del rimanente,
  Non vogliate negar l'esperienza,
  Diretro al sol, del mondo senza gente!
Considerate la vostra semenza:
  Fatti non foste a viver come bruti
  Ma per seguir virtute e conoscenza."

["O brothers!" I said, "who through a hundred thousand dangers have reached the West, deny not, to this brief vigil
of your senses that remains, experience of the unpeopled world behind the Sun.
Consider your origin; you were not formed to live like brutes, but to follow virtue and knowledge."]

In this narrative, which like a dream that interprets reality, discloses the unity of the European character in the spirit of world conquest that has carried down from Greek to modern times, one might be tempted to find an autonomous invention of character in the modern manner. It is only at the end of the story that its true meaning is laid bare. For five months Odysseus and his companions sail over the ocean; then they see a great mountain, but their joy is brief; the mountain is the Mountain of Purgatory, a cyclone rises up from it and the ship is wrecked. The providential order of the world has set a goal to human immoderation; the boldness of Odysseus has no validity of its own; the human character finds its measure not in itself but in a destiny which is a righteous judge. Yet despite that doctrine—and this, as we have said, is characteristic of Dante's portraits of men—he is able to preserve the autonomy of the character, and indeed Odysseus even seems to gain in concrete presence from such rigorous evaluation and interpretation. Down to the most extreme particularity of his former sensuous being, the individual man is preserved in the place of his ultimate fate: he is preserved in his physical as well as his spiritual being. Physical and spiritual—the disjunction may give rise to a misunderstanding: what has been preserved is not two different things, but the unity of a single personality.

Dante saw many men, his vision was clear and precise; he was no mere observer. And events that he did not see but only heard or read of, sometimes in the most abstruse terms, became living images for him: he heard the tone of his speakers, saw their movements, sensed their hidden impulses, and thought their thoughts. All these are one; and it is from that unity that he derives the figure. The gestures, the "manifestazioni plastiche," the plastic manifestations, as an Italian scholar calls them, are never an idle display of naturalistic observation; they have their ground and limits in the event being narrated, and though at the same time they manifest the person's physical being, such a concordance must follow inevitably from the concordance between the personality and the event. We are given no details as to the appearance of Dante or Virgil; none of their physical traits is described and the one passage where something of the sort is said—Beatrice's " 'alza la barba' ['lift up your beard']"—is very startling. But it is purely metaphorical, for it is quite certain that Dante never wore a beard. However, a picture of them pieces itself together from the many scenes in which they speak and move as the situation demands. And every single figure in the poem—the glutton Ciacco, rising up in the murky rain and sinking back again with revulsed eyes; Argenti biting himself; Casella coming to meet Dante with open arms; the slothful Belacqua who sits hugging his knees and barely raises his head at the unexpected sight of a mortal—all show that naturalistic observation is governed and limited by the very definite event that is being related and that if the man nevertheless stands there complete, in all his sensuous fullness, it can only be because he is fully encompassed in the event. The gestures are few, but Dante tends to describe them with elaborate precision; he does not suggest, but describes or analyzes the actual movement, and often even that does not satisfy him: he tries to make it still clearer, and to accentuate it, by a long spun-out metaphor, which compels the reader to linger. When at the beginning of the poem he turns round to look back at the wooded valley, he unfolds the image of the swimmer who "has escaped from the deep sea to the shore," and still panting looks back over the perilous waters; at the end of the *Paradiso* he likens his immersion in the vision of God to a mathematician's increasing concentration on an insoluble problem. Between those two images lie the hundred cantos with their infinite wealth of metaphors, designed more often to clarify a concrete situation than a feeling. Perhaps more clearly than any other element of the work, they show the range and intensity of Dante's perception; animals and men, destinies and myths, idylls, warlike actions, landscapes, naturalistic street scenes, the most common periodic occurrence connected with the seasons and with men's occupations, the most personal recollection—everything is there: croaking frogs in the evening, a lizard darting across the path, sheep crowding out of their enclosure, a wasp withdrawing its sting, a dog scratching; fishes, falcons, doves, storks; a cyclone snapping off trees at the trunk; a morning countryside in spring, covered with hoarfrost; night falling on the first day of an ocean voyage; a monk receiving the confession of a murderer; a mother saving a child from fire; a lone knight galloping forth; a bewildered peasant in Rome; sometimes very brief, half a line—"attento si fermò com'uom che ascolta [he stopped attentive like a man who listens]"—sometimes rolling on at length, so that a landscape, an incident, a legend unfolds in all its breadth, always in order to serve the movement of the poem. This metaphoric technique, as we know, is ancient; some of the figures have even been taken from Virgil and many preserve something of the Virgilian tone; but the spirit and purpose are different. Virgil's metaphors are ornamental; they support the development only in the most general way, by evoking a similar, parallel idea; if they were removed, the poetic flow would be disturbed and the harmony of the picture would be impoverished, but the reality of the happening—which in any case is a vague, fairy-tale reality—would not be impaired. And Dante is still farther removed from his contemporaries who, like Guinizelli for example in his "Voglio del ver la mia donna laudare," let their imagination roam, gathering up random scraps of all that is charming and resplendent, so losing their hold on the definite particular. Dante's metaphors are not parallel but concordant; they are intended not to ornament but to make clear; taken from the concrete, they lead to the concrete. That is why they are so much richer than those of Virgil and capable of performing a function that is more than lyrical; they are not only beautiful inventions—they serve to make reality more real; they help Dante to achieve the aim for which he invokes the help of the Muses: "sì che dal fatto il dir non sia diverso [so that my words may not be diverse from the fact]."

What is said here of the metaphors is equally true of another poetic form which Dante took from his ancient models: the metamorphoses. In the *Comedy* the body is preserved along with the spirit; but the self-realization achieved in the hereafter brings about outward changes which sometimes destroy the former sensuous aspect completely. The change applies only to the appearance, not to the personality; on the contrary, the new appearance is a continuation, intensification, and interpretation of the old one and thus first discloses the real individual. In Dante, accordingly, metamorphosis loses its ancient fabulous character; from the remote darkness of legend it enters into present reality, for in every living man a metamorphosis may lie hidden: what man can say that he might not become a suicide? This apparent change is most drastic among the suicides and thieves: the suicides have become bushes devoured and soiled by the Harpies; and the thieves undergo a strange transformation before Dante's eyes: set afire by snakebite, they either rise from their ashes or exchange aspects with a serpent. Well-known figures of Dante's time incur those transformations, which embody a judgment on their former life; that is why the metamorphosis ceases to be mythical and enters the sphere of reality; the person who laments or scoffs or hisses or spits in that metamorphosed body is a very definite man whom many of Dante's contemporaries had known and whom all could imagine as one of their fellow men. Because Dante's metamorphosis is an individual human destiny, it is far more concrete than in Ovid or Lucan; the meeting with Pier della Vigna or the episode of the two Florentine thieves who exchange shapes, are set forth with an intensity and precision, they convey a degree of reality which is without parallel in ancient literature, precisely because, just as with the metaphors, the remote beauty of poetic illusion has been replaced by concrete truth taken as judgment.

In Paradise all the souls have undergone a transformation which human eyes cannot penetrate; they are hidden by the radiance of their beatitude and Dante cannot recognize them; they themselves must say who they are, and they cannot express their emotions by human gestures; strictly speaking, personal emotion can only manifest itself here by an increase in radiance. The danger of depersonalization and monotonous repetition is evident, and many believe that Dante succumbed to it and that the *Paradiso* lacks the poetic power of the first two parts of the *Comedy*. But such a criticism of Dante's *ultimo lavoro* springs from the Romantic prejudice of which we have spoken above and shows that the critic has been unable to give himself to Dante's subject as a whole. The great similarity between the luminous manifestations, resulting from their common beatitude, does not exclude a preservation of the individual personality; the man is almost if not entirely hidden from the eyes, but he is there and finds means of making himself known. The disclosure is more tenuous and unmediated than in the other two parts; but it, too, has its root in the unique concordance between earthly life and ultimate fate, and the occasion for it, here again, is the meeting with the living Dante. Although the bodies are hidden, the luminous apparitions of the *Paradiso* have expressive gestures which accompany their memories of the former lives on earth; these are the different modes and movement of light, which Dante illustrates with an abundance of metaphors; the feminine souls of the moon appear as pearls on a white forehead; the souls of the sphere of Mercury gather round Dante like fish in clear water, swimming toward food that has been cast to them; an interruption of the dance when a new melody begins, the bells of the clock calling to Matins, the double circle of the rainbow: all interpret the phases of the dance in the sphere of the sun; as a shooting star falls to earth, so Cacciaguida's light descends from the cross of Mars upon his grandson, and the Triumph of Christ gives occasion for the unfolding of the most beautiful of all moonlit landscapes: "quale ne' plenilunii sereni . . . ," as in the calm full moons. . . . The readers who intone such passages in a dreamy chanting tone and the interpreters who do their best to strip them of all meaning or purpose and regard them as pure inspiration, mystical, anonymous, and unrelated to the physical or spiritual world, in short, the modern view of poetry as the *ens realissimum* of intuition, which neither can nor need be carried back to its sources—all that is far removed from the spirit of Dante; for it is the truth of the rational doctrine which creates the concrete image and lends it power, and one who (as most readers do) remembers the passage but forgets that it refers to the Triumph of Christ is like a child picking raisins out of a cake; he gets very little of the taste of the cake. Such readers dwell too much on the "pasture da pigliar occhi per aver la mente," the food to catch the eyes and so possess the mind; they forget or rather overlook the fact that what is essential is "aver la mente," to possess the mind; the sensuous manifestation, however beautiful, serves to communicate a rational thought, and it is only by way of the thought that one can judge whether the enchantment of the senses is sleight-of-hand or whether it is legitimate.

The same may be said of Dante's landscapes and chronological indications; they do not serve merely to bewitch the senses, and the mythical or astrological references in his chronologies are not a mere show of learning. Mythical erudition and sensuous enchantment both serve to bring out the reality, and that tangible reality—of morning or evening, a time of day or a season—is a mode or manifestation of the divine order. Just because it is always encompassed in the divine order, nature is imbued with spirit; it is a "natura sympathetica," at once comprehending the whole and shot through with the spiritual significance of the literal events that take place in it. And from that unity of action and setting even the most violent expression derives measure and justification; because a line such as this—"Urlar li fa la pioggia come cani [The rain makes them howl like dogs]"—is embedded in that unity, or concordance, there is measure even in its gruesome expressiveness.

Throughout the Other World the empirical reality is preserved; it fills us with delight or horror, but never surfeits us as is so often the case with the reality of our own lives; and never is the individual image contingent, blind, and fragmentary, the picture set before us is always a whole. Ordered and transfigured by the divine vision, earthly appearance becomes the true, definitive reality which, by its essence and the place in which it is manifested, discloses the plenitude of the divine order, so presupposing and encompassing everything else contained in it. The *Comedy* is an eminently philosophical work, not so much because of the actual philosophical doctrines set forth in it as because the spirit of those doctrines compels Dante to write philosophically. The subject, the *status animarium post mortem*, the state of the souls after death, constrains the poet, who holds the Christian belief in an individual justice for each man, to give concrete form to the idea of the individual; everything that is contingent or even temporal in his outward manifestation must be set aside, and yet the man himself, in his former unity of spirit and body, must be preserved in order that he may suffer or enjoy divine justice. Temporal relationships are at an end, and yet the a priori form of the individual, the fruit as it were of all his earthly acts and sufferings, is preserved. Very much in the manner of philosophy, which abstracts pure ideas from phenomena, this poetic work draws from earthly appearances the true personality which is body and spirit in one; it creates what might be called an ideal sensuous presence or a spirit endowed with a body that is necessary, concordant, and essential. All appearances are given their place in the true order of the other world, and that is the source of the *Comedy*'s necessary reality, of the "vital nutrimento," the vital nutriment, which Dante promises his readers.

Dante hoped for the favor of those "che questo tempo chiameranno antico [who shall call this time ancient]"—and his hope has been fulfilled. But it did not occur to him that his work would one day be admired, in large part, by people to whom the foundations of his faith and world view had become meaningless and alien. He could never have conceived of such a thing, for like all his contemporaries he was lacking in historical sense, he was incapable of reconstructing an epoch on the basis of its own realities and presuppositions, rather than interpreting it in terms of his own time. His relation to Virgil was not very different from our relation to himself, for the spiritual and cultural foundations on which Virgil's art had arisen had crumbled and become utterly foreign to him. But of that he was quite unaware; he remodelled Virgil as though Augustan Rome were separated from his own epoch only by the passage of time, as though certain events had taken place and a certain amount of knowledge had been amassed in the meantime, but not as though man's whole form of life and thought had changed. Virgil the ancestor speaks the language of his descendant and profoundly understands him, whereas it would seem to us—Anatole France expressed the idea with a learned though somewhat facile elegance—that if anyone had spoken to Virgil of Dante, he would not have understood him in the least, much less appreciated him. We possess at least a relatively better understanding of past or foreign cultures and are able to adapt ourselves to them rather than to take the opposite course like Dante; we are able, for a limited period and without binding ourselves, to accept strange forms and presuppositions very much as one accepts the rules of a game, and we do so in the hope of acquiring the feel of strange countries and their institutions and of learning to enjoy their art. In connection with Dante and a few others, no such transposition is necessary; anyone who understands his language and is capable of sympathy with human destinies can take in large parts of his work directly; the poem itself imperceptibly provides the necessary minimum of historical understanding. But there is another question that is more difficult to answer: can a modern reader, even if he is supremely learned and endowed with the highest degree of historical empathy, penetrate to Dante if he is utterly unwilling to accept Dante's mode of thought? Of course the greatest creations of the human spirit are not tied inseparably to the particular forms of thought and faith from which they sprang; they change with every generation that admires them, showing to each generation a new face without losing their intrinsic character. But there is a limit to their power of transformation; where the form of admiration becomes too arbitrary, they refuse to go along. To put it very cautiously, it seems to me that with regard to the *Divine Comedy* such a limit has almost been attained when philosophical commentators begin to praise its so-called poetic beauties as a value in themselves and reject the system, the doctrine, and indeed the entire subject matter as irrelevancies which if anything call for a certain indulgence.

The subject and doctrine of the *Comedy* are not incidental; they are the roots of its poetic beauty. They are the driving force behind the rich radiance of its poetic metaphors and the magical music of its verses; they are the form of the poem's matter, it is they which animate and kindle the poet's sublime fantasy; it is they which lend the vision its true form and with it the power to move us and enchant us. Firm in that belief, we conclude this part of our investigation with Dante's apostrophe to Fantasy:

> O imaginativa che non rube
> Talvolta si di fuor, ch'om non s'accorge
> Perchè dintorno suonin mille tube,
> Chi move te, se il senso non ti porge?
> Moveti lume che nel ciel s'informa
> Per sè o per voler che giù lo scorge.

> [O fantasy, that at times so snatch us out of ourselves that we are conscious of nothing, even though a thousand trumpets sound about us,
> Who moves you, if the senses set nothing before you? A light moves you which takes its form in heaven, of itself, or by a will that sends it down.]

The content of the *Comedy* is a vision; but what is beheld in the vision is the truth as concrete reality, and hence it is both real and rational. Consequently the language which communicates the truth is at once that of a record and of a didactic treatise. It is the language of a record, not of an epic: for the fantasy is not free to roam in a distant legendary land; rather, the speaker is a witness who has seen everything with his own eyes and is expected to give an accurate report: he has seen something more miraculous than any legend, and he does not say: "Muse, name to me the man . . . ," or "Once upon a time King Arthur held a royal feast at the Pentecost"; he begins: "In the middle of my life I found myself in a dark forest." The language is also that of a didactic treatise, for what is beheld in the vision is Being or truth; it is always rationally ordered, and until close before the threshold of the actual *visio Dei* it is accessible to disciplined rational discourse.

An almost severely accurate record of events and dogmatic instruction, rational to the point of pedantry—these are the determining factors in the style of the *Comedy*. They are never wholly distinguishable and as a rule they are thoroughly blended; there is no happening that does not illustrate the doctrine and no teaching that is not based on concrete happening. But fantasy, the essential element of poetry—and that applies equally to the epic fantasy which freely links, transforms, spins out events drawn from a remote legendary sphere, and to the lyrical fantasy which spurns rational limits in order to arouse and give free voice to that which knows no limits, to feeling—has lost its autonomy in the *Comedy*. The poem contains incomparable examples of both epic and lyrical fantasy, of richly diversified happening, and of deep feeling, eloquently expressed. But neither one is free or dominant. The event is recounted briefly and succinctly, seldom taking the form of a tale and never of a rambling legend; among others of its kind it always preserves its strictly appointed place and never ceases to be subordinate to a higher principle; and the strongest feeling is always described with precision, in just so much space, as though measured out; it is so wholly contained in the lines devoted to it, so quickly and definitively disposed of, that all lyrical resonance is cut off and it is impossible to linger on it.

# The Vistas in Retrospect

*Charles S. Singleton*

Our "recovery" of the Middle Ages in this more profound and intimate sense has been truly remarkable in the two-thirds of our century that now have run their course. We have learned, and are always learning better, to do what must always be done if any age of our past is to be understood *from within*: namely to transfer ourselves (*trasferirci*: the phrase, as we know, is Machiavelli's in a famous letter) to project ourselves imaginatively and sympathetically, into positions *within* medieval thought and feeling, and then, analogously, to project ourselves into those corresponding positions within a poem that is the living incarnation of them and their supreme expression in form. Recovery of an age, in this sense, and recovery of a poem, have, quite naturally, gone hand in hand.

Some day perhaps we shall realize that one of the most important inquiries that might be undertaken in Dante studies would be a searching review of the way in which we lost touch, so to say, with Dante and his time—and with his poem; for, to go over the record of our *loss* in this respect, and of the way it came about through the centuries, would mean to come into sharper awareness of what we must do to recover his time and his "world," and his poem that mirrors his time and world. To be sure, I suppose that in a general and vague sort of way we do understand how it happened, and will admit, to put it briefly, that this came about simply because a *nonchalance du salut* increasingly prevailed in our hearts and minds after Dante—indeed so strikingly soon after Dante. The phrase is Pascal's and in it he pronounced judgment on Montaigne and the spirit of his *Essais*;

---

From *Atti del congresso internazionale di studi danteschi, 20–27 (aprile 1965)*. © 1965 by Charles S. Singleton.

but we know it for a very useful phrase, one that we can apply also to Boccaccio and the spirit of his *Decameron*, for instance, close as Boccaccio and his human comedy are to Dante and his *Comedy* in time. And yet how incredibly distant in spirit! Giovanni of the *quiet heart*: perhaps if we translate Pascal's phrase to that and speak of *nonchalance du salut* as the matter of possessing a *quiet heart*, we shall have an even more useful phrase for saying what happened. For it did indeed come to pass that the unquiet heart of the Christian pilgrim, as we find it termed on the first page of a famous book of *Confessions*, gradually grew quiet in an age we call a Renaissance and quieter yet in another age we call the Enlightenment, and put us more and more out of touch with a Middle Age and its fundamental modes of thought and feeling, its pulse and heartbeat. The unquiet heart of the pilgrim, as Augustine means it, was in fact the living source and basis of the whole *symbolic* structure of medieval thought, of its *polysemous* ways, whereby, as we know, the event of an Exodus, as recounted in Holy Scripture, can be seen to point beyond itself (and point for *us*, since that Book was written for *our* salvation) to other inner events in the life of the individual Christian, pilgrim that he is in this life, as he seeks to depart from Egypt or a dark wood, and turn toward the Promise or the light of a Sun of Justice. God's Book is addressed to the unquiet heart, to a reader who has *chalance* of salvation and who knows that a journey to Him, a journey of the mind and heart, is an open possibility here and now, in this life—provided He, in His mercy, turn to a man and help him along the way. And yet, so soon after the *Comedy*, a mere generation, comes the *Decameron* with its "quiet heart," and a Boccaccio who no longer understands Dante's allegory of the unquiet heart, but reads him if he had written in the "quiet-heart" allegory of the pagans.

It is, all in all, a far longer story than may be told here, of course. But, in putting the matter thus in terms of *chalance du salut*, I am aware that I run the risk of being misunderstood: as if I were preaching a sermon of conversion to my present audience, trying to be a Savonarola here before you. I make haste, therefore, to clarify this matter—though what I have already said in terms of Machiavelli's *trasferirsi* might be clear enough. I do not speak of the necessity of a religious conversion in order to recover an age and a poem, but I do speak of a necessary conversion of our *imagination*, of that conversion, in fact, that each and every reader, if he is to have experience of *any* poem, must undergo, in the act of sympathetic reading. Perhaps I shall be clearer if I put it this way: it is quite conceivable to me (though I confess I do not know that it has ever happened) that an out-and-out atheist might achieve an understanding reading of the *Divine Comedy* through a willing suspension of disbelief and an imaginative and sympathetic *surrender* to the experience of the poem. Or I might turn the matter around and put it this way: it is also conceivable to me that a reader of the most ardent religious temper might, for purposes of gaining full experience of Boccaccio's hundred tales, convert himself temporarily to the quiet heart which that book requires of its reader, and achieve the *nonchalance du salut* which the whole framework of the *Decameron*, with its dedication to the idle ladies, is in fact trying to bring about from the outset.

## II

Dante's *Comedy*, as we were saying [elsewhere], is Christocentric, Christ shines through its center, if center be taken to mean that point in the journey where the wayfarer passes from Virgil's guidance to Beatrice's; for Beatrice's advent at the summit of the mountain bears the signs and signals of Christ's Advent, if we are alert readers and see those signals: *Hosanna, Benedictus qui venis*, and the image of a rising Sun and a cloud of glory and the Resurrection of the flesh as it shall be in the end, at the Judgment. All of which, of course, must be followed out in the living texture of the poetic event there at the summit to be fully *actualized* in our reader's experience, as we were putting it; but when it is, we come to see that in Beatrice's advent Christ's Advent is "remembered" in its triple dimension in time: as it was in history, as it is in the individual soul, and as it shall be at the Judgment. And we also come to see that three lines of meaning are thrown out from these three signals of three dimensions in time: thrown out and *back down the line of the action*. And in these lines two configurations of a movement toward justice are seen, the justification of an individual, the "whichever man" of a moral allegory, as he attains to this summit, to inner justice and Grace; and justification, in history, of the *civitas peregrinans in terris*, as it was brought to universal justice under the Romans, to which Christ came as to a place prepared; while the promise of a higher justice is thrown out and upwards, in anagoge, by the signal in the imagery of the Resurrection and of Christ's future advent.

All of which is now part of the published record of our experience of the poem at this great pivotal point, and I may, on this occasion, turn to that other point which I have also called a pivot, the end of Inferno and the beginning of Purgatory, and inquire if a similar experience does not await us there. Do we not see how Christ shines forth there too? And do not broad patterns of meaning become visible there also, in past and future time? How our reading of the poem might come into better focus on the answers to these questions I shall try to suggest in this paper, to see how we may recover a major pattern of meaning that apparently we have lost, judging from the silence of our commentaries and our *lecturae*. I do not mean that the details, the single elements, of the pattern, have not received their gloss *as details* along the unfolding line of the poem. Indeed, as I review them, it will at once be clear to all that it would be a presumptuous absurdity to claim that they have not been noticed in our *commenti*. Our gloss of the *details* of the pattern that I would focus on has been ample enough, perhaps, as we move from verse to verse, but we seem not to have seen these as details of a *pattern*, of a great vista of meaning that opens up in retrospect at the pivotal point I have named. And, as usual, it is the way in which this *happens* in the poem that interests us, who seek full experience of it as a *happening* in form.

Since the pattern of which I speak will be visible only from the end and "in memory," so to say, it seems well to recognize at once that Dante's poem may not claim a monopoly in the matter of this kind of disclosure of meaning. A novel (and it need not be a novel by Marcel Proust) or any narrative structure, must of necessity disclose its meaning gradually, and that meaning so disclosed is always understood in retrospect. Or, to be even simpler about a rather obvious fact, we may take the example of a single declarative sentence made up of so many words in sequence, and we might marvel or wonder, even as St. Augustine did, over our faculty of memory, how in memory we understand that simple sentence. For each word in turn is uttered and then is heard no more, ceases to exist as a sound, and so the next, and yet each passes into the memory of the listener and all the words are finally held there in the order of their sequence as uttered words, until the series forms a meaningful whole, and is recognized as complete because, from the end, the recognized completion, that is, the mind's eye can look back over the whole (which no longer exists anywhere save in memory) and comprehend it as a whole.

The example is simple enough to be banal (and clearly what is true of the sentence is true of musical structures, too, or of any meaningful form that unfolds itself in time) but the very simplicity of the example can help us to come into essential focus on the way in which the pattern in retrospect that I would have us see comes into view for us. But can we apply this miniature paradigm of the sentence in this regard to the whole poem and conceive of understanding the whole of it from the end, as we do the sentence? This one may well doubt, I think. Indeed it would seem more than a little presumptuous to assume that any reader, even one who lives with this poem for the better part of his life, would ever be able to comprehend the great structure from its last verse as one does the sentence from its last word. The poem is far too vast and complex a structure for that, and one always has the feeling somehow that it is taking the measure of us at the moment we try to take the measure of it. Indeed I doubt that we need think it even desirable to understand the poem as we would a simple sentence, from the end. For the full experience of the poem in the endless variety of its advancing narrative and its unfolding form is what matters most. That unfolding *is* the poem, the poetry of it is there, in the ever-changing perspective of a form *in fieri*. This is not to say, however, that we are unable, in the case of Dante's *Comedy*, to look back from the end of the experience and hold the whole of it in mind far better than we may do, say, with the *Orlando Furioso*. For the understanding reader of the *Commedia* does, in the end, attain to a vista in retrospect of a total unity and harmony, which is in itself one of the great experiences the poem holds for us. But it is but one experience among others and does not (as if it were some beatific vision) cancel out the many other experiences that are had along the way to the end.

The experience at the end is in a forward-looking focus and a gradual increase of vision until vision fails, and *we* are left looking up, as it were, to the stars, even as at the end of the other two *Cantiche*. We *must* look up, we may not look back. But not so at the two major pivotal points of the action, as I have called them. There we may look back. Indeed signals prompt us to look back, over the way we have come, over the "sentence" (to make use of our miniature paradigm) that we have followed out, and to see, in the broad outline of a journey down and a journey up, the pattern of meaning that has unfolded and may be known from the end.

Perhaps I may be permitted to add to my example of a sentence understood in memory another paradigm for this matter of understanding from the end, which I shall borrow from the second canto of the *Paradiso*, the figure of an arrow's flight, as it is given there in the first term of a simile, to represent the wayfarer's upward flight with Beatrice as he moves with her from the summit of the mountain to the first Heaven of the Moon: and the verses will probably be familiar to all readers for the figure they contain, a figure known as ***hysteron proteron***, "the last first":

> Beatrice in suso e io in lei guardava;
> e forse in tanto in quanto un quadrel posa
> e vola e da la noce si dischiava,
>
> giunto mi vidi

[Beatrice was gazing upward, and I on her, and in the time, perhaps, that a bolt strikes and flies and looses from the catch I saw that I had (arrived)]

(*Paradiso* 2.22–25)

The usual gloss to these verses has it that the figure of the arrow turned about so, the end first, aims to express the great velocity of Dante's upward flight. But this can hardly be so, since the arrow would not fly any faster whether viewed end first or not. Speed is indeed signified by the mere trajectory of an arrow here, if it be shot from any ordinary bow, since Dante presumably moves a great distance in soaring from the summit of the mountain (high as that may be) to the Heaven of the Moon, and covers that distance in the time it would take an arrow to hit its mark, which can, at most, not be very long. But what of the *way* the flight of the arrow is viewed, from the end? Why should it be turned about so? Surely we see that *hysteron proteron* here is expressive of something more important than speed: for it views the movement as teleological movement, as motion caused from the end, or the *telos*: that being the first Heaven, the proximate destination in this case; but it will finally be the last Heaven, where God is, to which all hearts and minds move that enter upon an *itinerarium* to Him.

My interest in this figure of an arrow's flight, at any rate, is in the paradigm it so graphically provides of a way of *seeing from the end*. In these verses no mysterious or supernatural *reversal* of an arrow's flight is implied, of course, nor would any reader be likely to take it so. It is the way the flight of an arrow is *viewed* that impresses us. The poet's eye—and our eye guided by his—looks back, from *a position at the end*, at the target, back over the forward flight of the arrow all the way from its beginning, sees from the end, the *telos*, which means watching a purposive movement complete itself from end to beginning. But if we try to conceive of purposive movement looked upon from the end as being an arrow's actual flight from bowstring to target, we realize that the trajectory of the arrow seen thus in retrospect can only be seen in memory, nowhere else. It has passed to the mind. Like the words of the sentence, the forward movement of the arrow is no more when it comes to "rest" at the target. Indeed, with these simple examples of sentence and arrow in mind, we may understand that all such vistas from the end, when we view them so, must be vistas in memory, and must be in the mind and nowhere else.

By way of these little paradigms now we may come to what I have termed a lost dimension of the poem, one that becomes visible from the pivotal point of the end of *Inferno* and the beginning of *Purgatorio*.

## III

To come into full view of that vista it becomes necessary first to follow out the "words" of its "sentence" (our paradigm will prove useful) in the due order of their sequence as it inscribes itself in our reader's memory, in order then to see from the end, or, to keep our other figure, to see the arrow hit the target, fly through the air, and leave the bowstring—*after* it has already done that. The words of our sentence, that is, the details of the series that I would focus on, are, in the first order of their occurrence in the narrative, so familiar to every reader of the poem, and to everybody in my present audience, that I must ask indulgence for reviewing them here.

The first "word" of the "sentence" comes in canto 5, and is the word "ruina," in a context of verses that could not be more familiar to us all:

> Io venni in luogo d'ogni luce muto,
> che mugghia come fa mar per tempesta,
> se da contrari venti è combattuto.
>
> La bufera infernal che mai non resta,
> mena li spirti con la sua rapina:
> voltando e percotendo li molesta.
>
> Quando giungon davanti a la ruina,
> quivi le strida, il compianto, il lamento;
> bestemmian quivi la virtù divina.

> [I came to a place where all light was mute and where was bellowing as of a sea in tempest that is beaten by conflicting winds. The hellish storm, never resting, seizes and drives the spirits before it; smiting and whirling them about, it torments them. When they come before its fury there are shrieks, weeping and lamentation, and there they blaspheme the power of God.]

Just so do we learn it, and no more of it do we learn here in this second circle of Hell: learn that when the "lussuriosi" are swept before the "ruina," whatever that may mean, their wailing increases. But why should a "ruina," be that what it may here in this circle, cause this to happen on the part of those who subjected their reason to their appetite and sinned in carnal love? Clearly the "ruina" causes increase of pain, of anguish, in them, and is part of their punishment. But to these questions we find no answer here. The poet has plainly left us with a mystery, one that we shall have to hold in our reader's memory and carry along in suspense, awaiting some possible enlightenment from a point further along.

That point comes, as we all recall, seven cantos later, when Virgil and Dante, having succeeded in getting past the Minotaur, descend into the seventh circle of Hell by walking down a kind of landslide which provides a way down the steep; and as he makes his way down this shifting path Dante's living feet dislodge stones, to the amazement of a group of Centaurs who stand watching the two wayfarers descend. Straightway the landslide is called a "ruina" in the verses that describe it and compare it to a famous landslip "di qua da Trento":

> Qual è quella ruina che nel fianco
> di qua da Trento l'Adice percosse,
> o per tremoto o per sostegno manco,
>
> che da cima del monte, onde si mosse,
> al piano è sì la roccia discoscesa,
> ch'alcuna via darebbe a chi su fosse;
>
> cotal di quel burrato era la scesa

[Like the landslip that struck the flank of the Adige on this side Trent on account of earthquake or lack of support, where from the mountain-top from which it started to the plain the rocks are so shattered that they would give some footing for one above, such was the descent of that ravine.]

Then, as Virgil and Dante descend, the master surmises that the latter's thoughts are turning on the "ruina" down which they walk, and himself terming it "ruina," as the narrative had done, says to him:

> "Tu pensi
> forse in questa ruina ch'è guardata
> da quell'ira bestial ch'i' ora spensi.
>
> Or vo' che sappi che l'altra fiata
> ch'i' discesi qua giù nel basso inferno,
> questa roccia non era ancor cascata;
>
> ma certo poco pria, se ben discerno,
> che venisse colui che la gran preda
> levò a Dite del cerchio superno,
>
> da tutte parti l'alta valle feda
> tremò sì, ch'i' pensai che l'universo
> sentisse amor, per lo qual è chi creda
>
> più volte il mondo in caòs converso;
> ed in quel punto questa vecchia roccia
> qui e altrove tal fece riverso."

> ["Thou are thinking, perhaps, of this ruined cliff that is guarded by that bestial rage I quenched just now; know then that the other time I came down here into the nether Hell this rock had not yet fallen. But surely, if I reckon rightly, it was a little before he came who carried off from Dis the great spoil of the highest circle that the deep, foul valley trembled on every side so that I thought the universe felt love, by which, as some believe, the world has many times been turned to chaos; and at that moment this ancient rock, here and elsewhere, was thrown down thus."]

Qui "e altrove." The reminder is pointed, and the careful reader will not fail to catch the signal in the "altrove" and recall the "ruina" of canto 5: recall it, to let all that we learn from Virgil about this second "ruina" cast light upon that first. For we are indeed told important things now about the second. For one thing, Virgil can report that this break-down of the cliff was not here when he passed through Hell before, which, as he has told us, was shortly after his death (in 19 B.C.), that is, just before Christ came to harrow Limbo, where Virgil was; and, for another, that the whole cavity of Hell was shaken by an earthquake that caused the "old rock" of that foul valley to collapse over this seventh Circle, here and "altrove," i.e., in the second Circle, we gather. Virgil, as a pagan in Limbo, knew nothing of the Crucifixion, of course, and can report that at the time the tremor shook Hell he thought the universe must be feeling love and (according to the speculation of the pagan Empedocles) reverting to chaos because of that. But our own Christian memories, which the poet knows he can count on, at once tell us what the real occasion and cause of this quake must have been, for, given Virgil's timing, it can surely be no other than that reported by Matthew, the quake that shook the earth when Our Lord died on the Cross—shook the earth and *rent the rocks*, according to the Gospel:

> et ecce velum templi scissum est in duas
> partes a summo usque deorsum et terra mota
> est et petrae scissae sunt.
>
> (Matt. 27:51)

And the rocks of Hell were also rent, apparently. Accordingly, from what Virgil can report, the two "ruine" seen so far were caused by the tremor that shook the whole earth when Christ gave up the ghost on the Cross. We can look back, even from this point, now, and wonder why the louder wailings of the "lussuriosi" as they pass the first "ruina"? Might it be that that serves as an eternal reminder to them of Christ's death and of the act of supreme Love which was manifested in that death (and these are great lovers all!)? We note that Virgil, in thinking to account for the quake, conceived its cause in terms of love, universal love, even if mistakenly, according to a pagan view. One thing is clear: "ruina" in canto 5 stands in a context of love, of carnal, sinful love. Could it be that these lovers feel increase of anguish and remorse when they are reminded of the Love that opened the door of salvation to all, either to those who had believed in the Redeemer who was to come, or those who believed in Him who had come ("i passuri o i passi piedi")? Looking back from what we learn of the second "ruina" encountered, we seem to glimpse some such meaning in the increase of punishment which the first causes these sinners. Even so, it still stands in a light of mystery.

"Altrove" may imply a plural of more than two, perhaps several, points at which the rock of Hell was rent, but this we do not come to know until, nine cantos later, we approach just such another point. We hear of it first in canto 21, from the devil Malacoda who, as we then see shortly thereafter, was actually deceiving Virgil in speaking of a "ruina" ahead, and was tricking him into proceeding along the bank of the "barattieri" with that fearful escort of devils he marshalls for the two travelers; for, as every reader remembers, Malacoda tells Virgil that the bridge of stone, which was formed by the "scoglio" along which he and Dante had proceeded across the several "bolge" thus far, is broken down over the next ditch (and this is true), but that the bridge formed by the next "scoglio" is not broken down (and this, as Virgil learns to his own embarrassment, is a lie); and, most significantly, in telling Virgil this, the devil speaks of the time when the collapse of the bridge occurred:

> Ier, più oltre cinqu'ore che quest'otta,
> mille dugento con sessanta sei
> anni compiè che qui la via fu rotta.

> [Yesterday, five hours later than now, completed a thousand, two hundred and sixty-six years since the road here was broken.]

"Qui" means over the next ditch, the sixth; and Malacoda is lying as noted. But nothing, in the three verses we have cited, or in their context, suggest that his dating of the breakdown of the bridge is anything but true. And indeed all readers are aware of the importance of the single terzina he utters here. First of all, what he tells us by it confirms (when we have done a bit of simple arithmetic) what we had already learned from Virgil to be the time when the rocks in Hell were rent, for his dating of that event points to the same time and cause: to that same quake which produced the other two "ruine." But Malacoda is far more precise than Virgil had been about the time of it, reckoning, as he does, down to the very hour: "yesterday, five hours later than this hour, 1266 years ago." And in our Christian memories we know what such a reckoning must mean, for Our Lord died on March 25, thirty-four years after the date of the Incarnation, that is, at the age of thirty-three and three months form His birth.

Then, two cantos further on, when Virgil and Dante escape from their escort of devils by sliding down the bank of the next "bolgia," the sixth, they find themselves among the hypocrites, who go their slow and painful round clad in leaden cloaks; and see stretched across the floor of the ditch a figure crucified with three stakes upon the ground in such a way that the heavy hypocrites must "weigh themselves" upon it each time they pass in their eternal round. This is Caiaphas, the arch-hypocrite whose false words counseled Christ's death on the Cross. Virgil marvels over him, for not only was he not here when Virgil passed this way before, but the manner and reason of his punishment, a crucifixion, surpasses Virgil's understanding. But we again, in our Christian memories, understand full well the reason and the justness of that punishment (and of the similar punishment of Annas who, we are told, is likewise crucified upon the floor further on in the circling ditch.

The sixth "bolgia" is thus seen to have a special connection with the Crucifixion; and if what Malacoda has told us proves indeed to be true, namely that even *one* of the bridges across this "bolgia" is broken down, then that seems to point up such a connection as particularly fitting. Were the rocks not rent in a circle where love, bad love, was punished? Why not here, where Caiaphas is crucified?

But Virgil must now learn that the devil is a liar and that the next bridge is not intact over the ditch, as Malacoda had said it was, but lies as a "ruina" (it is clearly termed that) which spills down the bank and into the ditch. And we readily conceive that the bridge of the other *scoglio* which the devil had said was broken down, is indeed such a ruin as this one, and that all the bridges over the circle of the hypocrites must lie as "ruine" in its bottom—though this is merely implied by the two instances we know of.

Nor, if such be the case, can we come to this greatest of the ruins caused by the earthquake at Christ's death without thinking of course of the other two. We know now of *three* ruins, three places where the rock of Hell was rent, and that number is scarcely ever without significance in this poem. Indeed, we may now glance back over the series and note a certain symmetry in the spacing of these ruins: the first is in the second circle of Hell, but that second circle is to be counted as the *first* of upper Hell, if we mean the area where *actual* sins are punished. Then the second ruin is over the first circle of lower Hell, which the seventh is, as explained in canto 11. And the third ruin is *almost* at the center of *Malebolge*, the eighth Circle of Hell, which is, in fact, the *central* circle of the three that make up lower Hell. And we observe that, strikingly enough, it is not the third *ruin* which is at the exact center of lower Hell, (i.e., the fifth "bolgia" of ten) but that it is Malacoda's *reckoning of the time* that comes at that exact center. Which clearly suggests that the timing he makes has somehow a central importance (and we shall see how).

To view the series of three "ruine" now in terms of understanding the simple sentence we had before us as paradigm, we may say that they stand in a most meaningful sequence in our reader's memory—and we may look back upon them from the third as from the end of the "sentence" (for the third "ruina" proves to be last that we are given to see in Hell). All are evidence of that rending of the rocks of Hell in the great moment of our Christian calendar when the Saviour died on the Cross. Hell thus bears witness to that Death which is our salvation from the second death: three "ruine" mark off that moment in the rock of Hell, register there three eternal reminders of it.

In his Letter to Cangrande, Dante styled his literal subject "the state of souls after death"; and remembering a distinction of differing dimensions of structure which that phrase can suggest, we may say that the three "ruine" are a part of that "state." They are there, they would be there, even if no living man ever passed this way to behold them—even if there were no such journey as his through Hell. Thus, as we look back over the series of three ruins and view the "sentence" they form, we know that we see them as an objective feature of the very structure of Hell and wholly meaningful as such. In them, as reminders, the Death on the Cross shows forth, the rock of Hell bears witness to that Death three times over. And we see now how, by looking back from beyond it, from the "end," we come to understand the first "ruina," in canto 5, where it was only a mysterious word when we first encountered it.

Now the three "ruine" as a feature of Hell are so well known to all readers that again I feel I must apologize for taking so much time to review them. But it seemed necessary to recall precisely the way in which the gradual disclosure of a line of meaning happens in the poem, for this, in miniature, is typical of the whole unfolding "revelation" of the structure along its narrative line.

In which connection (and since we have thought, and are thinking, of what our *commenti* to the poem do, or do not do, to illuminate it for us) I would raise a question which will also serve to clinch my point here in yet another way. What, I will ask, should those who gloss this poem for us, verse by verse, tell us, the reader, when we come to the first "ruina" in canto 5? That it comes as the merest word there and stands in darkest mystery, we have noted. Shall the *commento* proceed to clarify the mystery of it for us, then, by drawing upon knowledge of what lies ahead, upon the illumination that will come in retrospect? Should our *chiosatore* give us, in canto 5, a long gloss to explain all that we are eventually to know about the "ruine" of Hell, the time of their occurrence and their cause?

I can only hope that I am not alone in this learned company of "dantisti" in feeling that to such questions the answer must be a most emphatic no. Have we no respect for the mystery of a poem? Shall we anticipate a poem's ways of disclosing meaning, when the manner of that disclosure is the very life and essence of the *poetry*? Is there a surer way to defeat a poem, to keep it from *happening* as the poet intended it to do, than to barge in thus and tell the reader what he is only to know in the unfolding, and is only to understand from the end? Again, if you will bear with me, I find our example of a sentence useful. The "ruina" in canto 5 is the first word of a "sentence" which proves to be made up of three "words" when it completes itself in canto 23. Now to intervene at this the first word with a full gloss of the "sentence" is like hearing the first word of a sentence (out of metaphor) and interrupting, then and there, to explain what that word will mean when the other words that make up the sentence shall have been uttered. And yet our commentaries do this constantly: we have only to think of the three beasts of canto 1 to remember very well how little respect for the form of a poem and a gradual revelation of meaning through form most of our *commenti* display. The usual gloss to the three beasts in canto 1 attempts to give them names at once, names that are only disclosed as properly theirs by the unfolding form, far down the line from that first canto. And so forth.

What then (if I may go on about this particular problem for a moment) is our *chiosatore* to do? How can he respect the form? The answer seems clear: he must devise ways of commenting on the "sentences" of the poem from their "ends," must find ways of looking back over meaningful sequences of meaning from where understanding is possible, namely, from where these "wholes" may be seen as wholes, in retrospect. At such points his gloss, or sometimes his excursus, must invite the reader to stand for a moment and look back with him over these lines of disclosure, these vistas in memory, as they complete themselves. Or perhaps it is again useful to remember the flight of the arrow viewed from the moment it rests at the target. That seems finally the best paradigm of all. But I would now leave this series of three "ruine," all reminders of Christ's Death on the Cross, and pass to a far broader pattern or "sentence" which arises, as we shall see, out of these ruins and reminders, to provide us finally with that great vista in memory which in my beginning I said would open up to view, open up, that is, from the pivotal point which the end of the *Inferno* and the beginning of the *Purgatorio* proves to be.

## IV

This larger "sentence" has its point of origin in the time reference given by Malacoda, when from him we learn the day and the hour the rocks of Hell were rent, for his reckoning of the time of the quake with respect to the exact hour in Hell when he is speaking these words to Virgil proves to be the *one* explicit reference and the *one* fixed point of reference by which the time of the journey through Hell is disclosed. To be sure, in line with our reflection on glossing the poem above, most of our commentaries will have told the reader, in the notes to canto 1 or 2 or 3, that Dante enters Hell on Good Friday evening of the year 1300, and thus will have supplied him with what he was supposed to wait to have revealed to him (or so the poet seems to have wished it) as far along as canto 21 and the midpoint of lower Hell (and there from a devil)—dispelling thus the darkness and mystery of a matter that a gradual disclosure is to illuminate. Indeed, the gloss to canto 1 or 2 or 3 may even have taken the reader through the question as to whether the year is really 1300 or 1301 and, in this case or that, whether the day is an ideal Good Friday or an actual Good Friday, and if so, on which of several calendars, and whether it is March 25 or April 8, etc. But I have had my say about what I think of such procedures.

As the poet wished it, the reader is to come into awareness of the time of the journey, the days of the year and hours of the day (and so know just when it is that the wayfarer enters Hell) by looking back on this matter down the line of the three "ruine," all caused by the earthquake at Christ's death, back down that line, and on past it to what he was told in canto 1, namely, that it was spring and a season of bright hope when the wayfarer tried to climb the mountain, and that it was at dusk on the day when he entered Hell, with Virgil as his guide: so much then, and no more. That is, from canto 21, looking back over a series of three reminders of our Lord's death on the Cross, the reader is expected to see, from Malacoda's reckoning of the time the third occurred, to come into his *first* and full awareness that it was, in fact, on the anniversary of that evening when the rocks were rent and our Saviour gave up the ghost on the Cross that the wayfarer and his guide entered through the portal of Hell; for back down this retrospective vista of meaning the one fact is framed that is as an arrow leaving the bowcord (as will be seen from the end) in a trajectory that could not be richer in meaning for each and every Christian reader. For through the realization that this *itinerarium* began in such a moment, are we not all prompted to consider how fitting it was, and is, that any journey to God, the journey of "whichever man" to God, should begin at just such a time? But we, you or I, cannot begin our journey in the year 1300 or on any such precise date as, say, March 25 of that year, as the usual commentary, in its mistaken procedure, would have us know the time to be, there at the beginning of this man's journey, and thereby close the door of allegory to us. For this journey can be ours as an open possibility (in allegory) only if the beginning of it is not too precisely disclosed at the beginning, but only later, and then as framed in and through the "mystery" that we have followed out, a mystery that involves us all. In like manner is the name of the wayfarer withheld until it must "of necessity be registered," and by then the poem may be said to have completed two-thirds of its course. Even so in the matter of disclosing the time: where Malacoda gives us the reckoning, we are, by a count of the cantos of *Inferno*, just two-thirds of the way along the journey through Hell.

It was dusk, we remember, when the wayfarer entered Hell. Then beyond that point the poet gave certain time references which, as we see now, have accurately clocked the journey for us, so that counting back from Malacoda's reckoning, it is possible for us to know what the hour and the day and the year was when this journey began: for all now rests on a single fixed point of references, on the time of Christ's death on the Cross. We are looking back down the dimension of *journey* now, not of "state of souls"; and what I shall continue to call a "sentence" has its beginning in our knowledge now that it was Good Friday evening at dusk in the year 1300 when the journey began. But where does this "sentence" end? Not with Malacoda obviously, nor at the point where the wayfarers finally stand before Satan, for neither Satan, nor the bottom of Hell, is any positive terminus of the journey, but Virgil immediately declares that they must be on the way, for the way ahead is long, that they have now seen all of Hell. The way is indeed long, for it passes through the earth, and so viewed from our hemisphere, may be seen as one *descent*. Then beyond the fixed point of reference which Malacoda has given us in canto 21, yet other references are offered us so that we are finally able to say, when Virgil and Dante stand before Satan, that it is around six o'clock on the evening of Good Saturday. Then, when they have proceeded down Satan's body through the center of the earth (much to Dante's perplexity) and have come to stand on a little sphere of rock that is somewhat past the center, they are to be thought of as standing under the *southern* Hemisphere now, so that Virgil, telling the hour for the first time with reference to the position of the Sun, can explain that in this new hemisphere it is twelve hours earlier, that their "clock," so to speak, has been set back that much. Accordingly we are to conceive of the two wayfarers as beginning their long upward climb from that point, not on Good Saturday evening, but on Good Saturday morning around 7:30 [A.M.]; from which point on we are left to gather, from the rapid narrative, how much time is required for the climb out of Hell, and to see finally that this is equal to the time it took for the descent to the bottom. The two wayfarers issue forth from Hell, as we know, (know, not from the end of *Inferno*, but from canto 1 *Purgatorio*) just before dawn, which must mean, by this clocking, Easter Sunday morning.

Only in the first canto of Purgatory do we learn this, so that the time sentence we have followed out actually extends to Easter Sunday there, to an hour just before dawn. The awareness of that fact could not be more meaningful to us. Here too all signals point to resurrection, to newness of life. Here are "better waters" for the poet's ship to course, which now leaves "dead poesy" behind. And now, looking back, from the rich cluster of all these signals to the word "tomba" as it came toward the end of the climb forth from Hell, we see it take on a special significance. There it meant Satan's tomb, to be sure. But when the wayfarer issues forth from that tomb on an Easter Sunday morning just before dawn, the Christian reader can hardly fail to find a good deal of meaning in that fact.

Clearly all signs here point to a fresh beginning, the beginning that Resurrection can and must signify. And gradually, as day comes on and we realize (what we did not know with the last verse of *Inferno*) that the place at which we have come out to see the stars again is the shore of an island that is also a mountain—and a mountain that is to be climbed—and we know too, of course, that this must be Purgatory, since this is that second realm where the human spirit is purged—there begins to open to our view a most striking correspondence between this scene and the scene of canto 1 *Inferno*. The mountain which the wayfarer had tried in vain to climb at the beginning, in the prologue scene, is now seen to have been the prefiguration of this mountain, which rises before Dante and Virgil and which surely will now be successfully climbed. The sun will show the way, as Cato, guardian of these cliffs, tells them—and we shall hardly fail to remember the Sun on the prologue scene, a planet said to lead every man aright by whatever path. But, before the ascent of the mountain begins, Virgil, being so directed by Cato, must lead the living man to the lowest margin of the shore where rushes grow in the soft mud, and must there gird him with one of those "humble plants," which yield to the buffetting of the wind and waves and so can grow there where no other plant could survive. The rush is the symbol of humility, of course. The wayfarer must don the girdle of humility before he can ascend the mountain. That girdle will be his "golden bough," will give him access to this second realm and to successful ascent.

All our commentaries to this canto appear to agree on the symbolic significance of the rush—and how could they fail to do so, with all the pointers the poet has built into the canto to guide them? All see, too, that the verses which describe the girding on of the rush are reminiscent of Aeneas's golden bough, and therefore see the wayfarer's girdle of humility as that which he must have in order to ascend the mountain. The commentaries, that is, look *forward* from this point toward the journey that lies ahead, through the second realm. But we do not find them looking *back* from the girding on of the rush, to see what can be seen in retrospect from that point. Not one of them (to my knowledge) speaks of the rush as the *goal* of the journey through Hell, nor of the way in which such a goal connects with the whole symbolism of a journey that began on Good Friday evening when the wayfarer entered Hell, and that (down that line of "ruine" and the timing of Malacoda which we have followed out) bore at its "center" Christ's death on the Cross; an *itinerarium* which now makes a new beginning, and is rightly viewed as such. But it also is to be seen as an *end*, a terminus, a goal. It is, in fact, the goal of the journey through Hell, and standing at the point of the attainment of it we stand at the *target* of the entire journey through Hell, from which we may watch the "arrow" leave the bowstring and fly the whole trajectory of the "descent" through Hell. And yet that is not quite the way our image had it. If this *is* such a target, then we are supposed, as *hysteron proteron* had it, to watch the arrow strike that target, then fly through the air, then leave the bowstring: we are to see what can only be seen in memory, a revelation in retrospect, the disclosure of a configuration of movement *from the end*. Is such a revelation there to be experienced at this point in the journey?

It is, and most impressively, if our Christian memories hold the pattern, the vista, which the poet's unfolded form (as seen from the target) can now evoke. The timing, Good Friday evening to Easter Sunday morning, and the image of Our Lord's death on the Cross is enough to summon that pattern of meaning to mind now, as we see from the end, if we connect this particular time span of a journey with humility as the goal of that journey.

But how can such a pattern of meaning as may now be seen from this goal fail to be stored up in our Christian memories, there to be evoked, when it is one that is writ so large in Christian doctrine and indeed even so large in a canto of the *Paradiso* (the seventh)? It is the conceptual pattern of a *necessity*, the necessity of *Descent before Ascent*, of Descent to Humility before Ascent can begin, of the necessity of Christ's Descent to the Humility of His death on the Cross, in order that man might ascend to salvation. In all Christian memories, in Dante's time and for a thousand years before his time, the pattern of it is there, so fundamental and central a mystery of the Faith that the poet might feel certain it could not fail to be seen as a central pattern of his poem if he signalled it as we have seen him do. But since he caused Beatrice to expound it to the wayfarer in a canto of the *Paradiso* and thus rendered it explicit in his *Comedy*, we may briefly remind ourselves of the essential argument of it as he has her state it there.

Beatrice must answer a question which the soul of Justinian had aroused in Dante's mind in speaking of two "vendette" to be seen in Christ's death on the Cross. She begins with Adam's sin, which was a sin of pride and, as such, damned Adam and all his progeny; wherefore human kind "lay sick" for many centuries in great error until it pleased the Word of God to descend and assume that human nature which had withdrawn from its Creator through Adam's sin: to descend to death on the Cross. But at this point another question springs in Dante's mind: why did God choose that way of atonement? And now Beatrice must make a new beginning: Man is "disfranchized" by sin, she explains, and falls from God-given dignity as from Paradise (the Earthly Paradise from which Adam "fell"), and man may not regain that lost dignity (and Paradise) unless he renders full satisfaction for his sin. Now in Adam's sin our *human nature* sinned totally (peccò tota), and man could not atone for such a sin because he was unable, of himself, to descend low enough in order to compensate for the willful ascent in pride that was Adam's sin:

> Non potea l'uomo ne' termini suoi
> mai sodisfar, per non poter ir giuso
> con umiltate obediendo poi,
>
> quanto disobediendo intese ir suso.

[Man could never, within his limits, give satisfaction, for he could not go so low in humility, by a later obedience, as, by disobedience, he had thought to go high.]

Beatrice has thus brought the argument regarding Adam's sin and the impossibility of man's atonement for that sin into the focus of an ascent and a descent: an ascent that was sinful and had to be atoned for by a descent, which man was unable to make by his own power. And we recall how the argument proceeds from there: the word of God descended for man, the only begotten Son of God descended to the humility of the Incarnation, of Death on the Cross and Descent to the Tomb (and Descent to Hell, for the Harrowing). But of these "humiliations" it was Death on the Cross that was the supreme "Descent to Humility"; and it was this Descent that opened the door to our salvation, that we might ascend, even as Himself did ascend on the third day, on a Sunday just before dawn, which we celebrate as Easter on our Christian calendar. Thus precisely the time between Good Friday evening and Easter Sunday morning is the time of that great Descent to Humility which made ascent possible for us.

Had Malacoda not told the time as he did, we should not have known that the journey of the wayfarer through Hell took place during exactly that span of time, and that it thus fulfills a pattern that could not be more fundamental in Christian doctrine, since Christ Himself established it by His own Descent and Ascent, and without which there would have been no journeys to God, either the journey after death or the journey here and now, in our hearts and minds. To be sure the poet could well have found some other way by which to disclose the time of the journey. But he chose the way we have now followed out, in a gradual revelation through form, the way of a revelation that begins with the little word "ruina" planted in canto 5—and in a context of *love*. Out of the word "ruina" a "sentence" grew, which led into the awareness that the rock was rent in three places in Hell when Christ died on the Cross, together with all the meaning we have noted as coming into that line of signification in its unfolding. Then, from that line, came the full awareness that was given us at the end (at the third "ruina") namely, the time of the journey through Hell, and from this, finally, the disclosure that the journey had required exactly the time that had passed between the evening of the Crucifixion and the morning of the Resurrection. And this is known, not at the end of Hell, but at the beginning of Purgatory, where journey is completed in one if its phases and may begin another, where descent (including ascent from a "tomb") is completed and the ascent of the mountain, a successful ascent, may now begin. But it is finally the act of the girding on of the rush as the goal of the journey that can evoke that pattern in Christian memory which opens up to us only in retrospect from the end, which is the attainment of humility. For we should take note that, as the ideal first readers of the poem we must ever try to be, we simply do not know that the journey through Hell *is* a journey to humility until we come to the rush as to such a goal, a humility which Christ's death on the Cross made it possible for us to attain through His Descent and Ascent.

So it is that Christ may be seen to flash at the center of a vista that opens to us in retrospect, from the end. And so it proves to be at the other great pivot which comes at the end of the *Purgatorio*; for there, too, broad patterns of meaning will become visible from the end and goal (Justification), but which are not visible except from the end, looking back. We may, for a last time, remember the arrow which in fact flies from bowstring to target, but which we *see* strike the target and leave the bowstring, and see this only in memory.

Here, then, are dimensions of a poem that appear to have been lost and forgotten in our gloss on a great poetic structure. It is a great pity. And we have speculated as to how and why it happened, and need say no more on that. But, as I was also saying, a Centenary is a time to take stock of how we may recover these vistas and record the recovery in our gloss. Clearly, we shall do so by learning to look back, as well as forward, and to respect the unfolding of a form for the experience of poetry that it holds for us.

The Angel at the gate of Purgatory tells the wayfarer, as he enters, that he must not look back, that he who looks back goes out again. Curiously enough, it would seem that that warning must be turned about for the reader of the poem. He must be told that he who does *not* look back will deny himself vistas in memory, dimensions of meaning, that could not lie closer to the heart of Dante's poetry.

> Chè 'n quella croce lampeggiava Cristo,
> sì ch'io non so trovare essemplo degno.

[For that cross so flamed forth Christ that I can find for it no fit comparison.]

# The Prologue Scene

*John Freccero*

In the shadowy world of the prologue scene, things both are and are not what they seem. For all its familiarity, the scenery seems to have no real poetic existence independent of the allegorical statement it was meant to convey. Moreover, the statement itself, judging from the vast bibliography dedicated to it, is by no means obvious to the contemporary reader. The ambiguous nature of the moral landscape lends itself too readily to arbitrary allegorization, but scarcely to formal analysis. In this respect, the prologue is radically unlike any other part of the *Commedia* and matches the abortive journey of the pilgrim with an apparent failure that is the poet's own.

## The Region of Unlikeness

Any fresh interpretation of the prologue, if it is to contribute measurably to our understanding, must not only attempt an exploration of this well-travelled critical terrain, but also account for the presence, in this most substantial of poetic visions, of a region whose outlines are decidedly blurred. It is such an accounting that I hope to offer. My thesis is that the landscape in which the pilgrim finds himself bears a striking, indeed at times a textual, resemblance to the "region of unlikeness" in which the young Augustine finds himself in the seventh book of the *Confessions*. Moreover, the resemblance is not simply an isolated fact of purely historical interest but is also of some significance for an interpretation of the poem. If

From *Dante: The Poetics of Conversion*. © 1986 by the President and Fellows of Harvard College. Harvard University Press, 1986.

the point of departure, as well as the goal, of Dante's spiritual itinerary deliberately recalls the experience of Augustine in the *Confessions*, then it may be that we are to regard Dante's entire spiritual autobiography as essentially Augustinian in structure.

There is good evidence, apart from the prologue scene, for considering Dante's poem as a spiritual testament in the manner of Augustine. Toward the end of the *Purgatorio*, at a moment that is of great dramatic importance, Beatrice calls to the pilgrim by name:

> in su la sponda del carro sinistra,
> quando mi volsi al suon del nome mio,
> che di necessità qui si registra,
> vidi la donna

> [so on the left side of the chariot—when I turned at the sound of my name, which of necessity is registered here—I saw the lady]
>
> (30.61–64)

Thus, in defiance of medieval convention, the author identifies himself with his protagonist, insisting that he does so "di necessità." The apology is so pointed and the word "necessità" so strong that the passage seems to call for some interpretation. It happens that in the *Convivio* Dante had discussed the circumstances under which it might be considered necessary to speak of oneself. One of his examples, precisely the *Confessions*, is described in terms that seem almost to herald Dante's own "testament":

> Per necessarie cagioni lo parlare di sè è conceduto: e intra l'altre necessarie cagioni due sono più manifeste. L'Una è quando sanza ragionare di sè grande infamia o pericolo non si può cessare . . . L'Altra è quando, per ragionare di sè, grandissima utilitade ne segue altrui per via di dottrina; e questra ragione mosse Agostino ne le sue confessioni a parlare di sè, *chè per lo processo de la sua vita, lo quale fu di* [*non*] *buono in buono, e di buono in migliore, e di migliore in ottimo, ne diede essemplo e dottrina, la quale per sì vero testimonio ricevere non si potea.*

> [Speaking of oneself is allowed, when it is necessary, and among other necessary occasions two are most obvious: One is when it is impossible to silence great infamy and danger without doing so . . . The other is when, by speaking of himself, the greatest advantage follows for others by way of instruction; and this

> reason moved Augustine to speak of himself in his confessions, so that in the progress of his life, which was from bad to good, and from good to better, and from better to best, he furnished example and teaching which could not have been obtained from any other equally truthful testimony.

Critics have usually been content with rather generic explanations for Dante's mention of his own name in the *Purgatorio*, none of which seem as relevant as does this passage in the *Convivio*. It is clear from the beginning of the poem that Dante, like Augustine, intends his work to have exemplary force for "*nostra* vita." Elsewhere Dante makes this explicit, when he says that he writes "in pro del mondo che mal vive" (*Purgatorio* 32.103 [all further references to this text will be abbreviated as *Purg.*]). By naming himself at the moment of his confession, however, he gives to the abstract *exemplum* the full weight of *vero testimonio*, exactly as had St. Augustine before him. Furthermore, the three stages of Augustine's progress are described in the *Convivio* in terms that are partially echoed in the *Paradiso*:

> È Bëatrice quella che sì scorge
> *di bene in meglio*, sì subitamente
> che l'atto suo per tempo non si sporge.

> [It is Beatrice who thus conducts from good to better, so swiftly that her act does not extend through time.]
>
> (10.37–39; italics mine)

The phrase "di bene in meglio," for all of its apparent banality, has technical force, describing the second stage of the pilgrim's progress. Beatrice is virtually defined here as the guide for the second stage of spiritual progress in terms that the *Convivio* had used for the second stage of Augustine's conversion from sinner to saint: "di buono in migliore." It seems likely that in the *Convivio* Dante perceived in Augustine's life the same pattern of conversion that he was later to read retrospectively in his own experience.

Dante speaks of Augustine's life as giving an "essemplo," implying the transformation of personal experience into intelligible, perhaps even symbolic, form. We may observe in passing that it is the exemplary quality of the *Confessions* that distinguishes it from its modern descendants. Augustine's purpose is not to establish his own uniqueness (nor, therefore, innocence, in terms of the standards by which ordinary men are judged), but rather to demonstrate how the apparently unique experience was, from the perspective of eternity, a manifestation of Providence's design for all men. The scholarly debates about the historicity of Augustine's conversion scene, where a real garden in Milan seems to enclose the fig tree of Nathanael (John 1:48), are paralleled by the scholarly debates about Beatrice who, on one hand, was a woman of flesh and blood and yet, on the other hand, seems to be surrounded at Dante's confession scene with unmistakably Christological language and mystery. The point is that in the "then" of experience, grace came in intensely personal form, whereas in the "now" of witness, the particular event is read retrospectively as a repetition in one's own history of the entire history of the Redemption. For both Dante and Augustine the exegetical language seems to structure experience, identifying it as part of the redemptive process, while the irreducibly personal elements lend to the *exemplum* the force of personal witness. Together, *exemplum* and experience, allegory and biography, form a confession of faith for other men.

Conversion, a death and resurrection of the self, is the experience that marks the difference between such confessions and facile counterfeits. In the poem, the difference between the attempt to scale the mountain, the journey that fails, and the successful journey that it prefigures is a descent in humility, a death of the self represented by the journey through hell. Augustine alludes briefly to a similar *askesis* in order to describe his suffering during his stay in Rome:

> And lo, there was I received by the scourge of bodily sickness, and I was going down to Hell, carrying all the sins which I had committed, both against Thee, and myself, and others, many and grievous, over and above that bond of original sin, whereby we all die in Adam. . . . So true, then, was the death of my soul, as that of His flesh seemed to me false; and how true the death of His body, so false was the life of my soul.

The descent into hell, whether metaphorical as in the *Confessions*, or dramatically real as in Dante's poem, is the first step on the journey to the truth. It has the effect of shattering the inverted values of this life (which is death, according to Christian rhetoric) and transforming death into authentic life. The inversion of values is represented in Dante's poem by the curious prefiguration in the first canto of the ascent of the mountain of purgatory: the light at the summit, the mountain itself, the attempted climb. Although the landscape is analogous to the scenery that comes into sharper focus in the second *cantica*, all directions are reversed. What seems up is in fact down; what seems transcendence is in fact descent. Just as the reversed world of Plato's myth in the *Statesman* represented a world of negative values, so the reversed directions of the prologue stand for spiritual distortion. Augustine alludes in the seventh book to Plato's myth when he describes his spiritual world before his conversion as a "regio dissimilitudinis." Although Dante nowhere uses the phrase, he borrowed several of Augustine's topographical details to describe his own spiritual condition.

Augustine's journey to God, like Dante's is immediately preceded by a journey that fails, an attempt at philosophical transcendence in the seventh book of the *Confessions* that amounts to a conversion *manquée*. Lost in what he refers to as a "region of unlikeness," Augustine turns to the light of Platonic vision, only to discover that he is too weak to endure it. He is beaten back by the light and falls, weeping, to the things of this world. At that point in the narrative, the author asks himself why God should have given him certain books of neoplatonic philosophy to read before leading him to Scripture. He answers: "[So that] I might know the difference between presumption and confession; between those who saw where they were to go, yet saw not the way, and the way itself, that led not to behold only, but to dwell in the beatific country." The answer applies exactly to the dramatic purpose of Dante's prologue scene.

There are some excellent reasons for believing Dante meant that first ascent to be read as a purely *intellectual* attempt at conversion, where the mind sees its objective but is unable to reach it. After the pilgrim's fear is somewhat quieted, the poet uses a famous simile:

E come quei che con lena affannata,
   uscito fuor del pelago a la riva,
   si volge a l'acqua perigliosa e guata,
così *l'animo mio, ch'ancor fuggiva,*
   si volse a retro a rimirar lo passo
   che non lasciò già mai persona viva.
Poi ch'èi posato un poco *il corpo lasso,*
   ripresi via per la piaggia diserta,
   sì che 'l piè fermo sempre era 'l più basso.

[And as he who with laboring breath has escaped from the deep to the shore turns to look back on the dangerous waters, so my mind which was still fleeing turned back to gaze upon the pass that never left anyone alive.]

(1.22–30)

Charles Singleton has called our attention to the shift, in these lines, from the flight of an *animo*, the mind of the pilgrim, to the lagging of a *corpo lasso*, a tired body. He was primarily concerned with the radical shift in poetic tone, the beginning of what he referred to as Dante's vision "made flesh." It should be observed that such a shift, besides being a radical poetical departure, has a precise conceptual significance in this context. The whole reason for the failure of all such journeys of the mind resides precisely in that laggard body. The *animo* is perfectly willing, but it is joined to flesh that is bound to fail.

The phrase "l'animo mio ch'ancor fuggiva" has an unmistakable philosophical ring. For one thing, the word *animo* is decidedly intellectual, rather than theological in meaning, quite distinct from the more common *anima*. For another, the phrase recalls, or at least would have recalled to the Church fathers, the flight of the soul from the terrestrial to the spiritual realm according to the Platonists and especially to Plotinus. In the *Enneads*, the latter urges such a flight: "Let us therefore flee to our dear homeland. . . . But what manner of flight is this? . . . it is not with our feet that it can be accomplished, for our feet, no matter where they take us, take us only from one land to another; nor must we prepare for ourselves a team of horses or a ship . . . it is rather necessary to change our sight and look with the inner eye."

This flight of the soul by means of the "interior eye" was destined to have an interesting history. It is perhaps the ancestor of Dante's abortive journey. The point of it is that the Plotinian sage can safely ignore his body in his attempts at ecstasy. By chance this passage was well known in the Middle Ages, having been paraphrased, indeed almost translated, as Pierre Courcelle has shown, by St. Ambrose. In one of his sermons, he adds an interesting detail to Plotinus's exhortation: "Let us therefore flee to our true homeland. . . . But what manner of flight is this? It is not with our bodily feet that it is accomplished, for our steps, no matter where they run, take us only from one land to another. Nor let us flee in ships, in chariots, or with horses that stumble and fall, but let us flee with our minds (*fugiamus animo*), with our eyes or with our interior feet." It is not essential, for my purposes, to suggest that Dante knew this passage, although there is no reason why he could not have. The phrase "fugiamus animo" is not so bizarre that its resemblance to Dante's phrase could establish it as the poet's source. But even if Dante did not know it, the point can still be made that since Ambrose's phrase was meant to sound Platonic, it is likely that the similar phrase, "l'animo mio ch'ancor fuggiva," especially in a context of failure, was likewise meant by Dante to have philosophical rather than theological force.

The division between body and soul was of course a commonplace in ancient "flights" of the soul. For Christians, however, it was not the body per se that constituted the impediment, but rather the fallen flesh. It is not physical reality that the soul must flee, but sin itself. Before looking at

Augustine's view of the dichotomy, it might be well to show how a less original thinker saw the effect of the division of body and soul in the psychology of conversion. Gregory the Great provides us with the kind of theological context in which I believe we are to read the "animo" and "corpo" of Dante's verses. His remarks are suggestive, too, for a reading of the impediments that beset the pilgrim:

> Indeed, one suffers initially after conversion, considering one's past sins, wishing to break immediately the bonds of secular concerns, to walk in tranquillity the ways of the Lord, to throw off the heavy burden of earthly desires and in free servitude to put on the light yoke of God. Yet while one thinks of these things, there arises a familiar delight in the flesh which quickly takes root. The longer it holds on, the tighter it becomes, the later does one manage to leave it behind. What suffering in such a situation, what anxiety of the heart! *When the spirit calls and the flesh calls us back.* On one hand the intimacy of a new love invites us, on the other the old habits of vice hold us back.

This is the "flesh" that was ignored by Plotinus in his rather optimistic invitation to the soul to fly to the Truth.

To return to Ambrose's influential statement for a moment, we notice that he added the detail of the "interior feet" to Plotinus's remarks. No reader of Dante's first canto can fail to remember that after resting his tired body, the pilgrim sets off to his objective "sì che 'l piè fermo sempre era 'l più basso." In another essay, I attempt to explain the meaning of that verse in terms of the allegory of the "interior feet" of the soul. The "piè fermo" signifies the pilgrim's will, unable to respond to the promptings of the reason because of the Pauline malady, characteristic of fallen man whose mind far outstrips the ability of a wounded will to attain the truth. The fallen will limps in its efforts to reach God. Augustine, who uses the theme in a submerged way, was himself very probably Dante's direct source for the image of an *homo claudus*, unable to advance to the summit. In a passage from the *Confessions* paraphrasing precisely the Plotinian, then Ambrosian passage, Augustine insists upon the inability of a crippled will to complete the journey. He does so with an extended comparison of the movement of the limbs with the movement of the will:

> I was troubled in spirit, most vehemently indignant that I entered not into Thy Will and Covenant, O my God, which all my bones cried out unto me to enter, and praised it to the skies.

> And therein we enter not by ships, or chariots, or feet, nor move not so far as I had come from the house to that place where we were sitting. For, not to go only, but to go *in* thither was nothing else but to will to go, but to will resolutely and thoroughly; not to turn and toss, this way and that, *a maimed and half-divided will, struggling, with one part sinking as another rose.*

In this magnificent passage, Augustine uses Platonic words and turns them against the Platonists. The goal is not some world of Ideas, but the covenant of Jehovah. Moreover, the problem is not of the body as a purely physical impediment, but rather of the fallen and crippled will, shortcomings the Platonists had not considered. As Augustine was unable to achieve the ecstasy of the Platonists, so Dante's pilgrim is unable to reach the truth of the mind with a will that "sempre era 'l più basso." The parallel is close enough to suggest on Dante's part a conscious evocation.

Apart from the parallels between Dante's journey and Augustine's with respect both to the need for the journey and to the fatal flaws in the wayfarers, there are also parallels to be drawn with regard to the objective. The light of God, even as perceived with the neoplatonic eyes of the soul, proves too much for Augustine in the seventh book of his *Confessions*: "And Thou didst beat back the weakness of my sight, streaming forth Thy beams of light upon me most strongly, and I trembled with love and awe: and I perceived myself to be far off from Thee, in the region of unlikeness, as if I heard this Thy voice from on high: 'I am the food of grown men, grow, and thou shalt feed upon Me.'" In spite of his repeated attempts to reach the light, the weight of "fleshly habit" causes him to fall back, "sinking with sorrow into these inferior things—*ruebam in ista cum gemitu.*" Dante might well have been remembering that phrase when he described himself as beaten back by the wolf: "i' rovinava in basso loco." Augustine seems to hear the voice of God in the light that he sees. The synaesthetic effect is rhetorically appropriate in this interior journey, for all of the senses here stand for movements of the mind, moved by a single God in all of His various manifestations. It may not be purely coincidental that Dante also insists on a mystical synaesthesia in his experience. After he is beaten back to the dark wood, he describes it as the place "dove 'l sol tace." The implication is that the light which he saw before spoke to him with a voice that was divine.

Pierre Courcelle has traced Augustine's "vain attempts at Plotinian ecstasy" back to their neoplatonic sources. What emerges clearly from his study is that the ancients saw no need for a guide on such a journey. Plotinus explicitly says that one requires self-confidence to reach the goal, rather than a guide. This self-confidence was precisely what Augustine interpreted as philosophical pride, the element that in his view vitiated all such attempts. His own interior journey begins with an insistence upon his need for help: "And being thence admonished to return to myself, I entered even into my inward self, *Thou being my Guide*: and able I was, for *Thou wert become my Helper*. And I entered and beheld with the eye of my soul (such as it was), above the same eye of my soul, above my mind, the Light Unchangeable." Christian virtue, unlike Socratic virtue, is more than knowledge and vice is more than ignorance. The Platonic conversion toward the light is doomed to failure because it neglects to take account of man's fallen condition. To put the matter in Platonic terms, the pilgrim must struggle even to reach the cave from which Plato assumed the journey began. That struggle, the descent in humility, helps remove the barrier that philosophy leaves intact. God's guidance, represented dramatically in the poem by the pilgrim's three guides, transforms philosophical presumption into Christian confession. St. Bernard, an outspoken critic of philosophical presumption, speaks of the opposition between humility and pride in the itinerary to God. His remarks serve as an excellent illustration of how familiar Augustine's struggle was in the Middle Ages and of how readily the struggle lent itself to dramatization in terms that are strikingly like Dante's:

> "Who dares climb the mountain of the Lord or who will stand in His holy place?" . . . Only the humble man can safely climb the mountain, because only the humble man has nothing to trip him up. The proud man may climb it indeed, yet he cannot stand for long. . . . The proud man has only one foot to stand on: love of his own excellence. . . . Therefore to stand firmly, we must stand humbly. So that our feet may never stumble we must stand, not on the single foot of pride, but on the two feet of humility.

There can be scarcely any doubt that Dante's pilgrim climbs the mountain in the same tradition.

The final passage from Augustine's seventh book provides a series of images which offer the closest analogue to the landscape with which Dante begins his poem. The theme is humility, which provides a transition to the eighth book, from attempts at Plotinian ecstasy to the conversion under the fig tree. Speaking of Christ against the philosophers he says:

> They disdain to learn of Him, because He is gentle and humble of heart; for these things hast Thou hid from the wise and prudent, and hast revealed them unto babes. For it is one thing,

> from a wooded mountain-top (*de silvestre cacumine*) to see the land of peace and to find no way thither; and in vain to essay through ways unpassable, opposed and beset by fugitives and deserters, under their captain the lion and the dragon: and another to keep on the way that leads thither, guarded by the host of the heavenly General (*cura caelestis imperatoris*); where they spoil not who have deserted the heavenly army (*qui caelestem militiam deseruerunt*).

The Augustinian phrase, "de silvestre cacumine," may at first seem a trifle remote as an analogue for the "selva oscura," but if we read on in the *Confessions* we find that Augustine elaborates on the description of his former life with an alternate image: "In this so vast wilderness [*immensa silva*], full of snares and dangers, behold many of them I have cut off and thrust out of my heart." Of greater significance is the fact that elements of the former passage echo not only in the first canto of the *Inferno*, but perhaps also in the eighth canto of the *Purgatorio*. In other words, there seem to exist between the two authors not only analogies of detail but also of structure, for in these few lines Augustine distinguishes between success and failure in the journey to God by a series of oppositions that match the opposition between the journey of the prologue and the successful journey that it foreshadows. One need only paraphrase Augustine in Dantesque terms in order to make this apparent: it is one thing to be beset by wild beasts and quite another to be guarded by the "essercito gentile" (*Purg.* 8.22) of the "imperador che là sù regna" (*Inferno* 1.124 [all further references to this text will be abbreviated as *Inf.*]), safe from the chief deserter, "'l nostro avversaro" (*Purg.* 8.95).

A further word must be said here about the most famous image of the prologue scene, that of the "selva oscura." If we are in fact dealing in the prologue with an attempt at transcendence that is neoplatonic in origin, then the temptation is strong to identify Dante's "selva" with the prime matter of Plato's *Timaeus*, the traditional enemy of philosophical flights of the soul. The Greek word for matter, *hylē*, was rendered into Latin as "silva" by Chalcidius and the phrase "silva Platonis" became proverbial in the Middle Ages. Bernardus Silvestris uses the word with a force that sometimes suggests a totally unchristian equation of matter with evil: *silva rigens, praeponderante malitia, silvestris malignitas*. Some critics recently have attempted to associate Dante's "selva" with the Platonic "silva," thereby reviving a gloss that goes back to the Renaissance commentary of Cristoforo Landino. The gloss runs the risk, however, of leading to a serious misunderstanding. In the dark wood, we are not dealing with man's hylomorphic composition, but rather with *sin*. Landino's facile equation, "corpo, cioè vizio" will not do for the "selva," for it obscures the fundamental point of Christianity's quarrel with metaphysical dualism. Ultimately, to obscure the difference between "corpo" and "vizio" is to forget the doctrine of the Incarnation and this Dante was no more likely to forget than was Augustine, who spent much of his life refuting the Manicheans.

Nevertheless, it is possible to show that Dante used the opposition "selva–luce" in exactly the same way that he used the opposition "corpo–animo"; that is, as a Platonic commonplace used to signify a struggle of which the Platonists were unaware. The distinctive characteristic of the dark wood in Dante's poem is not that it is a *selva*, but rather that it is *oscura*, as the following textual parallel reveals:

| | |
|---|---|
| Già m'avean trasportato<br>i lenti *passi*<br>dentro a *la selva antica*<br>tanto, ch'io<br><br>non potea rivedere *ond'*<br>*io mi 'ntrassi*;<br><br>*ed ecco* più andar mi tolse<br>un rio | Nel mezzo del *cammin*<br>di nostra vita<br>mi ritrovai per *una*<br>*selva oscura*<br>. . .<br>Io non so ben ridir com'<br>*i' v'intrai*<br>. . .<br>*Ed ecco,* quasi al cominciar<br>de l'erta |
| Now my slow steps had carried me on into the ancient wood so far that I could not see back to where I had entered it, when lo, a stream took from me further progress<br>(*Purg.* 28.22–25) | Midway in the journey of our life I found myself in a dark wood. . . . I cannot rightly say how I entered it. . . . And behold, near the beginning of the steep<br>(*Inf.* 1.1–2, 10, 31) |

The resemblance can hardly be fortuitous. Dante's descent into hell and his ascent of the mountain of purgatory bring him to a point from which he can begin his climb to the light, his entrance into sanctifying grace, without fear of the impediments that blocked his way before. That new point of departure, the garden of Eden, was the home of man before the fall. Through Adam's transgression, the prelapsarian state of man was transformed into the state of sin. In poetic terms, Adam transformed the *selva antica* into a *selva oscura.* Although the "rio" forever separates the pilgrim from original justice and Matelda, he can, with the help of Beatrice, go far beyond:

> "Qui sarai tu poco tempo *silvano*;
> e sarai meco sanza fine cive
> di quella Roma onde Cristo è romano."

> [Here shall you be short time a forester, and you shall be with me forever a citizen of that Rome whereof Christ is Roman.]
> (*Purg.* 32.100–102)

To say that the pilgrim is a *silvano* is to say that he still inhabits the *selva* of human existence; only in the *selva* darkened by sin, what Dante called "la selva erronea di questa vita," does it become impossible to follow the path to the heavenly city.

Augustine chose to describe the impediments on his journey to the mountain top in terms of the wild beasts of the Psalms, the lion and the dragon. Dante, on the other hand, described them in terms of the three beasts of Jeremiah 5:6. I take these to be the basic wounds to the rational, irascible, and concupiscent appetites suffered by all men as a result of the fall (see [*Dante: The Poetics of Conversion*]). What is of particular poetic interest here is that in the text of Jeremiah, those three beasts are said to be enemies of all the sinners of Jerusalem. The question is, why should the three beasts associated with Jerusalem, the promised land, be the obstacles to the pilgrim in his climb?

The answer, I believe, resides in the fact that the pilgrim's goal is in a sense Jerusalem, or at least the heavenly Jerusalem, although he cannot know that until he reaches it, which is to say, until he assumes the perspective of the poet. Earlier I suggested that both Augustine and Dante used scriptural exegesis in order to structure their experience, superimposing (or discovering, they would insist) a biblical pattern of meaning upon their own history. Thus far I have tried to compare the shadowy world of the pilgrim with Augustine's region of unlikeness. There is nothing shadowy about the interpretative view of the poet, however, for, as Charles Singleton has shown, part of the poet's strategy is to introduce into both the prologue and the *Purgatorio*, superimposed upon the narrative, the *figura* which was considered to be the pattern of conversion. We have already cited the verses that relate the emergence from the dark wood to the crossing of a "passo" through the open sea. Again, as the pilgrim struggles up the slope of the mountain, the poet refers to him as being in a "gran diserto," as far from woods or water as can be imagined. Finally, when the wolf blocks the pilgrim's passage, Lucy, looking down from heaven, sees him as though he were standing before a flooded river of death, weeping and unable to cross. In the sea, desert, and river, any medieval exegete would discern the three stages of the exodus of the Jews, en route from Egypt to Jerusalem, the promised land.

In this respect too, Dante probably owed much to the Augustinian tradition. For the representation of his attempts at purely intellectual conversion, Augustine drew upon the traditional neoplatonic motifs of the conversion to the light. At the same time, he reinterpreted those motifs in the light of Revelation. On at least one occasion, the death of Monica, his allusion to the figure of exodus is explicit: "May they [God's servants] with devout affection remember my parents in this transitory light, my brethren under Thee our Father in our Catholic Mother, and my fellow-citizens in that eternal Jerusalem which Thy pilgrim people sigheth after from their Exodus, even unto their return thither." There may be as well an allusion to the exodus in the passage in the seventh book, which seems so important for Dante's representation: "For it is one thing, from the wooded mountain top to see the land of peace and to find no way thither." In the sixteenth century, the passage was annotated with a reference to Deuteronomy 32:48–52, where Moses is permitted by God to see the land of Canaan from the mountain, but not to reach it: "Yet thou shalt see the land before thee; but thou shalt not go thither unto the land which I give the children of Israel."

These references are admittedly too few to enable us to demonstrate that the presence of the figure of exodus is of importance in Augustine's narrative, but if Augustine was merely allusive with respect to the figure, commentators on his work throughout the Middle Ages were explicit. Courcelle's repertory of commentaries on the "region of unlikeness" provides many citations that are suggestive for the interpretation of Dante's prologue scene. Among them are several which specifically relate Augustine's conversion to the traditional biblical figure of conversion. Richard of St. Victor will serve as an example:

> The first miracle was accomplished in the exodus of Israel from Egypt (*In exitu Israel de Aegypto*), the second was in the exodus of Israel from the desert. Who will give me the power to leave behind the region of unlikeness? Who will enable me to enter the promised land, so that I may see both the flight of the sea and the turning back of the Jordan.

Richard makes clear, first of all, that Egypt is a state of mind, and, secondly, that even after leaving it, the soul must traverse a desert region which is precisely like the "gran diserto" in which the pilgrim is blocked: "Coming forth from the darkness of Egypt, from worldly error to the more secret places of the heart, you discover nothing else but a place of terror and vast solitude. This is that desert land, arid and unpassable . . . filled with all terrible things." In this desert place, where "all is confused, all is disturbed; where nothing is in its proper place, nothing proceeds in proper order," the impediments one encounters are the vices and passions (usually three-fold, according to Augustine's commentators) to which man is subject, since "vulnerati sumus ingredientes mundum [we are already wounded when we enter the world]."

### THE WINGS OF ULYSSES (*Inf.* 26.125)

The canto of Ulysses contains a striking instance of Dante's use of neoplatonic imagery to describe, not simply the flight of the soul to the absolute, but also the inevitable failure attendant upon any such journey when it is undertaken without the help of God. This instance of neoplatonic imagery is therefore analogous, perhaps even coordinate, to the imagery the poet uses to describe his own unsuccessful journey in the first canto.

Since Giorgio Padoan's essay of some years ago, there can no longer be any doubt that Dante's Ulysses is the Ulysses of medieval tradition, whose journey was considered to have a moral significance. The knowledge which is the object of his quest is of a metaphysical, rather than navigational, order. In Dante's reading, as in the reading of the neoplatonists, the voyage was an allegory for the flight of the soul to transcendent truth; one could extend Padoan's argument to suggest that Dante's Ulysses ends up a shipwreck rather than in the arms of some paradisiac Penelope in order to indicate what Dante thought of such purely philosophical excursions. It is this dimension of meaning that gives the episode its structural importance throughout the poem, beyond the limits of the canto in which it is contained. The ancient voyager is recalled at the beginning of the *Purgatorio* and again toward the end of the *Paradiso* precisely to mark the contrast between his abortive journey and that of the pilgrim. Dante's descent into hell enables him to reach the shore which Ulysses was able only to make out in the distance, a contrast that evokes once again, as we shall see, Augustine's distinction between philosophical presumption and Christian conversion.

At one point in his famous speech, Ulysses describes his journey in terms that directly allude to the traditional flight of the soul:

e volta nostra poppa nel mattino,
  de' remi facemmo ali al folle volo

[And turning our stern to the morning, we made of our oars wings for the mad flight]

(124–25)

Critics have seized on the phrase "folle volo" and have used it to characterize the daring of Ulysses' voyage. The adjective is particularly apt, as Rocco Montano has observed, for it can reflect both Ulysses' regret for the disastrous consequences of his voyage, as well as the author's moral judgment on the entire undertaking. However, the first part of the verse is of potentially much greater significance. By itself, the word "volo" might be taken as a simple rhetorical twist, a faint suggestion at best of Platonic flights. A careful look at the preceding metaphor, however, transforms the suggestion into a certainty. When Dante has Ulysses say "dei remi facemmo ali," he is echoing a classical metaphor, the "remigium alarum" used by Virgil to describe the flight of Daedalus. The metaphor was eventually endowed with meaning in a philosophical context, a meaning which is relevant to our understanding of the entire episode.

In the sixth book of the *Aeneid*, Virgil summarizes in a few words the story of Daedalus and Icarus. He then describes the temple built by Daedalus and the votive offering made to Phoebus:

Redditus his primum terris, tibi, Phoebe, sacravit
remigium alarum posuitque immania templa.

[Here first restored to earth, he consecrated to you, O Phoebus, the oarage of his wings, and built a vast temple.]

(*Aeneid* 6.18–19)

It is to Pierre Courcelle that we are indebted for the history of the neoplatonic interpretation of Daedalus's "wingèd oarage." In the article to which Padoan alludes in his essay, Courcelle shows that both the story of Ulysses and the flight of Daedalus were interpreted by neoplatonists to signify the flight of the soul: "il faut que l'âme prenne son vol pour regagner sa patrie." St. Ambrose refers to the myth of Daedalus to describe the liberation of the soul from matter and uses the phrase "remigium alarum," as does St. Augustine on several occasions. I should like merely to add to Courcelle's vast documentation a passage that lies outside the scope of his study but is exactly within mine, since it occurs in the only medieval neoplatonic commentary of the *Aeneid* which Dante was likely to have known. Bernardus

Silvestris simply echoed a long tradition when he identified the temple with contemplation and the "remigium alarum" with reason, but in doing so, he probably made that gloss directly accessible to Dante:

> Daedalus came to the temple of Apollo, that is, to the contemplation of sublime things with the reason. And journeying with the intellect he turned his attention completely to the study of philosophy, and there he dedicated the oarage of his wings, that is, the exercise of his reason and intellect (*alarum remigium i.e. rationis et intellectus exercitium sacravit*).

Just as Virgil's *remigium alarum* metaphorically transformed Daedalus's flight into a sea voyage, so the phrase, "de' remi facemmo ali" transformed Ulysses' voyage into a Platonic "volo." Ulysses' journey is an extended dramatization of an interior journey through what Padoan has called "le vie della sapienza"; the very oars that he used were traditional metaphors for the power of intellect.

I should like to underscore what I take to be an important implication of the phrase that Dante puts into the mouth of Ulysses. The "wingèd oarage" of tradition was usually associated with Daedalus, rather than Icarus. In Virgil's story it was mentioned in connection with a flight that was not "folle" at all, for Daedalus, unlike his son, reached his objective. This element is what the allegory of Ulysses has in common with the allegory of Daedalus: the return of Daedalus to safety ("*Redditus* his primum terris") and the return of Homer's Ulysses to his home made those stories excellent analogues for the Platonic *regressus* of the soul to its heavenly *patria*. The fact that Dante associated the "remigium alarum" of tradition with Ulysses' voyage seems to suggest that he was aware of an allegorical significance common to the two stories; yet, by describing the flight as a "folle volo," he seems deliberately to have turned the allegory against its authors. In spite of the opinion of most modern commentators, he may even have known of Ulysses' return to Ithaca through several indirect sources; he certainly knew that the "wingèd oarage" of the soul was usually associated with the return of Daedalus. Nevertheless, it is *because* he accepts the common allegorical significance and interprets it as a Christian must that his version of the story ends in shipwreck. If Ulysses is shipwrecked and if the wings of Daedalus seem rather to recall Icarus, it is because the *regressus* that both stories came to represent is, in Dante's view, philosophical presumption that is bound to end in failure. I should like to suggest that the voyage of Dante's Ulysses exists on the same plane of reality as its counterpart, the journey of the pilgrim; that is, as a dramatic representation of the journey of the mind. It is for this reason that Dante takes it as an admonition:

> Allor mi dolsi, e ora mi ridoglio
>   quando drizzo la mente a ciò ch'io vidi,
>   e più *lo 'ngegno* affreno ch'i' non soglio,
> perché non corra che *virtù* nol guidi.

> [I sorrowed then, and sorrow now again, when I turn my mind to what I saw; and I curb my genius more than I am wont, lest it run where virtue does not guide it.]
>
> (*Inf.* 26.19–22)

His insistence on the distinction between *ingegno* and *virtù*, between the motive power of his journey and his guide, contrasts sharply with the speech of Ulysses, in which "virtute e canoscenza" (120) seem almost synonymous, the single, somewhat exterior objective of the "folle volo." Just as the ancients equated knowledge and virtue, so too Ulysses seems to equate them, making no provision in his calculations for the journey within, the personal *askesis* upon which all such attempts at transcendence must be based. The distinction between Ulysses' journey and the journey of the pilgrim is not in the objective, for both are directed toward that mountain in the southern hemisphere, but rather in how the journey is accomplished. The difference is quite literally the journey through hell, the descent *intra nos* which transforms philosophical presumption into a journey of the mind and heart to God.

For Plotinus the power of intellect was a sufficient vehicle for the flight to the truth; the great neoplatonist specifically denied the need for any guide on such a journey. For Augustine, on the contrary, and for all Christian thinkers thereafter, the journey had to be accomplished "et per intellectum *et per affectum*." Such insistence on the volitive power of the soul is the constant theme of Augustine's polemic against neoplatonism in the *Confessions*. This polemic, I believe, lies at the heart of Dante's representation in the canto of Ulysses. Toward the beginning of the *Confessions*, Augustine uses the example of the prodigal son in order to illustrate his thesis that one moves toward or away from God with the will:

> For darkened affections is removal from Thee. For it is not by our feet, or change of place, that men leave Thee or return unto Thee, nor did Thy younger son look out for *horses* or *chariots*, or *ships*, or *fly with visible wings*, or journey by the *motion of his limbs*

that he might in a far country waste in riotous living all T
gavest at his departure.

Again, in the passage offered earlier as a background text for unc
Dante's "piè fermo" verse, some of these images of flight reappe

> And therein [Thy Covenant] we enter not by *ships*, or *ch*
> *feet*, nor move not so far as I had come from the house
> place where we were sitting. For, not to go only, but
> thither was nothing else but to will to go, but to will r
> and thoroughly; not to turn and toss, this way an
> maimed and half-divided will, struggling, with one p
> as another rose.

Each of Augustine's neoplatonic images of flight has its c
canto of Ulysses. Ulysses describes his navigation as a wi
the pilgrim the sight of the Greek hero recalls a celestial

> E qual colui che si vengiò con li orsi
> vide 'l *carro* d'Elia al dipartire,
> quando *i cavalli* al cielo erti levor

> [And as he who was avenged by the bears saw I
> its departure, when the horses rose erect to hea

Whatever else Dante may have intended to sugge
tuitous comparison, the fact remains that, like th
wings of Daedalus, the chariot of Elijah is on a f
presence of these comparisons, although strippe
banality by Dante's poetic power, neverthele
significance of Ulysses' voyage and generaliz
the limits of one man's experience. At first gl
*Confessions* just quoted and the episode of U
more in common than these images of fligl
Augustine, dramatic and powerful in Dante
Augustine's words can lead us back to a com
cal motifs to which, I believe, the figure of I

As Pierre Courcelle has shown, the n
tinian passage derive from a text of Plot
changed by St. Ambrose and quoted parti
passage reveals that Plotinus is in fact thir
reader on to the journey without a guide



> Those of the third category . . . perceive certain signs which remind them of their dear homeland . . . and, either they find their home again without wandering or delay, or more often, they lose their way in the fog or fix upon stars that sink in the sea. Again, they are sometimes held back by various seductions and miss the best time for setting sail. They wander for a long time and even risk shipwreck. It often happens to such men that some calamity, arising in the midst of their good fortune, like a tempest opposing their efforts, drives them back to the homeland of their desires and of their peace.

There is an undeniable, although somewhat generic, resemblance between these sea-going adventures of philosophical quest and Ulysses' own story. The reference to the navigational "fix" on stars that sink beneath the waters is perhaps less generic. It is paralleled by the apparently descriptive but probably significant detail mentioned by Ulysses:

> Tutte le stelle già de l'altro polo
> vedea la notte, e 'l nostro tanto basso,
> che non surgëa fuor del marin suolo.

> [The night now saw the other pole and all its stars, and ours so low that it did not rise from the ocean floor.]
>
> (127–29)

The point is that the ship is "off course," since the pole star, upon which all mariners must fix for guidance, has disappeared beneath the ocean floor. But the most startling detail of Augustine's allegory follows the paragraph just cited, and one that Padoan omitted; it may be the clue to why Ulysses should be sailing toward a *mountain*, rather than back to Ithaca:

> Now all of these men who, in some manner, are borne toward the land of happiness, have to fear and desperately to avoid a huge mountain set up before the port, creating a great danger to those entering. It shines so and is clothed with such a deceptive light that it seems to offer to those who enter a haven, promising to satisfy their longing for the land of happiness. . . . For what other mountain does the reason designate as fearful to those who are entering upon or have entered philosophical study than the mountain of proud vainglory?

At this point Augustine concludes his allegorical exposition and proceeds to apply the allegory of his own life. In his youth, he had fixed his eyes on stars that sank into the ocean and therefore led him astray. The study of various philosophies kept him afloat, but the attractions of a woman and the love of honor prevented him from flying "totis velis omnibusque remis [with full sail and all the oars]" into the embrace of philosophy. Finally, a tempest that he took to be adverse [his illness], forced him to abandon the career that was leading him toward the sirens and drove his shaky and leaking boat toward the haven of tranquillity.

The prologue of the *De beata vita* is a dramatic representation of the events recounted with apologetic intent in the *Confessions*. The attempts at Plotinian ecstasy are represented in the seventh book of the *Confessions* in largely traditional philosophical terms while in the prologue to the dialogue, under the influence of a long tradition of Homeric allegoresis, autobiography takes a more literary form. There is a similar relationship between the experience of Dante's pilgrim and that of Ulysses. For both men, the object of the journey seems to be the mountain in the southern hemisphere. Again, the pilgrim takes Ulysses' fate to be a specific admonition for himself. Ulysses dies shipwrecked before the looming mountain, but in the first canto of the poem the pilgrim seems to have survived, by pure accident, a metaphorical shipwreck of his own:

> E come quei che con lena affannata,
> uscito fuor del pelago a la riva,
> si volge a l'acqua perigliosa e guata,
> così l'animo mio, ch'ancor fuggiva,
> si volse a retro a rimirar *lo passo*
> che non lasciò già mai persona viva.

> [And as he who with laboring breath has escaped from the deep to the shore turns to look back on the dangerous waters, so my mind which was still fleeing turned back to gaze upon the pass that never left anyone alive.]
>
> (*Inf.* 1.22–27)

Ulysses' experience with the "alto passo" (*Inf.* 26.132) seems to be what one would expect of such a "varco folle." (*Paradiso* 27.82–83 [all further references to this text will be abbreviated as *Par.*]). It is the pilgrim's survival that is gratuitous, both on the mountain of the prologue and the mountain of purgatory. In the latter instance, just before he is girded with the rush of humility, he remembers Ulysses' pride:

Venimmo poi in sul lito diserto,
che mai non vide navicar sue acque
omo, che di *tornar* sia poscia esperto.

[Then we came on to the desert shore, that never saw any man navigate its waters who afterwards had experience of return.]
(*Purg.* 1.130–32)

The return is the element of the story that is given new meaning, in the Christian perspective. The mountain of philosophic pride, says Augustine, "swallows up into its depths the proud men who walk upon it and covers them over in its darkness, snatching from them that shining abode of which they had caught but a glimpse." For some that shipwreck was definitive; for others it was the prelude to a new life, "com'Altrui piacque."

At the beginning of this essay I suggested that Dante's borrowing from Augustine in the *Confessions* was not simply an isolated fact of purely historical interest but was also of some significance for the interpretation of the poem. If Dante chose to echo Augustine's attempt to reach the truth through philosophy alone, then the implication is that Dante undertook a similar attempt and also met with failure. For all of his efforts in the *Convivio* to define philosophic truth in theological terms, Dante's philosophical experience may have been as ultimately disillusioning for him as was Augustine's with the neoplatonists. Whatever that experience, we know that it was shared by Guido Cavalcanti, who seems to have remained obdurate in his philosophical presumption. In the fourth book of the *Confessions*, a deathbed conversion of a dear friend separates Augustine from one who was "of one soul with me." Although the roles are reversed, it is the same drama of conversion that seems to come between Dante and his "first friend" in the tenth canto of the *Inferno*.

The myth of Ulysses serves as an exemplar of philosophical pride and, as we have seen, an antitype of Dante's own philosophical experience. In concretely historical terms, however, Guido fulfilled the role of alter ego and antitype. Some of the words used by Augustine in his generic condemnation of the Platonists are repeated in intensely personal terms when Dante refers to his friend. In the seventh book of the *Confessions*, Augustine says that he was able to find in the teaching of the Platonists all of the prologue to the Gospel of John except for the doctrine of the Word made flesh. The philosophers "disdain to learn of Him because He is gentle and humble of heart." Similarly, in the *Inferno*, we learn that Guido "disdained" guidance for a descent into hell: "ebbe a disdegno" (*Inf.* 10.63). The past absolute tense with reference to a subject who is still alive requires us to understand "disdained" as a perfected action—disdained *to come*—rather than as some habitual attitude toward Virgil or Beatrice. In sense and in syntax, it is exactly equivalent to the refusal of the philosophers to learn from Christ's humility—*dedignantur ab eo discere*—as exemplified by His descent into hell. Like Ulysses or the pilgrim of the prologue, Guido was lost, perhaps definitively ("forse . . ."), by his philosophical presumption.

Beyond this biographical analogy, there is the more important analogy, or perhaps *homology*, of literary structure. As in all spiritual autobiographies, so in the *Confessions* and in the *Divine Comedy* there is a radical division between the protagonist and the author who tells his story. The question of the relative "sincerity" of such autobiographies is the question of how real we take that division to be. Augustine and Dante took it to be almost ontologically real, for it was their conviction that the experience of conversion, the subject matter of their respective stories, was tantamount to a death of their former selves and the beginning of a new life.

For Dante, the distance between protagonist and author is at its maximum at the beginning of the story and is gradually closed by the dialectic of poetic process until pilgrim and poet coincide at the ending of the poem, which gives a unity and a coherence to all that went before. From the outset, the poet's voice expresses the detached point of view toward which his pilgrim strives, while the journey of the pilgrim is history in the making, a tentative, problematic view constantly subject to revision, approaching certitude as a limit. It is at the last moment that the metamorphosis of the pilgrim's view of the world is completed, when he himself has become metamorphosed into the poet, capable at last of writing the story that we have read.

This metamorphosis accounts for much of the ambiguity in the characterizations of the *Inferno*. The critical uncertainties about whether Francesca is a heroine of spontaneous human love or merely a deluded medieval Emma Bovary, whether Ulysses embodies the spirit of the Renaissance or simply *mala curiositas*, whether Ugolino is a father suffering with Dostoyevskian dignity or a Pisan cannibal, arise from the dialectical relationship of the pilgrim's view to that of the poet. Further, it is no accident that we generally side with the pilgrim in his human response to these great figures, against the crushing exigencies of the poet's structure. The pilgrim's view is much like our own view of history and of ourselves: partial, perhaps confused, still in the making. But the poet's view is far different, for it is global and comprehensive, the total view of a man who looks at the world, his neighborhood, and indeed himself with all the detachment of a cultural anthropologist. The process of the poem, which is to say the progress of the pilgrim, is the transformation of the problematic and humanistic into the certain and transcendent, from novelistic involvement to epic detachment, from a synchronic view of the self in a dark wood to a diachronic total view of the entire world as if it were, to use Dante's powerful image, a humble threshing floor upon which a providential history will one day separate the wheat from the chaff.

The view from paradise is a spatial translation of what might be called a memory of universal history. The coherence of the whole poem may be grasped only with a view to its totality, a view from the ending, just as the coherence of the poet's life could be grasped only in retrospect, from the perspective of totality in death. Clearly the same may be said of universal history, whose coherence may be perceived only from the perspective of eschatology, when the evolution is finally concluded. In the linear time that is ours, such a perspective is impossible, for it implies a survival of our own death and the death of the world. For Dante, however, as for Augustine, there was a death which enabled the mind to grasp such totalities, not by virtue of linear evolution, but rather by transcendence: a death of detachment. To perceive the pattern of one's life in its totality was to see the structure or *figura* of God's redemptive act, the master-plan of all history. In the *Paradiso*, Dante describes the cognition of the blessed as he addresses Cacciaguida:

> come veggion le terrene menti
> non capere in trïangol due ottusi,
> così vedi le cose contingenti
> anzi che sieno in sé, mirando il punto
> a cui tutti li tempi son presenti;

> [even as earthly minds see that two obtuse angles can not be contained in a triangle, so you, gazing upon the Point to which all times are present, do see contingent things before they exist in themselves.]
>
> (*Par.* 17.14–18)

This "now" of the blessed, like a geometric *figura*, enables Cacciaguida to prophesy Dante's future without ambiguity. It provides the place to stand from which the pilgrim comes ultimately to see himself and the world around him under the aspect of eternity.

Augustine first saw the need to define that "present moment," the position from which one could see one's former self, in the totality that is present in God. He was also the first to see the metaphysical significance of what used to be referred to as "organic unity." For Augustine, as well as for Dante, a poem had to be understood as a unity, not because it was a "literary object," but rather because its significance could be grasped only when its process was completed. This was not simply a literary fact, but rather the outward sign of a spiritual reality. A passage from the *Confessions* makes clear how the progression to greater and greater totalities can lead from a poem to universal history:

> I am about to repeat a Psalm that I know. Before I begin, my expectation is extended over the totality; but when I have begun, however much of it I shall separate off into the past is extended along my memory . . . until the whole expectation be at length exhausted, when that whole action being ended, shall have passed into memory . . . the same takes place in the whole life of man, whereof all the actions of man are parts; the same holds through the whole age of the sons of men, whereof all the lives of men are parts.

Formal criticism helps us to see how the poem must be read in retrospect, but to see all of reality in that way requires a perspective more privileged than that of the critic. From such a perspective, the "present moment" of conversion, levels of meaning are not arbitrarily superimposed by the human mind, but are rather discovered to be exponential recurrences of the structure of God's Providence in history, life, and the whole universe. The passage from Augustine contains within it at once the essence of biblical allegory and the essence of Dante's spiritual autobiography, even to the stylistic level.

I should like to close with a verse to which I have already alluded. As he moves with the stars, Dante looks down upon "l'aiuola che *ci* fa tanto feroci" (*Par.* 22.151). For all the distance implied by the poetic fiction, the pronoun "ci" strains to have it both ways: to claim the perspective of eternity without a surrender of the poet's place in time. The synthesis of eternity and time is the goal of the entire journey: the vision of the Incarnation. At the end of the poem, the dramatic convergence of pilgrim and poet is matched by the conceptual convergence of humanity and the divine.

Augustine's autobiography, like Sartre's, is primarily concerned with words, but the ending of Christian autobiography is silence:

> For that voice passed by and passed away, began and ended; the syllables sounded and passed away, the second after the first, the

> third after the second, and so forth in order, until the last after the rest, and silence after the last. . . . And these Thy words, created for a time, the outward ear reported to the intelligent soul, whose inward ear lay listening to Thy Eternal Word.

So the literary unity of Dante's poem is no formal artifact, but is rather the testament of a spiritual journey from a region of unlikeness to likeness, from the "selva oscura" to "la nostra effige."

# The Imageless Vision and Dante's *Paradiso*

*Marguerite Mills Chiarenza*

In interpreting St. Paul's claim to have been rapt to the third heaven, St. Augustine developed a theory of knowledge which influenced the entire Middle Ages. For St. Augustine the problem was to define the third heaven and this involved discovering what was meant by the other two as well. He concluded that the three heavens are to be taken in a spiritual sense and represent three modes of vision. Briefly, the first mode is *visio corporalis*, knowledge through the senses of material objects; the second, *visio spiritualis*, is knowledge through the imagination in which, as in dreams, the senses are inactive but forms of physical objects are the means of representation; the third and highest, *visio intellectualis*, is intuition of spiritual substances *facie ad faciem*, without direct or indirect participation of the senses. Both spiritual and intellectual vision are immaterial but while intellectual vision is emphatically direct spiritual vision is mediated by images.

Francis X. Newman, to whom I refer the reader for a fuller discussion of St. Augustine's doctrine, has suggested most convincingly that the Augustinian modes of vision are a governing principle in Dante's imagery, that each of the *cantiche* tends toward a vision of God in one of the Augustinian modes and that the imagery of each reflects this tendency. Lucifer, the most corporeal object in the universe, parodies God in *Inferno*; the reflected image of the griffon in the *Purgatorio* is Dante's spiritual vision of Christ and, finally, in the *Paradiso* Dante sees God directly. Newman's suggestion is of particular significance for the *Paradiso* where Dante makes the unique claim to have followed in St. Paul's footsteps and to have seen God

From *Dante Studies* 90. © 1971 by the Dante Society of America, Inc.

face to face. And yet, except for the last cantos, Newman seems hesitant in his application of the concept of intellectual vision to the *Paradiso*:

> At the start of his flight, and, in fact, until its very conclusion, the pilgrim is still seeing (that is, knowing) with a mind conditioned to corporeal forms. For this reason, although the inhabitants of Paradise are properly incorporeal, they are given a perceptible shape of light—now not *ombre*, but *luci*—in order that the pilgrim may be prepared gradually for the final truly incorporeal vision.
>
> ("St. Augustine's Three Visions and the Structure of the *Comedy*," *MLN* 82 (1967), 72–73.)

Intellectual vision is by its very nature incongruent with poetry, for it is the denial of that of which poetry is made, images, and perhaps this is what leads Newman to imply that such an experience does not occur until the end of the voyage. However, what Dante claims in the *Paradiso*, to have seen God and lived, is as inconceivable as representing or mediating that which is by definition unmediated. Therefore, I would like to go further than Newman and suggest that the basic position of the poet in the *Paradiso* is revealed by his struggle to express a vision which was imageless from the start.

The *Paradiso* is possibly the greatest paradox in the history of poetry and it is small wonder that we are often distressed by a certain ambiguity found in the descriptions of its poetics. Nonetheless, if certain basic problems are clarified it is easier to arrive at some degree of precise statement. The two aspects of the *Paradiso* which lead to most confusion are, I think, the hierarchy represented there and the fact that the pilgrim's ultimate vision is of God. Both of these can lead the critic to distinguish stages in such a way as to imply that the poetics proper to the *Paradiso* are to be found only in the last cantos. If too much emphasis is placed on the division of the *cantica* in preparatory vision in the heavens and final vision in the Empyrean and if this division is then extended to the poetics of the *Paradiso*, the end of the poem becomes the true *Paradiso* and we are left with some thirty cantos which are not the *Purgatorio* and are not the *Paradiso*. To avoid this we must stress the declared superhuman quality of vision in these cantos and do away with definitions, such as *per speculum* [through a mirror] or *in aenigmate* [in a riddle or allegory], which make of it nothing more than a rarefied version of human experience.

The division of the *Paradiso* in vision in the heavens and vision in the

Empyrean is partially false. Clearly, the vision of God's face is to be distinguished from all other vision. But this vision transcends the poem, it does not end it. In the last verses Dante tells us that he did penetrate God's face and he tells us something of the effect it had on him, but he also tells us that this experience is lost to him as a man in whom memory fails and as a poet in whom *fantasia* fails—indeed failed already in the moment that vision was granted him. These last verses, not all of the Empyrean, are perhaps to be distinguished in that they represent the little that can be said of the ultimate vision. But all other vision in Paradise ends in the sum total of its parts, leaving only the mystery of God's nature to be known. What the poet can say of God's face is possible only because all conceivable vision has been exhausted. Vision in heaven is universal vision of truth which becomes a totality only when its separateness is transcended. This transcending of separateness is foreshadowed in the Empyrean but becomes a reality only as the pilgrim turns to God's face and, just before all experience, superhuman as well as human, is left behind, sees the unity implicit in the nature of truth, only to transcend even that unity in the vision of the Trinity and the Incarnation.

> Nel suo profondo vidi che s'interna,
> legato con amore in un volume,
> ciò che per l'universo si squaderna.

> [In its depth I saw that it contained, bound by love in one volume, that which is scattered in leaves through the universe.]
> (*Paradiso* 33.85–87 [all further references to this text will be abbreviated as *Par.*])

This image not only clarifies the content of Dante's vision but also, because he uses the book as his metaphor, it is a clue to his poetics as well. God's face is not the universe but in it is contained the universe in its truest form. In Medieval doctrine every creature has its truest existence in the mind of God, although its natural existence is external. As St. Thomas puts it:

> Effectus praeexistit virtute in causa agente; praeexistere autem in virtute causae agentis, non est praeexistere imperfectiori modo, sed perfectiori. . . . Cum ergo Deus sit prima causa effectiva rerum, opportet omnium rerum perfectiones praeexistere in Deo secundum eminentiorem modum. . . . Et sic quae sunt diversa et opposita in seipsis, in Deo praeexistunt ut unum, absque detrimento simplicitatis ipsius.

> [The effect preexists when virtue is acting in the cause; to preexist, however, in the virtue of the acting cause is not to preexist in a more imperfect way but in a more perfect way. . . . Since, therefore, God is the first effective cause of things, it is necessary that the perfections of all things preexist in God in a more distinguished way. . . . And therefore which things are different and opposite in themselves, they preexist in God as one, and without damage to simplicity itself.]

St. Augustine compares the difference between the natural existence of creatures and their existence in God to the difference between night and day and tells us that knowledge of a creature in itself compares to knowledge of it in God in the same way that no knowledge at all compares to knowledge in the creature.

> Multum quippe interest inter cognitionem rei cuiusque in verbo Dei et cognitionem eius in natura eius, ut illud merito ad diem pertineat, hoc ad vesperam. In comparatione enim lucis illius, quae in verbo Dei conspicitur, omnis cognitio, qua creaturam quamlibet in se ipsa novimus, non immerito nox dici potest: quae rursum tantum differt ab errore vel ignorantia eorum, qui nec ipsam creaturam sciunt, ut in eius comparatione non incongrue dicatur dies.

> [Indeed there is much difference between the cognition of each thing in the word of God and its cognition in the nature of itself, with the result that the former cognition deservedly belongs to day, the latter to night. For in relation to that light, which is beheld in the word of God, all cognition, by which we know any creature in itself, can be called, not undeservedly, night: which cognition on the other hand differs so much from the mistake or ignorance of these people who do not know the creature itself with the result that it is called, not inconsistently in this comparison, day.]

Dante's *terzina* is inspired by the doctrine of the double existence of creation, separate in the universe and unified in its Creator's conception. The unity of creation in God's mind is the pilgrim's final vision of the universe and represents the point at which the poem begins to be transcended. The pilgrim sees again all that he has hitherto seen, in its truest form. Dante tells us that he saw a repetition of his entire vision but does not describe it, for he has only human tools and to describe it would be literally a repetition. However, the image is far from being simply a statement of the whereabouts of the universe's conception, precisely because Dante chooses the book as his metaphor. When the universe is transcended, what was separate becomes unified just as all the pages when bound become the book. Dante does not represent the vision of always greater things ending in a thing greater still but the vision of all things followed and transcended by the vision of their unity. Vision of unity and totality are not a part of the poem but a result of it. The mind, the pilgrim's and the reader's, absorbs totality in its separate parts but is destined to transcend that separation. This principle is true of the poem also. The pilgrim does not see the last page of the book in God's face, he sees the book bound together, for when the poem is complete it is no longer a sequence but a unity. The reader transcends the pages to retain in his mind the poem, which was conceived by the author before it was written and is now transcended by him much the same as creation is conceived and transcended by God.

As the pilgrim turns to God's face all that is left to be seen of the universe is its unity. If vision until this moment is of spiritual substances, such as souls, and is defective only in its lack of unity, then it is intellectual in the Augustinian sense. It is direct intuition of spiritual substances even though not yet intuition of them in God. The notion that the highest form of vision is only to be found in the Empyrean seems, however, to be supported by the hierarchy represented throughout the heavens. Because of this some discussion of hierarchy will be necessary if we are to maintain that St. Augustine's highest mode of vision is the mode of all of the *Paradiso*.

Hierarchy, whose incongruous presence in the *Paradiso* is the source of some equivocation, is itself presented as an equivocation. It is presented, in fact, as an artificial structure which does not exist outside of the momentary need for it. The saints descend to various spheres which dramatize their place in a harmonious world of beatitude where the greater and the lesser are equally perfected, where qualitative difference does not diminish quantitative completeness, for "ogni dove in cielo è paradiso" and each position is unlimited. They stage this hierarchy because the pilgrim is not ready for a vision of totality. He must see the parts in order to see the whole. Because this hierarchy is not temporal in nature, time is so underplayed in the *Paradiso* that there is no way of accurately measuring it. The various entities must all appear to the pilgrim to give him the whole vision but their ordering is not a sequential phenomenon. They do not have to follow one another in taking their place, they simply must all be there. The poem, on the other hand, is constrained in a sequential form and, if it is to be read, verse must follow verse. In fact, while the pilgrim is speeding through the heavens at a velocity inconceivable to the human mind, time for the poet, the length of the third *cantica*, is the same as it was in the other two. This consideration leads us to confront the new relation between the pilgrim and the poet.

In the *Inferno* and the *Purgatorio* the poet's struggle is secondary to the pilgrim's and the danger is essentially in the voyage. In the *Paradiso* it is the poet who struggles while the pilgrim is safe. This is because the pilgrim was in possession of transhuman powers while the poet, who has returned to the human, is not. The pilgrim transcended time in Paradise, which from the start of his flight approached deletion. Human categories of perception were left behind with Purgatory. His vision was essentially "in un ponto solo," which *punto* substituted and annulled a kind of paraphrase which led up to it. The poet, however, must work exclusively with human categories and make the paraphrase take the place of the essential vision, that is, spend thirty-three cantos telling us that he approached the vision which he uses only a few verses to tell us he has forgotten. The pilgrim should not be seen as one who is passing from one stage to another in order to acquire his highest faculties but as one in whom these faculties are already activated and who is growing, through the accumulation of vision, not toward a new kind of vision but toward the supreme object of vision. If this growth appears to occur in stages it is because the poet is representing it. Whatever the pilgrim's limitations, which made certain concessions from heaven necessary, the poet's are far greater and his concessions to the reader greatly exceed those of heaven to him. We must not attribute all of the characteristics of the representation to the vision itself but must remember that what we read is twice mediated, first through memory for the poet and then through words for the reader. This mediation must not be confused with any mediation in the experience itself. My purpose is 1) to show that Dante denies mediation in the experience and 2) to illustrate partially how he copes with its necessity in the poem.

Just as Dante gives us a hierarchy but at the same time undercuts its value by denying its independent reality, so he makes the limitations to which he (who has returned to the human) is subject work in his favor. These limitations are memory and words. From the start he tells us that the vision is no longer accessible to him and that memory must take its place. If intellectual vision—unmediated, imageless knowledge of spiritual substances—is the subject of the *Paradiso* and memory which, like the imagination, functions through images is the source, then we should expect to find universal infidelity in the representation. Hugh of St. Cher tells us, in reference to St. Paul's intellectual vision, what happens when memory confronts spiritual intuition:

> Ad illud, Quomodo habuit (Paulus) in memoria post raptum quae vidit? Dicendum quia talem habuit cognitionem de praeviso, qualem habet caecus natus de coloribus, de quibus scit multa loqui, quia multa de eis audivit. Vel potest dici sicut dicit Hieron. in Prologo Apoc. de Ionne, *Qui res quas viderat, in similitudinem postea transformavit: sic Paulus res quas vidit transtulit in similitudinem et figuras, non quia per illas Deum a principio viderit, sed ut eas in memoria retinens nobis enarraret.* [Italics mine]
>
> [Moreover, how did Paul hold in his memory after his abduction the things which he saw? It must be said that he could do this because he had a sort of knowledge about what had been foreseen such as a man blind from birth has about colors, about which he knows how to say many things, because he has heard many things about them. Or it is able to be explained as Jerome explains it in the Prologue to John, "Who changed the things which he had seen afterwards into images: so Paul changed the things which he saw into images and figures, not because he saw God through these images at first, but so that holding these in his memory he might explain them fully to us."]

Dante is counting on us to know that memory will introduce images where there were no images. He tells us that we are reading only what his memory could retain:

> Nel ciel che piú della sua luce prende
> fu'io, e vidi cose che ridire
> né sa né può chi di là su discende;
> perché appressando sé al suo disire,
> nostro intelletto si profonda tanto,
> che dietro la memoria non può ire.
> Veramente quan t'io del regno santo
> nella mia mente potei far tesoro,
> sarà ora matera del mio canto.

> [I was in the heaven that most receives His light and I saw things which he that descends from it has not the knowledge or the power to tell again; for our intellect, drawing near to its desire, sinks so deep that memory cannot follow it. Nevertheless,

> so much of the holy kingdom as I was able to treasure in my mind shall now be matter of my song.]
>
> (*Par.* 1.4–12)

Thus, we are warned to look beyond what we are offered. Dante warns us and reminds us constantly of the limitations of the source, because if these limitations are forgotten, it will lose its truthfulness as a source.

What we have said of memory can also be said of words. Their insufficiency is declared from the beginning:

> Trasumanar significar per verba
> non si poria: però l'essemplo basti
> a cui esperienza grazia serba.
>
> [The passing beyond humanity cannot be set forth in words; let the example suffice, therefore, for him to whom grace reserves the experience.]
>
> (*Par.* 1.70–72)

Indeed words are one step further removed from the experience than memory itself. The poet can only communicate through verbal reference to experience derived from the senses, the denial of intellectual vision. Again, Hugh of St. Cher tells us, in terms very like Dante's, what happens when an attempt is made to communicate intellectual vision. He compares it to trying to describe the taste of wine to one who has never tasted it and can only refer the description to something else which he has tasted:

> Qui ergo non diligit, non intelligit, quid est dilectio; quia non habet ipsam dilectionem apud se nisi forte per auditum; sicut si aliquis diceret ignoranti vinum esse optimum potum, non imaginaretur vinum sed ei simile, ut medonem et cervisiam: tamen crederet se imaginari vinum.
>
> [Who therefore does not delight in it, he does not understand why there is delight; because he does not have the delight itself in himself except by chance through hearing; just as if someone were to say to an unknowing man that wine is the best drink, the unknowing man would not imagine wine but something similar to it, such as mead or beer: nevertheless, he would think that he was imagining wine.]
>
> (*Opera Omnia in Universum Vetus et Novum Testamentum* [Venice, 1703], 7)

As with memory, Dante uses the obviousness of the insufficiency of his means to his advantage, and creates his most revolutionary technique, that of using words and images not merely to point beyond themselves but to point against themselves as well.

As I will show, Dante tells us that his vision was intellectual throughout the journey in Paradise and, therefore, to acquire such vision is not a goal of the pilgrim. The representation of such vision is, however, a goal for the poet. He is human and must cope gradually with the elimination of mediatory images and will completely do away with them only when he is silent. Vision of God by a man in the flesh is parallel to the paradox of a poet attempting through images, which are incorporeal only in that they have no corporeal—or spiritual—substance but which are based on reference to the senses, to represent that which is by definition spiritually substantial and void of any reference to the senses. And yet Dante's imagery in the *Paradiso* is developed in two directions which tend precisely toward the fulfilment of the two attributes of intellectual vision, incorporeality and substantiality.

Light metaphysics is not the subject of this discussion, but since light plays a role in the representation of intellectual vision it will be necessary to make a few remarks, however general, on its function in the *Paradiso*. The pilgrim sees everything in Paradise in the form of light which is gradually intensified to the point of blindness. Light has the unique attribute of being the source of all vision though itself shapeless and invisible outside the objects it illuminates. In the *Paradiso*, however, it does not illuminate objects but shines forth from subjects. These are lights themselves, not shining on objects but reflecting their own vision. Everything in the *Paradiso* is a reflecting light and it is this light which Dante uses to represent substance, which light is not a passive reflection of an external source but an active reflection of internal vision. The souls are not represented as inferior versions of something else but as spiritual centers of energy and truths in themselves. In fact, the pilgrim does not see God indirectly in the souls but beatitude directly. The souls are, of course, dependent on God for their vision and their beatitude but this dependence in no way diminishes their substantiality, for God is reflected by the entire universe which could not exist without Him. For the souls not to reflect God would be to cease to exist.

The reflecting light characteristic of the *Paradiso* represents substantiality in Dante's imagery. To represent substantiality is a challenge for a poet, but for him to attempt to represent the other essential quality of intellectual vision—absence of reference to experience derived from the senses—is more than a challenge, it is a contradiction in terms. It means, in effect, to represent through images that which is by definition incompatible with images. Nevertheless, this is a theme of Dante's imagery already evident in the pilgrim's first encounter with the inhabitants of the heavens.

> Quali per vetri transparenti e tersi
> o ver per acque nitide e tranquille,
> non sì profonde che i fondi sien persi,
> tornan di nostri visi le postille
> debili sì, che perla in bianca fronte
> non vien men tosto alle nostre pupille;
> tali vid'io più facce a parlar pronte;

> [As through smooth and transparent glass, or through limpid and still water not so deep that the bottom is lost, the outlines of our faces return so faint that a pearl on a white brow does not come less quickly to our eyes, many such faces I saw, eager to speak;]
>
> (*Par.* 3.10–17)

These souls are compared to mirrors but, immediately, the traditional mirror, that of Narcissus, is negated:

> per ch'io dentro all'error contrario corsi
> a quel ch'accese amor tra l'omo e 'l fonte.

> [at which I ran into the opposite error to that which kindled love between the man and the spring.]
>
> (*Par.* 3.18–19)

Most interesting is the way in which these images stress immateriality in their very reference to material objects. They are calculated to suggest incorporeality, even imperceptibility. Their visibility is described only through their near invisibility: reflections not in a mirror but in glass or shallow water so clear as to offer virtually no reflection at all; a pearl whose color so blends into the forehead on which it is worn that it cannot even be seen at first glance. Dante tells the reader what he saw in terms of visual experience in which the eye fails. I will return to this passage to show how directly it introduces the concept of intellectual vision, but first I would like to illustrate briefly, through a few other images, how what is already present here at the beginning is developed in the rest of the *Paradiso*.

When the pilgrim enters the heaven of Mars the souls arrange themselves in the pattern of the cross. Dante's images at this point (*Par.* 14.91 ff.) are extremely complex and deserve a fuller analysis. For our present purpose, we should notice that now Dante does not describe the lights in terms of their individual visibility but only of the collective shape they form. It is as if, on the one hand, only the cross not the souls were visible; on the other hand, there is no material cross to be seen but only the souls in the shape of the cross. That of which the cross is formed is not described, all that we are told is that it is formed. We are given a shape formed of shapeless parts. Neither the cross nor the souls are directly more visible than light itself; what the pilgrim sees is the meaning which the souls wish to show him, the "venerabil segno" (101). That this cross is not a material shape but the spiritual shape it signifies, is reinforced by the fact that as the pilgrim looks at it, he no longer sees it but the mystery from which it is inseparable:

> Qui vince la memoria mia lo 'ngegno;
> chè quella croce lampeggiava Cristo,
> sì ch' io non so trovar essemplo degno;

> [Here my memory defeats my skill, for that cross so flamed forth Christ that I can find for it no fit comparison;]
>
> (*Par.* 14.103–5)

The spiritual value of his vision is further enhanced by his use immediately afterward of the metaphor, not so metaphorical for Dante, of the cross in each man's life:

> ma chi prende sua croce e segue Cristo,
> ancor mi scuserà di quel ch' io lasso.

> [but he that takes up his cross and follows Christ shall yet forgive me for what I leave untold.]
>
> (*Par.* 14.106–7)

The same can be said of the souls in the heaven of Jupiter who form the sign of the eagle (*Par.* 28.74 ff.), but here Dante has progressed one step further beyond the material form. The eagle is the final shape in a series of metamorphic images which remain visible only until they have been comprehended. Furthermore, these images represent letters, shapes indeed but as inseparable from their collective meaning as they are individually meaningless. This inseparability is all the more evident because the letters are not seen together but one by one so that when their meaning is read they have already disappeared leaving only their message, a verse from the Bible, whose author is God. When they have disappeared, their meaning, now in the form of the symbolic eagle, emerges, and again Dante could say he saw no eagle but only the meaning of justice shining forth from the formless souls of the just.

The cross and the eagle are images taken from the middle cantos of the *Paradiso* and show an obvious development from the first images of the *cantica*. Turning to the last canto of the poem and necessarily skipping countless other equally significant images, we find the famous image with which Dante ends his series of "anti-images":

> Qual è 'l geometra che tutto s'affige
> per misurar lo cerchio, e non ritrova,
> pensando, quel principio ond'elli indige
>
> [Like the geometer who sets all his mind to the squaring of the circle and for all his thinking does not discover the principle he needs, such was I at that strange sight.]
>
> (*Par.* 33.133–35)

The squaring of the circle crowns a series of abstract geometrical shapes describing the mystery of God's nature and is the one shape in the universe which can be defined but cannot be seen. We, like Hugh of St. Cher's *caecus natus*, can "say much of it because we have heard much about it," but we have no experience of it.

There are, then, stages in the development of Dante's imagery in the *Paradiso*. Three of them are those mentioned, in which we find, first, concrete shapes which can barely be perceived, then shapes in which symbolic meaning overshadows concrete form, and at last purely conceptual shape not found in the material universe. These stages lead the poet to the point at which he can go no further but must end his poem in order that it become literally imageless. This does not mean that the pilgrim's vision was not imageless from the start. His vision was peripheral at the beginning as he tended toward "un punto solo" at the spiritual center of the universe. But that it was peripheral does not mean that it was not direct spiritual intuition. In describing the impenetrable depth of God's mind Dante uses an image which becomes very eloquent if we remember that the souls in the moon, the first encountered in Paradise, were compared to shallow water in which the bottom is still visible:

Però nella giustizia sempiterna
  la vista che riceve il vostro mondo,
  com'occhio per lo mare, entro s'interna;
che, *ben che dalla proda veggia il fondo,*
  *in pelago nol vede*; e nondimeno
  èli, ma cela lui l'esser profondo. [Italics mine]

[Therefore the sight that is granted to your world penetrates within the Eternal Justice as the eye into the sea; for though from the shore it sees the bottom, in the open sea it does not, and yet the bottom is there but the depth conceals it.]

(*Par.* 19.58–63)

The difference between the pilgrim and the man whose faculties have not been elevated beyond the human is that the pilgrim approaches the spiritual creatures of the "gran mar dell'essere" without ever losing sight of the sea's bottom.

All of this might seem pure speculation if Dante did not make it explicit from the start, from that first encounter with the souls in the moon to which I must now return. In the moon the pilgrim is faced with a vision which seems designed to discourage the senses. The human mind knows incorporeality through spiritual and therefore unsubstantial vision. So incorporeal is the pilgrim's vision that, since his mind is still conditioned to human experience, he falls into the error of thinking it also unsubstantial and turns away looking for what he has taken to be an image. Beatrice corrects him with the words "vere sustanze son ciò che tu vedi" (27). Surely, by "vere sustanze" Beatrice does not mean corporeal substances, for she is speaking of souls, not bodies. She means spiritual substances. But it is not through Beatrice's words, unequivocable as they are, that we first realize the nature of what the pilgrim sees, it is through the image with which Dante describes the pilgrim's error:

per ch'io dentro all'error contrario corsi
a quel ch'accese amor tra l'omo e 'l fonte.

[at which I ran into the opposite error to that which kindled love between the man and the spring.]

(*Par.* 3.18–19)

The allusion is of course to the myth of Narcissus.

Twice already Hugh of St. Cher's discussion of intellectual vision has seemed relevant to Dante's poetic position in the *Paradiso*. It is perhaps most revealing with regard to the image of Narcissus which appears in Hugh's text as the image of the man, perhaps a philosopher or a mystic, who is so carried away with the flight of his imagination that he thinks he has transcended the senses altogether and does not realize that his vision is still mediated by images. Hugh is discussing the difference between spiritual and intellectual vision and poses the problem whether any man could so abstract himself from the senses as to see God as St. Paul did. The answer is that he could not, but he might think he had, for

> in contemplatione videt anima pulchritudinem per imaginem, quia adhuc videt eam per imaginationem, sed tantum intenta est pulchritudini illi, quod videtur ei quod videat eam non per imaginem . . . *sicut Narcissus se per imaginem comprehendens, quod esset imago nullo modo cogitabat.* [Italics mine]
>
> [in contemplation the soul sees beauty by means of an image because it still sees it through a mental image, but, being so much directed to that beauty, the soul seems to see it not by means of an image . . . just as Narcissus, catching hold of himself by means of an image, understood in no way that it was an image.]
>
> (*Opera Omnia in Universum Vetus et Novum Testamentum* [Venice, 1703], 7)

When Dante describes his error as the opposite of Narcissus's there can be no doubt that his Narcissus is the same as Hugh of St. Cher's, the man who mistakes an abstraction of the imagination for direct intuition or, what is the same, spiritual vision for intellectual vision. The pilgrim, who has been prepared on all levels of human experience, but only of human experience, when confronted with incorporeal vision assumes that it is also unsubstantial. His error is indeed the opposite of that of Narcissus for, while Narcissus mistook spiritual vision for intellectual vision, he mistakes intellectual vision for spiritual vision. While Narcissus failed to turn away from an image which he thought was substance, the pilgrim turns away from substance thinking it an image.

It is worthwhile comparing this episode to that of Casella in the *Purgatorio*:

> Io vidi una di lor trarresi avante
> per abbracciarmi, con sì grande affetto,
> che mosse me a fare il simigliante.

Ohi ombre vane, fuor che nell'aspetto!
Tre volte dietro a lei le mani avvinsi,
e tante mi tornai con esse al petto.
Di meraviglia credo, mi dipinsi.

> [I saw one of them come forward with so much affection to embrace me that it moved me to do the same. O empty shades, except in semblance! Three times I clasped my hands behind him and as often brought them back to my breast. Wonder, I think, was painted in my looks.]
>
> (*Purgatorio* 2.76–82)

Like the souls in the moon, Casella is the first soul the pilgrim meets in the new realm. Newman has pointed out that the encounter with Casella represents a kind of introduction of the pilgrim to spiritual vision, for the pilgrim, who has just come from the realm of corporeal vision, does not realize at first that Casella is but an "ombra vana fuor che nell'aspetto," almost a technical definition of an image. In the *Paradiso* the situation is similar, for the pilgrim has just arrived from Purgatory and again misjudges his new vision which is again described in terms which seem almost a definition, "vere sustanze."

There is a further relation between the episode of Casella and its counterpart in the *Paradiso* for, while the pilgrim's error in the *Paradiso* is described as the opposite of Narcissus's error, with Casella it is strikingly reminiscent of the myth as it appeared in the classics. Like the classical Narcissus the pilgrim sees an image which appears to be a man and, like Narcissus, he attempts to embrace it. His error is identical to the one Ovid described: "corpus putat esse quod umbra est." Had the pilgrim, or Narcissus, turned away from the image before him, there would have been no error. Perhaps the pilgrim's very caution in the *Paradiso* ("sovra il ver lo piè non fida," [27]), which causes him to turn from the souls, is a manifestation of his fear, when confronted with what does not even appear to have corporeal substance, of falling into his previous error. Yet, in the *Purgatorio*, the poet avoids any direct allusion to the myth of Narcissus. Had Dante's Narcissus been simply the one found in Ovid the image would have been appropriate to the *Purgatorio*. But this Narcissus has undergone a transformation in a tradition which treated him as the man who fails to turn away from an inferior experience toward the truth, a truth which has long since ceased to be the truth of the senses. As Narcissus appears in Hugh of St. Cher's version his error is clearly that of mistaking an image for spiritual, not corporeal, substance and such an error has little to do with the passage from corporeal to spiritual vision.

The encounter with the souls in the moon is clearly an introduction of the concept of intellectual vision. And yet there is one aspect of it which, on the surface at least, seems to go against such an interpretation, encouraging the reader to suppose the pilgrim is not yet ready for a truly incorporeal experience. This is the presence of faces in the description of the souls. In no other part of the *Paradiso* do souls bear any resemblance to the human form. This corporeality is mitigated by the fact that only faces, not bodies proper, are present and by the fact that they are barely visible. However, in speaking of outlines ("postille"), Dante is using terms inapplicable to spiritual substance which "nullam corporis similitudinem gerunt" and which we see "non utique intuentes lineamenta earum vel colores."

Of course, as we have had occasion to say, the poet deals in images and shows us only conceptually what he can have no hope of showing us directly. Still, the form of the human face, in this instance, cannot be understood merely as a necessary imperfection in the representation. It could if there were no emphasis on it, but it is the key image of the passage. Dante compares what he saw, a group of faces, to the reflection of faces in water or glass, and he speaks of a pearl worn on the forehead. The image of Narcissus is the image of a reflected face. Finally, the pilgrim's error consists, dramatically, in his turning his face away from the vision.

Dante's vision could be purely incorporeal but, if it were not direct it would not be intellectual. The whole passage is intended to introduce into the poem the experience of direct spiritual intuition and the image of the face is no exception. It represents the dramatization of the Pauline phrase which was commonplace in describing the directness of intellectual vision, "facie ad faciem," and which was inseparable from its association with the phrase that described all other vision, "per speculum in aenigmate." Everything in the episode works to replace the mirror by the face. In fact, the pilgrim does not yet understand the nature of his vision and consequently puts himself in such a position as to reject it. With the help of Beatrice he corrects his error so that he can then receive the vision granted him. In order to see face to face he must turn face to face.

Somehow the pilgrim's error and its correction do not seem vital to his development. Surely, once granted this vision, he should be able to recognize it. But sometimes the pilgrim must show the reader the pitfalls to be avoided by himself failing to avoid them. If recognition should be fairly simple for the pilgrim, it is not simple for the reader. On the one hand, the reader sees what might be described as images of images, on the other hand, he finds the concept of images strongly denied. Different from the pilgrim, no matter how much the images tend to negate their nature as images, the reader will have them before him for the entire duration of the poem. Because of this it is necessary that he understand from the beginning that they were not there for the pilgrim, that the vision the poet describes was imageless. Dante could have followed St. Paul and resorted to silence, for of such things "homini non licet loqui" and a poet cannot speak without images. Instead of this he chose to testify to his experience despite the fact that he could only offer an "essemplo," an imperfect rendering and a substitute for the experience itself. From the beginning of the *Paradiso* he confesses that it will be but an "ombra del beato regno," a shadow, a reflection, even an image. Yet from the very first heaven he shows us, through the pilgrim's initial error, that, though we shall see only images, he saw only substances. If he can make us accept this, then perhaps we will accept the climax of his claimed vision, substantial knowledge of God.

# Bestial Sign and Bread of Angels: *Inferno* 32 and 33

*John Freccero*

The episode of Conte Ugolino, virtually the last in the *Inferno*, has been considered through the centuries as one of the most moving accounts of human suffering and, by some readers, as one of the most grotesque. From the Renaissance to the time of Shelley, it has been read as an attempt to understand the most unfathomable of evils. The suffering of the children, like the slaughter of the innocents, represents the most radical instance of the irreducibility of evil, just as the mystery of salvation is represented, at a structurally corresponding place in the *Paradiso*, by the joy of the children in the celestial rose. This formal correspondence dramatizes the limits of salvation history, limits more familiar to modern readers, perhaps, in the form given to them by Dostoyevski. In *The Brothers Karamazov*, Ivan asks: "What of the *children*, Alyosha?" and, as if in answer, the novel ends with the anticipation of the Resurrection in the form of a love-feast, with the children gathered around the table recalling the former life. In the *Inferno*, Dante confronts both the stumbling block of children's suffering and, as we shall see, the traditional Christian answer. The episode is thus neither merely anecdotal nor simply another infernal monstrosity; it is rather a paradigm of death and salvation, stripped of comforting illusions and conventions, and so epitomizes the theme of the entire poem.

At the same time the episode is a paradigm of political understanding, representing a model of what civic life has become within a purely secular order. Seen from the perspective of the *Inferno*, Dante's own political philosophy, expressed in his treatise *On Monarchy*, seems an optimistic dream.

---

From *Dante: The Poetics of Conversion*. ©1986 by the President and Fellows of Harvard College. Harvard University Press, 1986.

it may be said that Ugolino's condemnation to the circle of political traitors functions as a political palinode, an Augustinian and very nearly despairing view of the possibilities for social peace in the political order. Augustine defined the city as a group of human beings joined together by the love of the same object. Since there were for him only two ultimate objects of love, God and the "self" (however illusory), it followed that there were only two cities: the City of God and the city of man. Similarly, I will suggest, in the episode of Ugolino the alternatives are narrowed down to two in man's relationship to his fellow man: communion or cannibalism.

Finally, the episode has been something of a scandal in the history of Dante criticism, for Ugolino's story ends with a verse whose meaning has been the subject of much debate. Unlike other interpretive problems in the text, however, this crux is part of its own theme, rather than the accidental product of semantic history. The critical stumbling block of Ugolino's last words marks the intersection of Dante's theme with his poetics and so constitutes one of those interpretive moments that the attentive reader comes to expect in a poem whose story, at one level, is its own genesis. Like virtually all of the sinners in hell, Ugolino does not grasp the import of his own words and so demands, on our part, an ironic reading, a *mystificatio* that permits us to see Dante's eschatological hope in Ugolino's eternal despair. The succession of such ironic moments in the characterizations of the *Inferno* adds up to the allegory of that *cantica*. At the same time, the debates of the critics in this and in other cantos reproduce its ironic tensions, translating them into an allegory of interpretation. We shall see that the significance of Ugolino's story is revealed by the struggle of his critics to arrive at that significance.

To begin with the theme itself, there are several indications that Dante intends it to be read, not only as a human and familial horror, but also as political tragedy. In the first place, we are in lowest hell, in the circle of treachery, where Ugolino is specifically identified as a traitor to his city, Pisa. He begins his story by explaining (33.15) why he is such a neighbor, "tal vicino," to Ruggieri. Ugolino's dream, in which he is cast as a wolf and his children as whelps, is politically emblematic—we recognize in the animal an emblem for the Guelf party. This allusion to contemporary Italian factionalism is reinforced by the identity of the traitors. Ugolino thinks of himself as a man who *was* a count: "i' fui conte Ugolino" (13). His bitter enemy is and remains forever Archbishop Ruggieri: "questi è l'arcivescovo Ruggieri" (14). Ugolino's eternal hatred seems to be as much directed against the office as against the person who held it. The two men stand for enemy institutions in Dante's day: the Church, in the person of the archbishop, and the Empire, in the person of the count. Finally, Ugolino's story evokes the narrator's invective against the city of Pisa, calling it a "New Thebes" (89). The ancient city, raised from dragon's teeth and nurtured in parricide and fratricide, is Dante's model for the city of man throughout the *Inferno*, the crystallization of the disease that afflicts all of mankind.

Confirmation of a political dimension of meaning in the episode is provided for us in the sixth canto of the *Purgatorio*, when Sordello and Virgil embrace at the mention of their city, Mantova. The embrace occasions the narrator's bitter tirade in a passage which has become a set-piece for Italian political rhetoric to the present day. It pictures the body politic as wracked by the disease of violence and compares the city of Florence to a sick woman, unable to find relief from her pain as she tosses and turns in a featherbed. The image that Dante uses to describe the illness recalls the infernal situation:

> e ora in te non stanno sanza guerra
> li vivi tuoi, e l'un l'altro si rode
> di quei ch'un muro e una fossa serra.

> [and now in you your living abide not without war, and of those whom one wall and one moat shut in, one gnaws at the other!]
> (82–84)

Thus, the savage hatred Ugolino expresses for his eternal enemy is not only a reenactment of Tydeus's hatred for Menalippus in the story of Thebes, but is also a dramatization of the disease that affects contemporary society. Ugolino and Ruggieri are enclosed in a single ditch; the passage from the *Purgatorio* serves in retrospect to give that situation a universal dimension of meaning, making of it an emblem of the Italian political order.

In the tangle of violence for which Ugolino and Ruggieri are the paradigm, vengeance is the law. Where every person is a god unto himself, the existence of another is perceived as a menace to be combated to the death. At the same time, this precarious uniqueness or individuality is continually threatened by the increasing resemblance of each to each. The social consequence of this struggle is a generalized violence, a parody of the city, such as is represented in the *Inferno*. Virtually every episode of the *cantica* reveals this alienation in physical proximity. This may explain why so many of the souls in hell are represented in pairs or groups, even when only one speaks to the pilgrim or to his guide. It is as if the heroic uniqueness of Ulysses, for example, were deliberately undercut by the silent presence of Diomede, who is physically indistinguishable from him, just as the thieves, for all of their individual virtuosity, are literally interchangeable. So too, in the episode under consideration, even the syntax seems to stress reciprocity, in spite of the fact that Ugolino's claim to justice rests on the distinction between himself and his enemy.

Reciprocity seems to govern phrases such as "l'un capo a l'altro era cappello [the head of the one was a hood for the other]" (32.126), while phrases such as "io vidi *due* ghiacciati in *una* buca [I saw two frozen in one hole]" (125) underscore the political irony, a unity in multiplicity. At the same time, the horrible isolation of Ugolino is reinforced by reflexive verbs that serve to distance him from his reified enemy: "si rose" (130) and "tu . . . ti mangi" (134). As in the Augustinian description of sin, to assert one's subjectivity is to treat the other as object, reified as though he were a piece of bread, and the consummation is literal: "come 'l pan per fame si manduca [as bread is devoured for hunger]" (127). Ugolino and Ruggieri are alone together, with their master-slave roles, "maestro e donno" (33.28), symmetrically reversed. In his dream, Ugolino was hounded by Ruggieri; in infernal reality, he is a dog to Ruggieri's flesh. The rule of reciprocity finds its counterpart in the attitude of the pilgrim, who says that he will repay Ugolino for what he has suffered (32.136). The implication is that Ugolino's portrait in the *Inferno* is what he deserves, despite his protestations. The horror alluded to in the ending of 32 builds up the suspense and carries us to the next canto; it is literally occasioned by the ghastly scene which the pilgrim witnesses, but perhaps also contains an allusion to the greater horror recounted in the tale: the suffering and death of innocent children. Ugolino and Ruggieri are damned for the same crime, of which the children are the innocent victims:

> Che se 'l conte Ugolino aveva voce
> d'aver tradita te de le castella,
> non dovei tu i figliuoi porre a tal croce.
> Innocenti facea l'età novella,
> novella Tebe, Uguiccione e 'l Brigata
> e li altri due che 'l canto suso appella.

> [For if Count Ugolino had the name of betraying you of your castles, you ought not to have put his children to such torture. Their youthful years, you modern Thebes, made Uguiccione and Brigata innocent, and the other two that my song names above.]
>
> (85–90)

The phrase "tal croce" is more than a figure of speech here. The innocent victim placed on a cross by an act of treachery cannot but recall in this, of all poems, the archetypal Victim and the Crucifixion.

Although critics have not noticed it until recently, the Christological language that is used to describe the children seems the most salient feature of the story. Apart from the word *croce* in the passage just cited, perhaps the clearest allusion to the passion of Christ is in verse 69: "Padre mio, che non m'aiuti?" echoing the words of Christ on the cross: "My God, my God, why has thou forsaken me?" The children's words are the last words spoken by the Savior before his death. The Christological suggestion is equally strong in verse 61 where the children, with devastating naïveté, offer themselves to their father:

> "Padre, assai ci fia men doglia
> se tu mangi di noi: tu ne vestisti
> queste misere carni, e tu le spoglia."

> ["Father, it will be far less painful to us if you eat of us; you did clothe us with this wretched flesh, and do you strip us of it!"]
> (61–63)

They echo at once the eucharistic sacrifice and the words of Job: "The Lord giveth and the Lord taketh away. Blessed be the Name of the Lord." It must not be supposed that the allusions to Christ's passion are merely pietistic embellishments to contrast with the infernal horror story; they are in fact the key for the whole dramatic interpretation. The point of the language here is that the suffering of the children is of a sacred order, carrying with it a redemptive possibility. To accept such suffering with total selflessness and no thought of vengeance is to put an end to the otherwise eternal series of violent acts, making possible a communion that was not possible before. The spirit of their words offers the hope of a shared grief and a reconciliation to their father, but he sees in their death only a spur to his infernal retribution, thereby repeating in hell the pattern set forth in his dream. His tragedy is a failure of interpretation, as well as an inability to accept the suffering of his children.

The Christological pattern is not only linguistic, but narrative as well, for anyone with an acquaintance with biblical typology. To speak of a sacrifice of a son in the presence of a father who only half understands the gesture is inevitably to recall, if only by contrast, the moment of the foundation of Israel in the story of Abraham and Isaac. To a Christian interpreter, that story is the foreshadowing of the Redemption; the sacrificial animal substituted at the last moment for Isaac is the prefiguration of the *Agnus Dei*. The language of Ugolino's children recalls at once the naïve obedience of Isaac and the resignation of the Savior. As so often in the poem, Dante seems to have collapsed both the figure and its fulfillment into a single historical event which is both itself and part of the pattern of salvation history. The generational struggle of fathers and sons, resolved in the covenant that founded Israel in the story of Abraham and Isaac, finds a new representation in contemporary Pisa, where it ends in Theban failure.

Because Ugolino's story ends as an emblem of political as well as human failure, Dante refers to Pisa as a new Thebes. Every city, every covenant has its foundational myth, cast in terms of the smallest social unit, the family. Israel has its Abrahamic sacrifice and Thebes, by contrast, has the story of Oedipus. Dante's "*novella* Tebe" may be said to be Theban tragedy in a New Testament perspective, where the Christological promise is no longer a messianic dream but is rather a bitter and despairing memory. The story of Abraham and Isaac represented an alternative to the repeated succession of fathers and sons in the Theban story, where the temporary survival of one generation seemed to demand the destruction of the other. Abraham is prepared to give up his lineage in the sacrifice of his son, and Isaac is ready to give up his life. In this mutual surrender to the will of God, a compact is formed, a third term that founds the new nation. The Christ event was believed by Christians to represent a new and eternal covenant, replacing the Abrahamic for all time and making communion possible.

In this perspective, the story of Ugolino is a sign of a second, perhaps definitive failure of men to live in peace according to a covenant. Insofar as the Abrahamic typology is evoked in violent contrast, the story is reminiscent of the Jewish legend of the woman who was forced to sacrifice her seven sons during the Roman persecution: "Go and tell Father Abraham: Let not your heart swell with pride! You built one altar, but I have built seven. . . . What is more, yours was a trial; mine was an accomplished fact." The bitterness in Dante's story is reserved, however, not for a messianic promise unfulfilled, but rather for the failure to understand the promise implicit in Abraham's words: "The Lord will provide."

For all the sympathy that the portrayal of Ugolino has aroused in readers of the poem, beginning with De Sanctis in the nineteenth century, there can be little doubt that he is condemned by Dante not only as a traitor but also for his inability to grasp the spiritual meaning in the letter of his children's words. In another context, he says of himself that he turned to stone at the sound of the nailing of the door—that *duritia cordis*, as well as his subsequent blindness, both Pauline signs of the interpretive obtuseness of non-believers, blind him equally to the spiritual significance of his children's words. He begins by not taking their offer seriously and ends, if we are to trust the traditional and unsophisticated reading of his last words, with a bestial literalism. That unspeakable ending transforms the potentially Abrahamic situation into Theban horror, suggesting quite literally that no matter how great is Ugolino's love for his children, the father's survival, for however brief a time, depends on the destruction of his sons, whose bodies he treats as he does that of his enemy. In the absence of a covenant, it is every man for himself and a man for himself is a beast.

Ugolino's failure is an inability to interpret the Christian hope contained in the words of his children. In the episode, he is portrayed primarily as an interpreter, first of his dream and then his life, but the meaning he reads is always death. His dream seems to foreshadow his capture and ends with a grim prophecy: "con l'agute scane / mi parea lor veder fender li fianchi [and it seemed to me I saw their flanks ripped by the sharp fangs]" (35–36). He infers from this incident in his dream no more than can be learned from any of the prophecies in hell: that is, that he and his children will die. Finally, when the children beg him for help, he is struck silent in incomprehension.

Ugolino's inability to understand his children's words is matched by the inability of Dante critics to understand his last words: "Poscia, più che 'l dolor, potè il digiuno [then, hunger was stronger than grief]" (75). A traditional reading sees in the verse an allusion to cannibalism, confirming a legend that surrounded the death of the historical Ugolino and the children. Another group of critics rejects that reading, preferring instead to interpret the verse as an allusion to Ugolino's death, construing it as follows: "Hunger succeeded in killing me, whereas grief did not." In other words, they interpret Ugolino exactly as *he* interpreted his own dream—the ripping of flanks by teeth as simply a prophecy of death. However interesting the theme of death may be as literary motif, it is a banality in the afterlife; something more is contained in Ugolino's words although it is *unspeakable*. In the same way, we can see that something more was contained in Ugolino's dream than he realized upon his awakening—not simply a message of death, but an inverted drama of damnation.

The point of Ugolino's story in hell is not simply that he died. He tells us specifically that it is the *how* of his death that is significant:

> Che per l'effetto de' suo' mai pensieri,
> fidandomi di lui, io fossi preso
> e poscia morto, dir non è mestieri;
> però quel che non puoi avere inteso,
> cioè *come* la morte mia fu cruda,
> udirai.

> [How, by effect of his ill devising, I, trusting in him, was taken and thereafter put to death, there is no need to tell; but what you cannot have heard, that is, how cruel my death was, you shall hear.]
>
> (16–20)

The specific nature of his grief is, however, unspeakable. When Ugolino says, at the beginning of his story, "tu vuo' ch'io rinovelli disperato dolor" (5), he is echoing Aeneas's words to Dido in the second book of the *Aeneid*, with the first and most important word omitted, precisely the word "unspeakable": "*Infandum*, Regina, iubes renovare dolorem." The omission of that word in Dante's allusion seems to underscore its import in this even more terrible context. Nevertheless, as we shall see, the absence of this sign is itself significant. On closer inspection, the whole of the episode seems very much concerned with signs and their interpretation. As it begins, in canto 32, the pilgrim sees Ugolino gnawing his enemy as if he were eating bread, but recognizes that his eating has a significance, as a *sign* of hatred: "O tu che mostri per sì bestial segno / odio sovra colui che tu ti mangi [O you who by so bestial a sign show hatred against him whom you devour]" (133–34). The bestiality of the gesture is somewhat tempered by the fact that it appears to be a dramatization of a Pauline figure describing the absence of charity: "But if you bite and devour one another, take heed or you will be consumed by one another" (Gal. 5:15). It is important to notice that in this introduction, the contrast between "hunger" and "hatred" is tantamount to the difference between eating and speaking, between bestial reflex and paralanguage. The action, whether reflex or sign, remains the same, and Dante underscores the ambivalence of the gesture with a paradoxical description: *bestiale*, because eating is natural to beasts; *segno*, because in this case, eating has human significance. The binary opposition between hatred and hunger is thus the opposition between significance and nonsignificance, between language and nature.

This opposition reappears in Ugolino's dream as does the "bestial segno." The dream, on the surface of it, seems an action of beasts, the wolf and the whelps ripped apart by the fangs of the dogs. On interpretation, however, the dream has the meaning of a sign that prefigures both death and, in the symmetrical inversion characteristic of the thematics of vengeance, the form of damnation. Ugolino says of his dream that "del futuro mi squarciò il velame" (33.27). The "rending of the veil" echoes the rending of the veil of the temple at the Crucifixion and so constitutes one more recall to Christ's Passion, yet it should be noticed that the specifically prophetic quality of the dream could be perceived only after death; that is, after it was too late. At his awakening, Ugolino understood only its most generic meaning: he and his children would die. In this respect, the dream resembles all of the infernal prophecies. Like the ancient oracles, they are accurate in detail to an extent that can be appreciated only after the future has come to pass, at which point they cannot help. The specific significance of Ugolino's dream is that it prefigures the form of his damnation, but that is something he can know only in hell. The ironic distance between his earthly reading of his dream and the infernal reality, between the generic message of death and the specific form of infernal cannibalism, corresponds exactly to the critical dispute about the meaning of his last words in the text. Ugolino's dream, as we shall see, is Dante's allegory for the reading of his own text.

Most significantly, the gesture of biting human flesh reappears when Ugolino sees himself mirrored in the faces of his children and bites his hand in a gesture of desperation: *dolore.* The children apparently misunderstand its nature as a sign and take it to be instead an attempt to eat himself:

> ambo le man per lo dolor mi morsi;
> ed ei, pensando ch'io 'l fessi per voglia
> di manicar, di sùbito levorsi
>
> [I bit both my hands for grief. And they, thinking I did it for hunger, suddenly rose up]
>
> (58–60)

Once more, the opposition is between significance and non-significance, between *dolore* and hunger. The action is ambivalent in exactly the same sense as the *bestial segno,* for the children interpret it as a natural desire for food, while their father means it to express his grief. It is at this point that they offer themselves and, by their surrender and innocence, offer as well a redemptive hope. Unlike their father's pain, their *dolore* would be assuaged by their offer. Because their father is a literalist, however, he cannot understand the spiritual significance of their apparently literal statement.

There is a certain condescension implied in Ugolino's suppression of the sign of his grief: "Queta' mi allor per non farli più tristi [then I calmed myself in order not to make them sadder]" (64). The irony, if I am correct in my reading, is that in the passage that follows, he exercises the same discretion, this time to spare the feelings of the pilgrim, by suppressing all mention of what must be assumed to have been the very same action: the biting of flesh that was symbolically, but no less really, his own: "then, hunger was stronger than grief." Although the gesture has been suppressed, the same binary opposition is involved between significance and non-significance, but this time it is clear that we have moved into the realm of the purely biological, not *grief* but *hunger* motivated the reappearance of the same action. We are spared the details by the particular form of ellipsis known as *reticentia*, used in rhetoric to avoid mentioning horrible or obscene details. Perhaps the most famous Dantesque use of the same figure occurs in the words of Francesca: "Quel giorno piu non vi leggemmo avante." At the thematic level, there is no point in suppressing the fact of death here in the afterlife; it is something worse than death that is suppressed by Ugolino. The absence of the sign, in this series of oppositions, must be construed as a sign. There is a very strong implication that in the last moment, he accepts quite literally the offer of his children and simultaneously moves into bestial muteness or, perhaps, noise:

> Quand' ebbe detto ciò, con li occhi torti
> riprese 'l teschio misero co' denti,
> che furo a l'osso, come d'un can, forti.

> [When he had said this, with eyes askance he again took hold of the wretched skull with his teeth, which were strong on the bone like a dog's.]
>
> (76–78)

Moving away from the purely thematic, we may say that both Ugolino and Francesca exist only as exemplars of their own stories; in short, as literature. The passage from literature to life, from significance to biology, is the functional equivalent, in both stories, to the disappearance of the character.

The movement from *dolore* to *digiuno* in the last lines of Ugolino's story marks the waning of his consciousness and his humanity. It is at this point that language is extinguished and that nature takes over. Ugolino ceases to exist as a speaker and thus as a character. Yet that mute unconsciousness is not the same as death: it is animality. Throughout the canto, the opposition has been between significance and non-significance, between the human and the bestial. Ugolino's last words do indeed report the triumph of biology over language and, in the long run, that triumph is indeed physical death, as the earthbound significance of his dream was death. In the context of hell, however, such a statement would be pure redundancy—in the long run, death is *always* the end term of life. Much more significant is the fact that the intermediate stage of the final entropy in terms of the oppositions set forth in the canto is *bestiality*, the mid-point between humanity and reification, as hunger is the intermediate stage between *disperato dolore* and death. To say that hunger overcame grief is to say that Ugolino moved one step from humanity and one step closer to death by becoming a beast to the flesh of his children. Thereafter, the final step, far from being dreaded, would seem precisely the relief that Ugolino has himself previously sought: "ahi dura terra, perché non t'apristi? [Ah, hard earth! why did you not open?]" (66). Whatever the sensibilities of the modern critic, in hell at least, there are some things worse than death.

The words of the children, we recall, held out a redemptive possibility —their literalism is of a different order. To discover it, we have simply to oppose and recombine the terms of the oppositions that we have established: the "savage repast," *fiero pasto*, has its counterpart in the sacred feast, the *agape*. If the first is a sign of despair and hatred, then the second is a sign of hope and love: the Eucharist is the eating of a living body, *come 'l pane per fame si manduca*. As the Eucharist is the opposite of the corpse, so communion is the opposite of cannibalism and the bread is not only the "bread of angels," but also of peace in the human community, *panis concordiae*. Eating food is an action in the biological order, whether the food is bread or human flesh. When it becomes significant behavior in hell, Dante calls it a *bestiale segno*. The opposite of that phrase would in fact be "divine food," or, to use the phrase that Dante uses elsewhere, the *pane degli angeli*. What seemed at first to be simply an oxymoric phrase invented by Dante to describe the lowest degradation of the highest powers turns out to be the logical opposite of the central mystery of Christianity: not bestial, but angelic; not simply a sign, but a presence. The children's offer is sacramental, a sign that presents what it represents. To Ugolino, as to the reader, a literal reading of their words suggests cannibalism.

I have suggested that throughout Ugolino's narrative, the action is the same, alternately ascribed to the realm of biology or to the realm of signification. The same dichotomy is expressed in medieval terms by Dante's text in the opposition of physical hunger to spiritual hunger. The offer of the children to their father is the same as Christ's offer to his disciples: a spiritual eating of the *living* bread, which absorbs the recipient into the mystical body of Christ. In the seventh book of the *Confessions*, the voice of God says to Augustine, "I am the food of grown men; grow, and thou shalt feed upon me; nor shalt thou convert me, like the food of thy flesh into thee, but thou shalt be converted into me." Ugolino's children, whether they understand it or not (the understanding of the children whose words lead to the conversion of Augustine in the eighth book, for instance, is irrelevant to the efficacy of their words), offer their father their suffering as an example, the promise of ultimate deliverance and the eschatological hope for the unity of the human community. The Eucharist, the central mystery of Christianity, is the message that Ugolino cannot understand. His death by starvation is a dramatic reenactment of the interpretive failure as it is represented in the New Testament.

In the sixth chapter of the Gospel of John, Christ offers the Jews two kinds of bread, the letter and the spirit. They come not for a sign, but for bread. They associate the miracle of the loaves and fishes with the manna that came down from heaven to assuage the hunger of the Jews in the desert, but Jesus says, "Moses did not give you the bread from heaven, but my Father gives you the true bread, which gives life to the world . . . so that if anyone eat of it he will not die. I am the living bread." The Jews ask the same question that might be asked of Ugolino's children: "How can this man give us his flesh to eat?" He replies, "He who eats my flesh and drinks my blood has life everlasting and I will raise him up on the last day." The Jews are left in perplexity: "This is a hard saying. Who can listen to it?" The "scandal," as Jesus calls it, the stumbling block of the cross, is the same as the crux in our text. Christ's words retrospectively gloss the natural hunger of the Jews in their exodus as a figure for the spiritual hunger for the Christian comfort, just as the children gloss Ugolino's grief, as he bites his own hand, as a figure for his spiritual hunger. Ugolino's "sensible" reading of their offer, like the "sensible" reading of Jesus' words (or Freud's reading in *Totem and Taboo*), interprets it as though it were an invitation to cannibalism. It is this literalism, this *letter* that, in the end, "kills" Ugolino spiritually. Once more, Dante glosses the Bible's words with an historical situation, substituting literal starvation for the metaphoric hunger of the Jews. Without that background text, the episode seems merely a grotesque anecdote.

The meaning of this chapter of the Gospel of John has occasioned centuries of debate, but on one point medieval thought was unanimous: the foundation of the Eucharist was at the same time the foundation of the Church, the mystical body of Christ. Henri de Lubac has shown that the phrase "mystical body" was in fact first used to describe the presence of Christ in the sacrament, in an age when there was no contradiction between "mystical" and "real," and only later applied to the Church. For our purposes, the important point is the association between the Eucharist and what might be called its "political" dimension of meaning. It suggests that the political overtones in the story of Ugolino are likewise intrinsic to its theme. When Ugolino bites his own hand from grief and subsequently turns on the flesh of his children, the analogy between the members of his body and the "members" of the mystical body makes the same point as the eucharistic sacrifice. Moreover, it provides us with the necessary link between his behavior toward his enemy in hell and his behavior on earth: gnawing the head of his neighbor is analogous to gnawing his own hand, for both he and Ruggieri were members of the human community.

At the same time, the mystery of the Eucharist is a mystery of interpretation. The word *mysterion* itself, in one of its acceptances, in fact refers to the hidden relationship between the sign and its significance in the indissoluble unity of the sacrament. It is in this sense that the word comes to be synonymous with the word "allegory," the search for the "mystic" sense. In a tradition that goes back to St. Augustine, the indissoluble unity of the letter and the spirit is what Christ offers his disciples when He calls himself the *living bread.* For the Jews who do not understand Jesus' words, like Ugolino who does not understand his children's words, the flesh is dead. Augustine says: "They understand it in the sense of dead bodies that are torn apart or that are sold by butchers, not in the sense of bodies quickened by the spirit." In the same paragraph, he makes it clear that the analogy holds in the realm of signs as well: "Whence comes to us the sound of words, if not from the voice of the flesh? How could Jesus' words have come to us had they not been written down? And these are works of the flesh, thanks to the spirit that causes it to move as an instrument."

Ugolino and his children are at opposite ends of the drama of salvation and, at the same time, at the opposite ends of signification. The children, in their apparent naïve literalism, offer themselves as food and in so doing, present themselves as a sign for which the text offers no explicit signification. In symmetrical opposition, the last words of Ugolino offer us a signification for which there is no apparent sign. Critics who refuse to see in this *reticentia* anything but death are forced to read it as pure tautology and are at the same time blind to the eucharistic meaning of the children's offer. They are undoubtedly correct for any *literal* reading of the episode, but that is the point: a literalist who refuses to acknowledge the spirit that animates the text reifies it as a cannibal reifies the human body. The letter alone is dead.

The central interpretive problem of the canto of Ugolino turns out to be its theme: Ugolino's critics dramatize the difficulty they seek to resolve. Put most simply, the problem is the allegorical problem of the relationship of the spirit and the letter, of the Word and the flesh. To read only death in Ugolino's words is at the same time to misunderstand his children's offer.

Just as Ugolino misreads his own dream and then acts out his misreading, so the critics continue to trope the text itself. The resolution of the difficulty lies beyond the limits of signification, however, for it implies the search for a sign which presents its own representation. Between that Incarnation and the noise of teeth against bone, there is only the constant referentiality of the poem, pointing continually beyond itself.

# The Language of Faith: Messengers and Idols

*Giuseppe Mazzotta*

The practice of reading, . . . leads the reader into the center of an imaginative maze, to the awareness of an impasse where the primary plot of the pilgrim's ascetic experience harbors within itself a counterplot, the sense that the explicit moral weight of the text is drawn within the possibility of error. The question must now be asked whether this view of the poet, and the reader, cast in a condition of exile, where everything appears uncertain, open-ended and tentative, is simply the reflection of too modern a critical temper suspicious of firm answers, an interpretative heresy of sorts in projecting on to the text strictly subjective preoccupations. The question is not a gratuitous exercise of the mind doubting, as it were, its own doubts. It must be raised because the dramatic action of the *Divine Comedy* depends, to a large extent, on the persistent presence of guides and the occasional intervention of messengers who point the way to the pilgrim, remove obstacles from his journey, and whose primary role is to dramatize the fact that this is not the journey of a man entirely left to himself. The pilgrim is ostensibly unlike Ulysses whose mad flight is the emblematic story of a voyager who relies exclusively on his own intellectual powers and leads himself and his companions to a tragic end.

What is true for the pilgrim is equally true for the poet's own sense of history, shaped, as it is, by the steady acknowledgments of guides, prophets and mediators who bear and interpret God's Word to man. The readers are reminded that they have the Old and New Testament and "'l pastor de la

---

From *Dante, Poet of the Desert: History and Allegory in the* Divine Comedy. © 1979 by Princeton University Press.

Chiesa che vi guida; / questo vi basti a vostro salvamento" (*Paradiso* 5.76–78 [all further references to this text will be abbreviated as *Par.*]); in spite of the contingent crisis of authority, pope and emperor ideally ought to be guides to the world (*Purgatorio* 16.91 ff. [all further references to this text will be abbreviated as *Purg.*]); and if these two "suns" have eclipsed each other and have left the world in a state of blindness, St. Francis and St. Dominic are the two "princes" of the Church, "che quinci e quindi le fosser per guida" (*Par.* 11.36), veritable angels who herald and preach God's love and wisdom. Dante himself frequently takes a prophetic posture and calls for the reform of the Church: at the top of Purgatory, Beatrice, for instance, promises the imminent advent of a "messo di Dio," the "cinquecento, diece a cinque" (*Purg.* 33.43–44.) who will come to kill the Whore dallying with the Giant.

To suggest, therefore, as I have done, that the reader is left alone in a space of contradictory and indeterminate choices, is, on the face of it, to lapse into what might be called a heresy of reading, the doctrinal error of extrapolating, unaided, one's own truth from the poem. In *Inferno* 9 and 10, where heresy is punished, Dante dramatizes precisely this error and juxtaposes to it the virtue of faith in God's Word as the perspective from which the spiritual interpretation of the poem can be attained. The question of interpretation, thus, must be reexamined from the point of view of the language of faith: by focusing on the messengers and interpreters of God's Word (without giving, however, a full inventory of their role and occurrence in the poem), this chapter will map out first the relation between heresy and faith, and secondly it will describe the prophetic content of Dante's own message. Prophecy is, in a real sense, the language of faith, the way faith speaks; but I shall also argue that, for Dante, prophecy itself is vulnerable to the possibility of turning into blasphemy. He systematically opposes heresy to faith, idolatry to prophecy, and yet he is also aware that the line which separates belief from unbelief is precarious, that metaphoric language is never impervious to those interpretive errors which he unequivocally condemns in his treatment of heresy.

In *Inferno* 9, on the threshold of the city of Dis, the pilgrim is about to enter the circle of the heretics, but experiences what to him is a veritable impasse. The three Furies, handmaids of Hecate (43–44) and guardians of the gates, obstruct his passage by calling on Medusa to appear and, by the power of her gaze, transform him into a stone (52–54). Virgil, who in the preceding canto had failed to persuade the devils to allow them to enter Dis, now quickly instructs his disciple not to look, turns his head backward and shuts the pilgrim's eyes with his own hands (55–60). An angel, "da ciel messo" (85), comes and, by a touch of his wand, opens the gates for the pilgrim and his guide. In the middle of this action, the poet interrupts the narrative and urges the readers to look under the veil of the "strange verses."

> O voi ch'avete li 'ntelletti sani,
> mirate la dottrina che s'asconde
> sotto 'l velame de li versi strani.

> [O you who are of sound understanding, look at the doctrine that is hidden beneath the veil of the strange verses.]
>
> (61–63)

Since the early commentators, the passage has been subjected to the allegorical reading the poet calls for. Iacopo della Lana, for instance, interprets Medusa as the emblem of heresy; Boccaccio sees her as the image of obstinacy that blinds man; by virtue of her etymology, "quod videre non possit," she has been taken to be the allegory of *invidia*; other critics gloss the Furies and the threatened apparition of Medusa as abstract figurations of remorseful terror and despair; some others explain Medusa as the sin of *malitia* and the angel as the allegory of imperial authority. From this political perspective, since the immediate context of the scene is the civil war ravaging Florence, one might infer that Dante is dramatizing the crisis of what has come to be known as an Averroistic political vision. The scene, actually, is so complex that no single critical formula can account for its metaphoric and doctrinal density. Its primary concern, I would like to suggest, is heresy, a sin that for Dante involves the failure of understanding and imagination, and which he equates with the madness of those who produce poetic and philosophical discourses but have no faith in God.

The phrase *intelletti sani*, I submit, calls immediate attention to what might be called the heresy of reading and translates a commonplace of biblical exegesis. The Church Fathers, denouncing the error of the heretics who expounded the doctrine of the Bible in any sense but that imparted by faith and the Holy Ghost, consistently use the formula *sanus intellectus* to qualify a faithful interpretation of Scripture. The heretics apply their own *sensus proprius* or *bovinus intellectus*, and fall into an illusory subjectivism which disrupts the prophetic integrity of the biblical text. Those with a *sanus intellectus*, on the contrary, interpret the doctrine for what it is and do not hold false opinions in matters pertaining to Christian faith. The same phrase, *intelletto sano*, is employed in this precise sense in *Convivio*. In the fourth treatise, while giving a systematic critique of Frederick the Second's false opinion that nobility resides in fine manners and wealth, Dante appeals to those with *intelletti sani* who would discern the falseness of the emperor's doctrine. In the subsequent commentary on the line, the phrase is glossed as meaning that "tempo è d'aprire li occhi a la veritade," and *sano intelletto* means a mind which is not petrified and knows "quello che le cose sono." This particular meaning, and the metaphor of opening the eyes, clearly carried over in *Inferno* 9, has an extraordinary dramatic aptness because heresy, as we shall now see, is a sin that forfeits and darkens the sanity of the intellect.

Indeed, even at first glance the circle of the heretics appears to be literally the graveyard of that philosophy that believes in the perishability of the soul along with the death of the body. The sinners, Epicurus and his followers, "che l'anima col corpo morta fanno" (*Inferno* 10.15 [all further references to this text will be abbreviated as *Inf.*]), Frederick the Second (and the irony of the name, Federico, is transparent), Cavalcanti and Farinata, by a stark *contrappasso* are buried in tombs to live out, as it were, the eternal death they upheld in life. In a real sense, this is the exact reversal of the value that Dante assigned to the Epicureans in *Convivio.* In its fourth treatise, Dante describes, using Cicero as his source, the philosophical schools of active life (namely the Stoics, the Peripatetics and the Epicureans) as the three Marys who go to the tomb, the receptacle of corruptible things, where the Savior, that is to say, beatitude, is buried. But the "monimento" is empty, and an angel of God, who had rolled the stone away, tells them that Christ has risen and has gone before them into Galilee where those who seek can find him. Quite overtly, this is the story of understanding seeking faith, an explicit turning around of the formula *fides quaerens intellectum* which in the philosophical context of *Convivio* is viewed as a legitimate and positive undertaking. But in *Inferno* 10, Epicurus, instead of seeking the risen Christ in Galilee, has remained at the tomb, the "monimenti," as Dante, echoing the passage of *Convivio*, calls it (*Inf.* 9.131), and he literally dwells in it.

We can, perhaps, account for this shift of views from *Convivio* to the *Divine Comedy*. If in *Convivio*, where philosophy is celebrated as the sovereign source of authority, Athens is the celestial city, in the *Divine Comedy*, Dante juxtaposes Jerusalem to Athens. There is a great deal of irony in Virgil's words, "Tutti saran serrati / quando di Iosafat qui torneranno / coi corpi che là sù hanno lasciati" (*Inf.* 10.10–12). From this perspective of the valley in Jerusalem, where the Last Judgment and the resurrection of the flesh will take place, philosophy leads as far as the tomb and no further. In

*Convivio* philosophy may even offer consolation to death; in *Inferno* 10, the tomb is the scandal against which philosophy stumbles.

Dante's way of experiencing the opposition between Athens and Jerusalem is by no means unusual. When St. Paul preaches in Athens that God is not like gold or stone, a representation by the art and imagination of man, and announces the resurrection of the dead, the Athenians laugh at him (Acts 17:22 ff.). Later on, his belief in life after death is dismissed as sheer madness: "Paul, you are mad; much learning is turning you mad" (Acts 26:24). The distance that separates philosophical reason from the madness of faith is also the brunt of Tertullian's *De praescriptione haereticorum*. When Tertullian asks "quid ergo Athenis et Hierosolymis? quid academiae et ecclesiae? quid haereticis et Christianis?" he answers that the two have nothing to do with each other. Tertullian's position, to be sure, depends largely on the assumption that faith believes what is rationally impossible; for Dante, it is not that reason is insignificant or absolutely inept in matters of faith. Reason, left to itself, is found wanting because it can grasp neither the mystery which belongs to faith nor the wisdom of God who chooses foolish things, in the language of St. Paul, to confound the wise. Confronted with death conquered, the empty tomb of Christ, Epicurus remains entrenched in his own unbelief, and *Inferno* 10 bears witness to the wreckage of his philosophy: his philosophical quest of *Convivio* is exposed as madness, the doctrinal error that litters the path to God's wisdom.

It has not been clear to scholars, however, why heresy, a philosophical error, should be punished in the sixth circle of *Inferno*, between the sins of incontinence and those of mad bestiality. The critical confusion stems from the fact that in his exposition of the moral structure of Hell, Virgil says nothing about heresy, and also from the fact that in Aristotle's ethical system there is no rationale to view it even as a sin. In his pagan frame of reference, heresy is simply a perversion of the speculative intellect, which results neither from any infirmity of the will nor from the impulses of the flesh. On the other hand, for Dante it must be stressed that sin always involves the various functions of the will. Because of the apparent contradiction, W. H. V. Reade concludes his examination of the problem by stating that Dante "did not know what to say about the moral causes of heresy." In effect, Dante develops his figuration of heresy along the broad lines of Thomas Aquinas's conception. In an elaborate passage of the *Summa*, Aquinas views heresy as a sin of choice (the word comes, he says quoting Jerome and Isidore, from the Greek *hairesis* meaning choice); as a misinterpretation of Scripture, it is a denial of the truth on which faith is founded and, in this sense, it designates an intellectual error. But it is also more than a sin of opinion: it is an act that involves the flesh and arises, as Aquinas puts it, "from pride or covetousness or even some illusion of the imagination which according to Aristotle is a source of error." A more careful reading of the pattern of allusions and metaphors obliquely woven in the folds of *Inferno* 9 and 10 will show that Dante gives an essentially Thomistic account of heresy, one in which the affections are engaged, much as the intellect was, and like the intellect, they are threatened by a veritable madness.

The Furies' call for Medusa to appear dramatizes in a primary way a case of madness: the epithet "sani" (*Inf.* 9.61) signals that whatever we are witnessing verges on *insania*. Medusa's own story, as told by Ovid, is an experience of mad love. Among the early commentators on the passage, Boccaccio and Buti rightly recall the Ovidian account of the myth: once a beautiful maiden, Medusa was raped by Neptune in the temple of Minerva, the goddess of wisdom, who avenges the violation by turning Medusa's golden curls into snakes and, eventually, by giving Perseus the mirrored shield by which he can kill her. In several mythographic glosses, the Gorgons (56) are interpreted as women who disrupt the sanity of the mind. In Fulgentius's *Mythologicon*, the first of the three sisters stands for "mentis debilitas"; the second, "terrore mentem spargit"; the third, "mentis intentum, vero etiam caliginem ingerit visus." (The description in its entirety reads: "But let me explain what the Greeks, inclined as they are to embroider, would signify by this finely spun fabrication. They intended three Gorgons, that is, the three kinds of terror: the first terror is indeed that which weakens the mind; the second, that which fills the mind with terror; the third, that which not only enforces its purpose upon the mind but also its gloom upon the fact.") Further, both John of Garland and Arnulf of Orleans explain the metamorphosis into stone by Medusa as the allegory of the *stupor* that she engenders in the mind; this gloss, it may be pointed out, is obliquely picked up by Benvenuto da Imola, who interprets the pilgrim's threatened petrification as meaning to be "stupidum."

A number of other dramatic elements in *Inferno* 9 suggest this motif of madness. The three Furies are conventionally etymologized as the three affections, namely, wrath, cupidity and lust, which "stimulis suis mentem feriant"; Tisiphone (48), Juno's messenger, is also said to bring "insania." But there is a more compelling allusion that gives madness a central place in the canto: the fearful summons to Medusa to appear. Medusa, to be sure, does not appear; nonetheless, her name is to the pilgrim a shock of recognition, literally a ghost issued from his own past, and her name reenacts the *amor insanus* that Dante celebrated in his *Rime petrose*. In a powerful piece of literary criticism, John Freccero has recently shown that the *Rime petrose* are textually recalled in the rhyme scheme, "alto . . . smalto . . . assalto" (50–54), to dramatize the memory of the pilgrim's erotic fascination with the stonelike woman of that poetic sequence. The myth of Medusa, I would like to add, explicitly governs one of those poems. In "Così nel mio parlar voglio esser aspro," the poet, installed in an eerie spiritual landscape, recounts the tortures of his obstinate passion for the *Donna Petra* and the condition of his mind which has been shattered by the madness of his vain pursuit.

> Non trovo scudo ch'ella non mi spezzi
> nè loco che dal suo viso m'asconda:
> chè come fior di fronda,
> così de la mia mente tien la cima.

> [I cannot find a shield that she does not shatter, nor a place to hide from her look; like the flower on the stalk, she occupies the summit of my mind.]
>
> (14–17)

As I have shown earlier [elsewhere] the lover is an unsuccessful Perseus, without a shield and unable to sustain the lady's glance. This myth of the woman as Medusa is countered by another myth that runs through Dante's imaginative contrivance. The poet obliquely casts himself as Pygmalion: like Pygmalion, who, by the intervention of Venus, breathes life into the statue, the idol he wrought with his own hands, the poet wishes to instill life into the loved lady, who is a "dura petra / che parla e sente come fosse donna. [The hard stone that speaks and feels as if it were a woman."] The lady, however, will remain an unresponsive stone, and the poet's love is a hopeless obsession which borders on death.

This effort to give life to what is only a stone is placed in *Inferno* 9 within a context of magic and witchcraft. It ought to be remarked that Pygmalion's transformation of the statue into a human being is understood by the Ovidian mythographers as a magic mutation. More importantly, *Inferno* 9 opens with an allusion to Erichtho, the sorceress, who, as it is told by Lucan, conjures the shades from Hades to foretell the future events in the civil war at Pharsalia, and whose necromancy involves Virgil himself. The Furies, the grim shapes howling in the night, are identified as the handmaids of Hecate (43–44), the goddess of the lower world, who presides over demons and phantoms, and who is said to have taught sorcery and witchcraft. In Latin love lyrics, where the focus is the enchantment of love, it may be added, Hecate's magic spells are invoked to engender or cure the incantations and delusions of love. Even the angel "da ciel messo" (85), who opens the gates of Dis with his wand, bears overtones of magic. Ever since the early commentators, he has been identified as Mercury, Jupiter's faithful messenger from Statius's *Thebaid.* In *Inferno* 9, to be sure, the angel is the emblem of divine eloquence, the bearer of God's message, who defeats the devils and lets the pilgrim continue his journey. Dante, in effect, alludes to and revises his source, the *Thebaid*, where the messenger's function is to summon back the dead soul of Laius to foment the civil war of Thebes.

These allusions in the canto to magic heighten the sense of the madness of the pilgrim's experience. Like madness, which violates the rigor of the intellect and mistakes one thing for another, magic creates deceptive semblances and false figments of the mind. This metaphoric link between magic and madness did not escape Isidore of Seville, who, quoting the same passage of Erichtho in Lucan's *Pharsalia* which Dante recalls in lines 22 to 27, views magic precisely as the practice in which "the mind, though polluted by no venom of poisoned draught, perishes by enchantment." For Dante the links between the two are such that they invest the very substance of *Inferno* 9. As magic designates the tampering with the natural order, it discloses Dante's madness and unnatural passion for the *Donna Petra*; as the demonic art of conjuration of the dead, it further discloses as pure illusion the poet's idolatrous attempt in his past to give life to what is only a stone and an insubstantial form.

In the case of Epicurus, who is blind to the fact that Christ's empty tomb is a sign of his resurrection from the dead, philosophy goes mad; in *Inferno* 9 it is the poetry of the *Rime petrose*, which attempts to give life to a stone, that retrospectively is seen to suffer the same fate. This is not the classical madness of poetry, the powerful frenzy that is traditionally said to possess and engender poetic divinations. It is the spiritual derangement of the imagination, as Aquinas understands it, that operates all sorts of "magic" changes: it believes it can transform death into immortality, and make of a stone the monument for one's own self. These errors of the imagination are given an ironic twist in the two cantos of the heretics: the monument is an illusory and hollow emblem of death; the poet's attempt to give life to the *Donna Petra*-Medusa is reversed into a threat to reduce the pilgrim to a veritable tomb, like the one inhabited by the heretics, to petrify his intellect and make him blind.

The metaphor of blindness is crucial, actually, to the question of heresy, and it sustains the unfolding of both cantos 9 and 10 of *Inferno*. In canto 9, Medusa herself blinds those who gaze at her; Virgil shuts the pilgrim's eyes; the poet enjoins his readers to open their eyes. In canto 10, Hell is referred to as "cieco carcere" (58–59), and the sinners, we are told, see the faraway future, but are blind to the present. The question of blindness figures so prominently in the exchange between Cavalcanti and the pilgrim that we must look at it closely in order to assess its exact significance for the problem of heresy.

The passionate partisan exchange between Farinata and Dante about the civil war ravaging Florence (*Inf.* 10.22 ff.) is interrupted by Cavalcanti's anxious query about his son Guido:

> Dintorno mi guardò, come talento
> avesse di veder s'altri era meco;
> e poi che 'l sospecciar fu tutto spento,
> piangendo disse: "Se per questo cieco
> carcere vai per altezza d'ingegno,
> mio figlio ov' è? e perché non è teco?"
> E io a lui: "Da me stesso non vegno:
> colui ch'attende là, per qui mi mena,
> forse cui Guido vostro ebbe a disdegno."
> Le sue parole e 'l modo de la pena
> m'avean di costui già letto il nome;
> però fu la risposta così piena.
> Di sùbito drizzato gridò: "Come?
> dicesti "elli ebbe"? non viv' elli ancora?
> non fiere li occhi suoi lo dolce lume"?
> Quando s'accorse d'alcuna dimora
> ch'io facëa dinanzi a la risposta,
> supin ricadde e più non parve fora.

[He looked round about me as if he had a desire to see whether someone was with me, but when his expectation was all quenched he said weeping: "If you go through this blind prison by height of genius, where is my son and why is he not with you?" And I answered him: "I come not of myself; he that waits there is leading me through here perhaps to that one whom your Guido held in disdain." His words and the nature of his punishment had already told me his name, so that I replied thus fully. Suddenly erect, he cried: "How did you say, 'he held'?

> Does he no longer live? Does not the sweet light strike his eyes?" When he perceived that I made some delay before replying he fell back again and was seen no more.]
>
> (55–72)

The phrase "cieco carcere" translates, as is generally acknowledged, "Carcere caeco" from *Aeneid* 6.734. But the importance of the context which the phrase evokes has not, to my knowledge, been stressed. It occurs, in effect, at the very center of Anchises' exposition of the theory of the reincarnation of the souls. The souls destined to return to the light, Anchises says, are held in a blind prison, but after their guilt is washed away, they drink of the waters of the river Lethe and return to the world. As the Virgilian context is evoked, it is ironically turned around. For these heretics do not believe in the immortality of the soul, and Cavalcanti is no Anchises speaking to a son who has providentially descended to Hades and will return back to the light; at the same time, from Dante's Christian perspective the Virgilian notion of the eternal return of the souls is deflated and emptied of any validity.

This ironic twist of the passage of the *Aeneid* is not an isolated occurrence; actually, it is extended to cover the whole of Cavalcanti's speech. The very phrase "altezza d'ingegno," which is his humanistic perception of the pilgrim's descent, shows the old man's peculiar blindness to the vanity of the intellect, a blindness which Dante dispels by replying that he is not undertaking the journey on his own but is guided by Virgil to that one whom Guido held in disdain. The use of the past absolute, as Pagliaro has shown, is mistakenly construed by the sinner as an intimation that his son has died. The mistake is primarily Dante's strategy to sanction Guido's spiritual death, or at least suggest the uncertainty of his future. For, ironically, Cavalcanti's questions, which ostensibly ask whether Guido is alive, in reality allude to the philosophical reasons for his spiritual loss. Just as in *Inferno* 9 Dante recalled the rhyme scheme of his own poetry, here he echoes the same rhyme scheme, "nome," "come," and "lume," which Guido, with the important variation of "lome" for "lume," had deployed in "Donna me prega," his philosophical meditation on the nature of love.

Love, in Guido's formulation, proceeds from the darkness of Mars, the sphere of the irascible, and dwells, stripped of any moral quality, in the sensitive faculty. If the *Divine Comedy* dramatizes the perfection of love stretching from the Intellectual Light through the layers of Creation, Cavalcanti's poem projects love as a tragic experience, which robs the human self of any rationality and makes intellect and love radically heterogeneous entities. Practically following Isidore's etymology, "A Marte mors nuncupatur," Cavalcanti sees love as war, the activity of Mars, which ends in death, "di sua potenza spesso segue morte." This view of love as war and death is heightened by Dante in both cantos 9 and 10 of *Inferno*: in canto 9, the recall of the *Petrose* is framed within two allusions to civil wars, the *Pharsalia* (21 ff.) and the *Thebaid* (88 ff.). In canto 10, the explicit focus is the civil war of Florence. In a sense, Dante draws the internal strife of the cities within the moral category of heresy, for civil war perverts the bond of love that alone orders the city. As such, the metaphors of civil war expose the tragic reality that lies under Cavalcanti's view that love shatters the intellect. The celebration of love as death is a veritable heresy, as the phrase "dolce lume" implies.

Editors of the *Divine Comedy* still debate whether "lume" or the variant "lome" is the proper *lectio* of the text. I contend that Dante deliberately changes Guido's "lome" into "lume" in order to graft onto the allusions to "Donna me prega" an echo from Ecclesiastes, "*dulce lumen* et delectabile oculis videre solem" (11:7). Together these allusions afford the perspective from which he indicts Guido's intellectual errors. There are at least two medieval texts, I would like to suggest, which give cogency to this strategy. St. Jerome interprets the passage of Ecclesiastes as an invitation to man to rejoice in his youth, but warns not to think that the words of the preacher are meant "hominem ad luxuriam provocare, *et in Epicuri dogma corruere*." More importantly, Ecclesiastes 11:7 is used by Aquinas in an article which probes whether blindness of mind (*caecitas mentis*) is or is not a sin. His authorities are St. Augustine, who asserts that "all love to know the shining truth," and Ecclesiastes, which says that "light is sweet and it is delightful for the eyes to see the sun." On the other hand, Aquinas acknowledges that Gregory places "blindness of mind among the vices originating from lust." His conclusion is that blindness of mind is a privation of intellectual vision which can occur for three reasons. The most important one, for our purpose, is the first, which concerns the light of natural reason "of which a rational soul is never deprived, though its proper exercise may be hindered as in the insane and the mad." Against what is possibly Cavalcanti's nostalgia for the delights of life, Dante obliquely insinuates, by the allusion to *dulce lumen*, that Guido and his poem are wrapped in the darkness of the Epicurean heresy and that the poem dramatizes a veritable madness of love which eclipses the mind.

In view of the foregoing, it is appropriate that heresy should be placed midway between the sins of incontinence and those of mad bestiality, for it is a sin that involves the passions and also implies a violence against the intellect. It is a sin that entails the bankruptcy both of that philosophical discourse which literally leads man to the tomb but cannot show him how to transcend it, and of that poetic imagination which erects illusory monuments to eternity. More important, heresy is an interpretive perversion: as Dante transposes the patristic commonplace *intelletti sani*, to his own text, he claims that his own poem demands the same interpretive discipline accorded to the Bible; by that phrase, the poet directs the readers to look beyond the blinding appearances of deceitful and insubstantial forms, which mask death. He asks that we read not with a human eye, which as St. Augustine already knew is always bound to doubt and contemptuous disbelief, but with a mind sustained by the light of faith. The messenger from Heaven, who in *Inferno* 9 comes to open the gates of Dis, is precisely the faithful interpreter of God who removes the obstacles from the pilgrim's ascent and opens the way to God.

The centrality of faith to the allegorical interpretation of Scripture can hardly be exaggerated. Biblical exegetes state it succinctly by formulas such as "allegoria fidem aedificat" and "littera gesta docet, quid credas allegoria." Accordingly, Dante makes faith the prerequisite for understanding and the virtue which is radically opposed to heresy. While in the symbolic world of heresy there is only death and the madness of illusory changes, faith ostensibly affords the perspective from which language can have a precise signification, and the contingent and the eternal are fused together. In this sense, Dante's indictment of heresy is not an arbitrary theological choice: he is bent, actually, to show that faith has a necessary value over and against the errors of heresy. We must look at the story of St. Dominic in *Paradiso* 12 to probe Dante's sense of faith further.

St. Dominic marries faith (61–63), and he appears as the knight of faith who stands at the center of the Church Militant to uproot the heretics and nurture the vineyard of the Lord (100–103). He achieves this by his being a preacher, a reliable messenger who proclaims God's Word to the end of the earth so that the whole world may be gathered into the truth of the Logos. In *Paradiso* 11, actually, both Francis and Dominic are introduced as the two guides of the Church (31–36) and, by echoing Ubertino da Casale's definition, they are referred to as veritable angels, "L'un fu tutto *serafico* in ardore; / l'altro per sapienza in terra fue / di *cherubica* luce uno splendore." In the wake of St. Gregory, Aquinas defines the cherubim as fullness of knowledge and the seraphim as the zeal of charity. The two hagiographies of Francis and Dominic, in effect, enact the interdependence of will and intellect and, from this point of view, retrospectively show and remedy the double *obduratio* of heart and mind which heresy embodies.

The interdependence of *Paradiso* 11 and 12 is reflected, as is well known, in the rhetorical structure of the cantos. Each hagiography is recounted in exactly forty-six lines; in canto 11, at line 51, St. Francis's birthplace is linked, by an etymological pun on Assisi, with the rising sun; in canto 12, line 52, Dominic's place at Calagora is associated with the setting sun, as if to suggest that the whole world is held within the compass of their light. In *Paradiso* 11, the Dominican St. Thomas delivers the eulogy of St. Francis, while in the successive canto the Franciscan Bonaventure celebrates the accomplishments of St. Dominic. Reversing the practice of the two fraternal orders on earth, each speaker praises the virtue of the opposite order and attacks the moral erosion of his own. By such strategies, Dante elicits the picture of the genuine fellowship of the Church bent on questioning itself and confronting its own need of spiritual reform in order to carry out the providential mission with which it is invested.

If by focusing on preachers Dante implies the necessity for the proclamation of faith so that the Word of God may be heard, he also gives a representation in *Paradiso* 12 of how language sustained by faith achieves its full sense. The canto is deliberately organized to evoke a significant and providential design of history:

> Come si volgon per tenera nube
> due archi paralleli e concolori,
> quando Iunone a sua ancella iube,
> nascendo di quel d'entro quel di fori,
> a guisa del parlar di quella vaga
> ch'amor consunse come sol vapori,
> e fanno qui la gente esser presaga,
> per lo patto che Dio con Noè puose,
> del mondo che già mai più non s'allaga:
> così di quelle sempiterne rose
> volgiensi circa noi le due ghirlande.

> [As two bows, parallel and like in color, bend across a thin cloud when Juno gives the order to her handmaid, the one without born of the one within, like the voice of that wandering nymph whom love consumed as the sun does vapors, and makes the people here presage, by reason of the covenant that God made with Noah, that the world shall never again be flooded; so the two garlands of those sempiternal roses circled round us, and so did the outer correspond to the inner.]
>
> (10–20)

The overt dramatic purpose of the passage is to describe the dance of the two garlands of saints in the shape of two concentric and equidistant semicircles of the rainbow. It also functions as an expedient to set apart and, at the same time, provide a smooth transition from one hagiography to the other. Yet, the mythological and biblical allusions to the rainbow are thematically relevant to the central topics of the canto. The rainbow appearing after the flood is the prophetic sign of history as the alliance between man and God. As a sign of the restored peace, it both contrasts with the motif of the war that St. Dominic will wage on the heretics and prefigures the final peace that will come at the end of that war. This technique of prefiguration, of signs that foretell future events, invests the whole structure of the canto.

Critics have pointed out that the allusion to Iris echoes the first book of Ovid's *Metamorphoses* (271 ff.) where she draws water from the teeming earth and feeds it into the clouds to produce the flood which will punish the wickedness of the world. In this sense, one might add, there is an important symmetry at work in the passage: Iris prepares the flood, while Noah's rainbow appears when the flood is over to mark the covenant between man and God. But there is another reference to Iris in Ovid's *Metamorphoses* which critics have neglected and which is also recalled in *Paradiso* 12. In book 11 of *Metamorphoses*, Ovid recounts the death of Ceix and his wife Halcyon's prayer to Juno that the fate of her husband may be disclosed to her. Juno sends Iris to the House of Sleep:

> "Iri, meae" dixit "fidissima nuntia vocis
> Vise soporiferam somni velociter aulam
> extintique iube Ceycis imagine mittant
> somnia ad Alcyonem veros narrantia casus."

> [She said: "Iris, most faithful messenger of mine, go quickly to the drowsy house of Sleep, and bid him send to Alcyone a vision in dead Ceyx's form to tell her the truth about his faith."]

Iris, "a rainbow through the skies," descends to Morpheus, the artificer of dreams, who counterfeits a dream to reveal to Halcyon her husband's shipwreck. The story sheds considerable light on canto 12 of *Paradiso*. One could point out the presence of "iube" in the passages of both Ovid and Dante (12); moreover, like Iris, the messenger of Juno and her "nuntia vocis," Dominic is "*messo* e famigliar di Cristo" (73); like Iris, who is "fidissima," Dominic is consistently linked to faith. Further, the Ovidian passage focuses on the prophetic powers of dreams and establishes the difference between Morpheus, who sends true visions, and Phantasos, who takes on deceptive shapes. In *Paradiso* 12, there are two prominent prophetic dreams. The first concerns the saint's mother who dreamt she would bear a black and white hound (58–60); the second concerns his godmother who receives a prophetic dream disclosing Dominic's future mission in the service of the Church (64–66). But in contrast to Ovid's story, in which the dream reveals the widowhood of Halcyon, in Dante, the godmother, emblem of spiritual regeneration, dreams of the marriage between Dominic and Faith.

This pattern of prophetic signs is extended to two other characters in the canto. As St. Bonaventure points out from among the blessed "Natàn profeta" (136) and Joachim "di spirito profetico dotato" (141), Dante seems to imply that prophecy is the language of faith. Prophecy is not simply the prediction of events to come. The prophet, for Dante, is one who is engaged in *reading* the signs of the times and who, sustained by faith, bears witness to his own words with the reality of his life. This was exactly the conduct of the Hebrew *nabi*, who would, for instance, marry a prostitute in order to give credence to his denunciation that Israel was unfaithful to her God. Accordingly, faith is a condition whereby words are bound to things (44) and, far from being obstacles obscuring their sense, they contain a univocal and proper meaning. The extensive presence of etymology in the canto explicitly dramatizes this fact of language. Dominic, for instance, is interpreted as the possessive of *Dominus* (67–70); his father is interpreted as "veramente Felice" (79), and we are told that his mother Giovanna, correctly interpreted, was really what the word means (80–81). Words, as the metaphor of etymology and derivations suggests, are not equivocal designations prone to misunderstanding and entangling us in interpretative contradictions. There is the possibility of order and sense, and the presence in the canto of the grammarian Donatus reinforces this point. He is praised for deigning to set his hands on the "prim' arte" (138), grammar, which is to be understood as the effort to rescue language out of the historical chaos into which it has plunged since the Fall, arrange it according to standards of order, and return it to the prelapsarian origin of history. This effort, it must be remembered, was Dante's own in his unfinished *De vulgari eloquentia*. In this sense, grammar is the first art, the ground in which the split between words and things, which characterizes the language of the fallen world, is healed and correct interpretation is envisioned.

This celebration of order in the language of faith is ostensibly refracted in Dante's own hagiographic representation in *Paradiso* 11 and 12. The biographical mode which he deploys implies that the legends, for all the stylized features that conventionally characterize these narratives of sainthood, are not just empty words but point to, and are charged with, the reality of life. The preaching of the Word, it would seem, is "faithful" in the measure in which one's own life is involved and Christ's life is reenacted. This motif is the overt dramatic substance of the hagiographies of both Dominic and, even more explicitly, of Francis.

# Casella's Song

*Teodolinda Barolini*

Art, as mankind's supreme collective accomplishment, pervades the *Purgatorio*. Like the women who are insistently invoked throughout this canticle, art is the emblem of the *Purgatorio*'s fundamental problematic: the transcending of an object of desire that is intrinsically worthy but earthbound and subject to time. All aspects of artistic endeavor are represented and find expression in the *Purgatorio*: music, the pictorial and plastic arts, poetry. Of these, however, poetry is the most thoroughly explored; this one canticle contains the episodes of Casella, Sordello, Statius, Forese Donati, Bonagiunta da Lucca, Guido Guinizelli, and Arnaut Daniel, to mention only those episodes that may be categorized by name. Poetry has a central role in the *Purgatorio* because this is the canticle where even poets must rearrange their priorities; by the same token, this is the only one of the three realms where poetry can truly come into its own as a theme. In the *Inferno* it is only valuable in so far as it is exploitable; in the *Paradiso* it is out of place, surpassed.

In the first two cantos of the *Purgatorio* Dante rehearses the canticle's theme of detachment with respect to a woman (Cato's wife, Marcia), a friend (Casella), and the *amoroso canto* that Casella sings. All three inspire a love that is in need of being redirected upward, away from the earthly catalyst. Of particular interest is Casella, the first of many "old friends" in this canticle, and his song, "Amor che ne la mente mi ragiona," which, as the *Comedy*'s first autocitation, also establishes Dante as the first lyric poet

---

From *Dante's Poets: Textuality and Truth in the* Comedy. © 1984 by Princeton University Press.

of the *Purgatorio*. If we look at the three episodes that contain autocitations in the *Comedy*, we notice that they are all linked to encounters with friends: in *Purgatorio* 2 Casella sings "Amor che ne la mente"; in *Purgatorio* 24 the recital of "Donne ch'avete intelletto d'amore," although executed by Bonagiunta, is part of the larger episode of Forese Donati; in *Paradiso* 8 "Voi che 'ntendendo il terzo ciel movete" is quoted by Charles Martel. Autocitations, or poetic reminiscences, are thus linked to personal encounters, or biographic reminiscences, so that the literary and literal moments of the poet's life are fused together in a highly suggestive pattern.

In the same way that the personal encounters of the *Comedy* have furnished clues to Dante's actual biography—for instance, by allowing us to date the canzone "Voi che 'ntendendo" with respect to the year in which Charles Martel visited Florence—so the *Comedy*'s autocitations may furnish clues to a more internal poetic biography. The linking of all three self-quotations to episodes that relate to Dante's previous life is a signpost; as those meetings reflect an experiential history, so the autocitations reflect a poetic history. In that they are depositories of a poetic past, deliberately inscribed into a poetic present, the autocitations are markers of a space in the text, a space defined as the relation between their previous existence outside the poem and their new existence within it. Why did Dante choose these specific poems for inclusion in the *Comedy*? Why did he place them where he did? Such questions face us with authorial decisions whose unraveling yields a definitive autobiography of the poet's lyric past, Dante's final statement regarding the way he wants us to perceive his poetic development, from its origins to the engendering of the great poem. . . .

## "AMOR CHE NE LA MENTE MI RAGIONA"

The autocitation of *Purgatorio* 2 has received considerable attention of the kind we are here concerned with; Casella's song has been studied in the context of the episode and in the light of its past associations. The canto has also generated a great deal of speculation regarding such issues as the reasons for Casella's delay on the banks of the Tiber, his identity, and whether a "doctrinal" song like "Amor che ne la mente" may be sung—this despite the fact that in *Purgatorio* 2 it is sung. Marti answers this last question by drawing on musicological data which shows that the canzone form was still set to music in Dante's time; he also points out that Casella would in any case have few qualms about singing "Amor che ne la mente," since he would be unlikely to consider it a doctrinal poem. Indeed, the poem makes its appearance in canto 2 in two guises. Vis-à-vis Casella, a musician who died before the composition of the *Convivio* and whose sphere of interest seems to have been far removed from that work's concern with transforming eros into ethos, the canzone "Amor che ne la mente" functions according to its literal sense in the *Convivio* gloss, as a love poem. Thus Casella, who is unacquainted with the *Convivio*, sings the canzone in response to a specific request from the pilgrim for an "amoroso canto":

> E io: "Se nuova legge non ti toglie
>    memoria o uso a l'amoroso canto
>    che mi solea quetar tutte mie voglie,
> di ciò ti piaccia consolare alquanto
>    l'anima mia, che, con la sua persona
>    venendo qui, è affannata tanto!"
> *'Amor che ne la mente mi ragiona'*
>    cominciò elli allor sì dolcemente,
>    che la dolcezza ancor dentro mi suona.

> [And I: "If a new law does not take from you memory or practice of the amorous song which used to quiet all of my desires, with this let it please you to console my soul somewhat, which coming here with its body is so wearied!" "Amor che ne la mente mi ragiona" he began then so sweetly, that the sweetness still rings inside of me.]
>
> (*Purgatorio* 2.106–14)

The emphatic presence of "dolcemente" and "dolcezza" in lines 113–14 further underscores the status of "Amor che ne la mente" as a love lyric, since, from the canzone "Le dolci rime d'amor" to the discourses of *Purgatorio* 24 and 26, "sweetness" is considered by Dante to be the external sign and stylistic prerequisite of love poetry as a genre. The inclusion of the code word *dolce* thus confirms that Casella has complied with the pilgrim's request; he sings what he presumes to be nothing more than a love song.

This stress on the love lyric serves to place *Purgatorio* 2 in direct contrast to *Inferno* 5, opposing the present verbatim citation of the *amoroso canto* to its former misquotation. A number of textual correspondences—the simile of the doves with which *Purgatorio* 2 ends, the use of expressions that echo *Inferno* 5 ("persona" for "body" in line 110 is a Francescaism; "affannata" in line 111 recalls "O anime affannate"), and especially the reference to the love lyric as "that which used to quiet all my desires" (108)—evoke the lovers of *Inferno* 5 and put them into purgatorial perspective. As—erotically—fulfillment of desire at the level of canto 5 is a narcissistic illusion ("lust") that leads to the *bufera infernal*, so—textually—love poetry at the level of canto 5 lacks the upward momentum that will redeem its physical point of departure. With respect to Dante's poetic autobiography, *Inferno* 5 represents a stage in which the poet operates entirely within the confines of a tradition and its authorities, a stage of nonexploratory stasis in which desire is prematurely satisfied.

If desire in the *Inferno* is eternally misplaced, in the *Purgatorio* it functions dialectically as both the goad that keeps the souls moving upward and the source of the nostalgia that temporarily slows them down. *Purgatorio* 2 is a paradigm for the rest of the canticle in this respect, dramatizing both these aspects of purgatorial desire in the lull created by the song and Cato's subsequent rebuke. Whereas formerly scholars tended to underline the idyllic qualities of the interlude with Casella, effectively ending their readings with the poet's strong endorsement in line 114 (where he says that the song's sweetness still reverberates within him), recently they have stressed Cato's rebuke as a correction—and indeed condemnation—of previous events. Thus, Hollander judges Casella's song severely, as a secular poison in contrast to the canto's other song, the Psalm "In exitu Isräel de Aegypto." Freccero, on the other hand, views the episode in a more positive light, claiming that "The 'Amore' celebrated here marks an advance over the 'Amore' of Francesca's verses in the same measure that the *Convivio* marks an advance over the *Vita nuova*." These views should be integrated as two facets of the same problematic within the dialectical structure of the canto: the quotation of "Amor che ne la mente" does indeed mark an advance over the misquotation of *Inferno* 5; Cato's rebuke simultaneously suggests that it too is in need of correction.

The target of the criticism that Dante levels at an earlier self in *Inferno* 5, and that he to some extent revokes or palliates in *Purgatorio* 2, cannot be simply the *Vita nuova*; rather, we must remember that the *Vita nuova* encompasses both the experiments of a poet overly subjected to his models and the moment in which he frees himself from them. "Amor che ne la mente mi ragiona" marks an advance over "Amor, ch'al cor gentil ratto s'apprende" in the same way that submission to Lady Philosophy implies forsaking the physical eros of the tradition ("ch'al cor s'apprende") for the rationally propelled eros of the *Comedy* ("che ne la mente mi ragiona"). Moreover, the textual misuse that characterizes *Inferno* 5 is no longer present in *Purgatorio* 2, where it is deflected not only by Cato but by the pilgrim himself; line 108, "che mi *solea* quetar tutte mie voglie," indicates—both in its use of the past tense and in its echo of another distancing verse, "Le dolci rime d'amor ch'i *solia* / cercar" (italics mine)—that he recognizes the limits of love poetry.

On the other hand, there is no doubt that a correction of "Amor che ne la mente" is implied by Cato's rebuke. On the literal level—Casella's level—the rebuke addresses the episode as a whole, and includes the vain attempt to re-create the ties of friendship in the same form in which they existed on earth (emblematized in the thrice-failed attempt to embrace), as well as the temporary succumbing to the blandishments of love poetry. Appearances by Cato frame the meeting with Casella, offering proleptic as well as retrospective corrections. Indeed, Casella's beautifully nostalgic projection of his love for Dante from the earthly past to the purgatorial present—"Così com' io t'amai / nel mortal corpo, così t'amo sciolta [As I loved you in the mortal body, so do I love you freed from it]" (88–89)—is undermined by Cato even before it is spoken. In the preceding canto, Cato repudiates Virgil's all too human attempt to win favor by mentioning his wife, "Marzïa tua, che 'n vista ancor ti priega, / o santo petto, che per tua la tegni [your Marcia, who in her look still prays you, o sainted breast, to hold her for your own]" (1.79–80). As in his reply to Virgil Cato rejects all earthly ties to his wife, placing her firmly in the past definite ("Marzïa piacque tanto a li occhi miei / mentre ch'i' fu' di là [Marcia so pleased my eyes while I was over there]" [85–86]), so later he reminds Dante and Casella that the earthly ties of friendship are less important than the process of purgation awaiting them.

Although Casella views the canzone he sings as a simple love song, we who have read the *Convivio* are obliged to take its allegorical significance into consideration as well. A textual signpost noticed by critics is the pilgrim's use of the verb *consolare* in his request to Casella: "di ciò ti piaccia consolare alquanto / l'anima mia . . ." (11.109–10). Echoing as it does Boethius's title, *consolare* is a verb that figures prominently in the *Convivio* chapter where Dante announces the true identity of the *donna gentile*. Given its connection to Boethius and Lady Philosophy, it may be profitable to briefly consider the history of this word in the *Vita nuova* and *Convivio*.

*Consolare* first occurs in the prose of *Vita nuova* 38 (and in the accompanying sonnet "Gentil pensero") where it refers negatively to the thought of the *donna gentile*: "Deo, che pensero è questo, che in così vile modo vuole consolare me e non mi lascia quasi altro pensare? [God, what thought is this, which in so vile a way wants to console me and almost does not let me think of anything else?]" (38.2). If we were to take *consolare* as the sign of Boethius, its presence here would support the notion that the *donna gentile* is

Philosophy as far back as the *Vita nuova*. But the next appearance of *consolare* demonstrates that originally Dante did not always connect the word with Philosophy; he uses it in "Voi che 'ntendendo" to refer not to the thought of the *donna gentile* as one would expect, but to the consoling thought of Beatrice ("questo piatoso che m'ha consolata" of line 32 is the thought that used to go, as in "Oltre la spera," to view Beatrice in heaven). Thus, at a purely textual level *consolare* does not necessarily signify Philosophy and does not necessarily involve Boethius. It is only in the allegorical gloss to "Voi che 'ntendendo" that Dante for the first time deliberately links the notion of consolation to Philosophy. In *Convivio* 2.12, where *consolare* is repeated in various forms six times ("consolare," "sconsolato," "consolarsi," "consolato," "consolazione," "consolarme"), there is no trace of the negative valence the word bore in *Vita nuova* 38. There, in the context of Beatrice's victory, the consoling thought of the *donna gentile* is "vile"; here, in the context of the *donna gentile*'s victory, consolation is ennobled by being presented in Boethian terms.

By the time, then, that we reach "di ciò ti piaccia consolare alquanto / l'anima mia" in *Purgatorio* 2, "consolare" has overtly Boethian associations. It also carries with it a history of signifying (with one exception) consolation from an incorrect source, whether the source be labeled the *donna gentile* or Lady Philosophy. As a canzone devoted to the wrong lady, "Amor che ne la mente" is corrected in the *Comedy*: first, in *Purgatorio* 2, by Cato's rebuke; then, within the larger context of the autocitations, by being placed below "Donne ch'avete." The canzone from the *Vita nuova* is located above the canzone from the *Convivio* in order to demonstrate that—chronology notwithstanding—the praise song for Beatrice must be ranked spiritually and poetically above the praise song for Lady Philosophy. In terms of his inner poetic itinerary as reconstructed in the *Comedy*, Dante views the earlier canzone as an advance over the later one.

This point is further conveyed through a consideration of the form and structure of "Amor che ne la mente." It has frequently been noted that "Amor che ne la mente" is closely modeled on "Donne ch'avete." It contains the same number of stanzas (five) and is organized on the same principles: in both, an introductory stanza is followed by a graduated series of stanzas dedicated to praising various aspects of the lady (general praise in the second stanza, praise of her soul in the third, and praise of her body in the fourth) followed by a *congedo*. Moreover, the rhyme scheme of the *fronte* of "Amor che ne la mente" repeats that of "Donne ch'avete." Such precise metrical and structural correspondences draw attention to a more basic resemblance; both belong to the *stilo de la loda* or praise-style, in which the poet eschews any self-involvement in order to elaborate an increasingly hyperbolic discourse regarding his lady. The marked similarities between the two canzoni have led critics to suggest that the later poem was conceived as a deliberate attempt to outdo the former. If Dante once intended that his praise of the new lady should surpass his praise of Beatrice, in confirmation of his changed allegiance, then the hierarchy of the *Comedy*'s autocitations serves as a reversal that reinvests "Donne ch'avete" with its original priority.

In *Purgatorio* 2 we witness a scene in which newly arrived souls are enchanted by a song to a new love, a song that is the textual emblem of their misdirected newcomers' enthusiasm. The *Convivio*'s misdirected enthusiasm for Lady Philosophy is thus replayed on the beach of Purgatory; the singing of "Amor che ne la mente" in *Purgatorio* 2 signals the re-creation of a moment spiritually akin to the poem's first home, the prose treatise, where indeed Philosophy's sweetness is such as to banish all care from the mind: "cominciai tanto a sentire de la sua dolcezza, che lo suo amore cacciava e distruggeva ogni altro pensiero [and I began so to feel her sweetness, that her love drove away and destroyed all other thoughts]" (2.12.7). To my knowledge, no one has noted that the drama of *Purgatorio* 2 exactly reproduces the situation of the first stanza of "Amor che ne la mente," in which the lover is overwhelmed by the sweetness of Love's song:

> Amor che ne la mente mi ragiona
> de la mia donna disïosamente,
> move cose di lei meco sovente,
> *che lo 'ntelletto sovr'esse disvia.*
>   *Lo suo parlar sì dolcemente sona,*
> che l'anima ch'ascolta e che lo sente
> dice: 'Oh me lassa, ch'io non son possente
> di dir quel ch'odo de la donna mia!'

> [Love which in my mind reasons so desiringly about my lady often tells me things about her *which cause my intellect to go astray. His speech sounds so sweetly* that the soul which listens and hears says: "Alas that I am not able to utter what I hear about my lady!"]
>
> (1–8; italics mine)

Here too we are faced with a verbal sweetness—"Lo suo parlar sì dolcemente sona," echoed in the *Comedy* by "che la dolcezza ancor dentro mi suona"—whose effect is debilitating; as in the *Comedy* the rapt pilgrims are unable to proceed up the mountain, so in the poem the listening soul—"l'anima ch'ascolta e che lo sente"—loses its powers of expression. In both passages, beauty causes the intellect to go temporarily astray.

Line 4 of "Amor che ne la mente"—"che lo 'ntelletto sovr'esse disvia"—thus provides the paradigm that synthesizes all the facets of this discussion: the souls go off the path (temporarily) as they succumb to the sweetness of the song in *Purgatorio* 2; Dante went off the path (temporarily) when he allowed himself to be overly consoled by the sweetness of Philosophy in the *Convivio*. Lady Philosophy was indeed a mistake. On the other hand, the location guarantees salvation; like the serpent which routinely invades the valley of the princes, the distractions of the *Purgatorio* have lost their bite. For all that they are new arrivals, easily led astray by their impulsive attraction to the new delights—erotic or philosophical—which cross their path, the souls of *Purgatorio* 2 are incapable of erring profoundly. For them, as for their more advanced companions on the terrace of pride, the last verses of the *Pater noster* no longer apply. As in the case of the *donna gentile* episode of the *Vita nuova*, the Casella episode functions as a lapse, a backward glance whose redemption is implicit in its occurrence.

# Chronology

| | |
|---|---|
| 1265? | Born in Florence. |
| 1266 | Guelph victory at Benevento over Ghibellines. |
| 1274 | Meets Beatrice, believed to be daughter of Folco Portinari. |
| 1277 | Engaged to Gemma di Manetto Donati. |
| 1283 | Between this date and 1295 marries Gemma and has three children. |
| 1290 | Beatrice dies. |
| 1292–93 | Begins study of philosophy; *Vita nuova.* |
| 1295 | Enrolls in Guild and enters political life. |
| 1300 | Becomes prior for bimester from June 15 to August 15. |
| 1301 | Opposes extension of troop consignment to Boniface VIII in July. In October sent with two other emissaries to Pope in Rome. Takeover of Florence by exiled Black Guelphs in November. |
| 1302 | Ordered to appear to answer charges; sentenced to death on March 10 when he fails to do so. Begins exile from Florence under pain of death. |
| 1304–7? | *De vulgari eloquentia* and the *Convivio.* |
| 1310? | *De monarchia.* |
| 1314 | Completes *Inferno.* |
| 1315 | Rejects possibility of pardon; settles in Verona with Can Grande della Scala. |
| 1319? | Moves to Ravenna with Guido Novella da Plenta. Completes *Purgatorio* and part of *Paradiso.* |
| 1321 | Dies in Ravenna in September. |

# Contributors

HAROLD BLOOM, Sterling Professor of the Humanities at Yale University, is the author of *The Anxiety of Influence*, *Poetry and Repression*, and many other volumes of literary criticism. His forthcoming study, *Freud: Transference and Authority*, attempts a full-scale reading of all of Freud's major writings. A MacArthur Prize Fellow, he is general editor of five series of literary criticism published by Chelsea House.

ERNST ROBERT CURTIUS (1886–1956) was one of the most distinguished literary historians of his time. He taught at the universities of Marburg, Heidelberg, Bonn, and Berlin. In addition to his famous *European Literature and the Latin Middle Ages*, his wide-ranging work included studies of French literature and of James Joyce.

CHARLES S. SINGLETON was Professor of Humanistic Studies at The Johns Hopkins University. His translation of *The Divine Comedy*, with commentary, has become the standard scholarly edition in English.

ERICH AUERBACH (1892–1957) was Sterling Professor of Comparative Literature at Yale University. His work on the Middle Ages has been highly influential. His best known works are *Dante als Dichter der dirschen Welt* and *Mimesis: The Representation of Reality in Western Literature*.

JOHN FRECCERO is Rosina Pierotti Professor of Italian at Stanford University. He is the author of several important articles on Italian literature, including "Medusa: The Spirit and the Letter." A collection of his essays is forthcoming.

MARGUERITE MILLS CHIARENZA is Professor of Hispanic and Italian Studies at the University of British Columbia at Vancouver.

GIUSEPPE MAZZOTTA is Professor of Italian at Yale University. His works include *Dante, Poet of the Desert* (1979) and *The World at Play in Boccaccio's "Decameron"* (1986).

TEODOLINDA BAROLINI is Associate Professor of Italian at New York University.

# Bibliography


Abrams, Richard. "Illicit Pleasures: Dante Among the Sensualists (*Purgatorio* 26)." *Modern Literary Notes* 100 (1985): 1–41.

———. "Inspiration and Gluttony: The Moral Context of Dante's Poetics of the 'Sweet New Style.'" *Modern Literary Notes* 91 (1976): 30–59.

Anderson, William. *Dante the Maker*. London: Routledge & Kegan Paul, 1980.

Auerbach, Erich. "Farinata and Cavalcante." In *Mimesis: The Representation of Reality in Western Literature*. Translated by Willard Trask. Princeton: Princeton University Press, 1953.

———. *Dante, Poet of the Secular World*. Translated by R. Manheim. Chicago: The University of Chicago Press, 1961.

Barbi, Michele. *Life of Dante*. Translated by Paul G. Ruggiers. Berkeley and Los Angeles: University of California Press, 1954.

Barolini, Teodolinda. *Dante's Poets: Textuality and Truth in the Comedy*. Princeton: Princeton University Press, 1984.

Bergin, Thomas G. *Dante. Riverside Studies in Literature*. Boston: Houghton Mifflin, 1965.

———. *Dante's* Divine Comedy. Englewood Cliffs, N.J.: Prentice-Hall, 1971.

———. *From Time to Eternity: Essays on Dante's* Divine Comedy. New Haven: Yale University Press, 1967.

Boyde, Patrick. *Dante Philomythes and Philosopher: Man in the Cosmos*. Cambridge: Cambridge University Press, 1981.

Charity, A. C. *Events and Their Afterlife: The Dialectics of Christian Typology in the Bible and Dante*. Cambridge: Cambridge University Press, 1966.

Cosmo, Umberto. *A Handbook to Dante Studies*. Translated by David Moore. Oxford: Blackwell, 1960.

Davis, Charles T. *Dante and the Idea of Rome*. Oxford: Clarendon Press, 1957.

———. "Dante's Vision of History." *Dante Studies with the Annual Report of the Dante Society* 93 (1975): 143–60.

Durling, Robert M. "Deceit and Digestion in the Belly of Hell." In *Allegory and Representation*, edited by Stephen J. Greenblatt. Baltimore: The Johns Hopkins University Press, 1981.

Fergusson, Francis. *Dante's Drama of the Mind: A Modern Reading of the* Purgatorio. Princeton: Princeton University Press, 1953.

Ferrucci, Franco. *The Poetics of Disguise: The Autobiography of the Work in Homer, Dante, and Shakespeare*. Translated by Ann Dunnigan. Ithaca, N.Y.: Cornell University Press, 1980.

Foster, Kenelm. *The Two Dantes and Other Studies*. Berkeley: University of California Press, 1977.

Freccero, John. "Casella's Song (*Purgatorio* 2.112)." *Dante Studies with the Annual Report of the Dante Society* 91 (1973): 73–80.

———. *Dante: The Poetics of Conversion*. Cambridge: Harvard University Press, 1986.

———, ed. *Dante. Twentieth Century Views*. Englewood Cliffs, N.J.: Prentice-Hall, 1967.

Gilson, Etienne. *Dante the Philosopher*. Translated by David Moore. New York: Sheed & Ward, 1949.

Hollander, Robert. *Allegory in Dante's* Commedia. Princeton: Princeton University Press, 1969.

———. "*Vita nuova*: Dante's Perceptions of Beatrice." *Dante Studies with the Annual Report of the Dante Society* 92 (1974): 1–18.

Leo, Ulrich. "The Unfinished *Convivio* and Dante's Rereading of the *Aeneid*." *Medieval Studies* 13 (1951): 41–64.

Mazzaro, Jerome. *The Figure of Dante: An Essay on the* Vita nuova. Princeton: Princeton University Press, 1981.

Mazzeo, Joseph Anthony. *Medieval Cultural Tradition in Dante's* Comedy. Westport, Conn.: Greenwood Press, 1960.

Mazzotta, Giuseppe. *Dante, Poet of the Desert: History and Allegory in the* Divine Comedy. Princeton: Princeton University Press, 1979.

———. "Dante and the Virtues of Exile." *Poetics Today* 5 (1984): 645–667.

Quinones, Ricardo J. *The Renaissance Discovery of Time*. Cambridge: Harvard University Press, 1972.

Reade, W. H. V. *The Moral System of Dante's* Inferno. Oxford: Clarendon Press, 1909.

Shapiro, Marianne. "The Fictionalization of Bertran de Born (*Inferno* 27)." *Dante Studies* 92 (1974): 107–16.

Shoaf, R. A. *Dante, Chaucer, and the Currency of the Word: Money, Images, and Reference in Late Medieval Poetry*. Norman, Okla.: Pilgrim Books, 1983.

Singleton, Charles S. Commedia: *Elements of Structure. Dante Studies* 1. Cambridge: Harvard University Press, 1954.

———. "The Irreducible Dove." *Comparative Literature* 9 (1957): 129–135.

———. *Journey to Beatrice. Dante Studies* 2. Cambridge: Harvard University Press, 1957.

———. *An Essay on the* Vita nuova. Cambridge: Harvard University Press, 1958.

Thompson, David. "Figure and Allegory in the *Commedia*." *Dante Studies with the Annual Report of the Dante Society* 90 (1972): 1–11.

Whitbread, Leslie George. *Fulgentius the Mythographer*. Columbus: Ohio State University Press, 1971.

Williams, Charles. *The Figure of Beatrice: A Study in Dante*. New York: Farrar, Straus & Giroux, 1961.

# Acknowledgments

"Dante" by Ernst Robert Curtius from *European Literature of the Latin Middle Ages* by Ernst Robert Curtius, © 1953 by the Bollingen Foundation. Reprinted by permission of Princeton University Press.

"Justification" by Charles S. Singleton from *Dante Studies 2: Journey to Beatrice* by Charles S. Singleton, © 1958 by the Estate of Charles S. Singleton. Reprinted by permission.

"The Presentation" by Erich Auerbach from *Dante: Poet of the Secular World* by Erich Auerbach, © 1961 by the University of Chicago. Reprinted by permission of the University of Chicago Press.

"The Vistas in Retrospect" by Charles S. Singleton from *Atti del congresso internazionale di studi danteschi* (April 20–27, 1965), © 1965 by the Estate of Charles S. Singleton. Reprinted by permission of The Johns Hopkins University.

"The Prologue Scene" by John Freccero from *Dante: The Poetics of Conversion* by John Freccero, © 1986 by the President and Fellows of Harvard College. This essay originally appeared in *Dante Studies* 84 (1966), © 1966 by the Dante Society of America. Reprinted by permission of the State University of New York Press.

"The Imageless Vision and Dante's *Paradiso*" by Marguerite Mills Chiarenza from *Dante Studies* 90 (1971), © 1971 by the Dante Society of America. Reprinted by permission of the State University of New York.

"Bestial Sign and Bread of Angels" by John Freccero from *Dante: The Poetics of Conversion* by John Freccero, © 1986 by the President and Fellows of Harvard College. This essay originally appeared in *Yale Italian Studies* 1 (1977), © 1977 by *Yale Italian Studies*. Reprinted by permission of the Yale Italian Department.

"The Language of Faith: Messengers and Idols" by Giuseppe Mazzotta from *Dante, Poet of the Desert: History and Allegory in the* Divine Comedy by Giuseppe Mazzotta, © 1979 by Princeton University Press. Reprinted by permission of Princeton University Press.

"Casella's Song" (originally entitled "Autocitation and Autobiography") by Teodolinda Barolini from *Dante's Poets: Textuality and Truth in the* Comedy by Teodolinda Barolini, © 1984 by Princeton University Press. Reprinted by permission of Princeton University Press.

# Index


Abraham and Isaac, 125–26, 127
Achilles, 44
Adam, 25–26, 87–88
Advent, 59
*Aeneid* (Virgil), 35, 73, 91, 128, 144
Ambrose, Saint, 82, 83, 95
"Amor che ne la mente mi ragiona" (Dante), 151–58
"Analysis Terminable and Interminable" (Freud), 10
Annas, 67
Antigone, 39
Argenti, Filippo, 48
Ariosto, Ludovico, 61
Aristophanes, 43
Aristotle, 1–2, 21, 22–23, 28, 31, 139, 140
Arnulf of Orleans, 140
Attic comedy, 43
Auden, W. H., 3
Auerbach, Erich, 1, 2–3, 5, 6, 33–55
Augustine, Saint, 58, 60, 77–104, 131–32, 133, 146
Averroistic heresy, 137

Bambaglioli, Graziuolo de', 12
Barbi, Michele, 14
Beatrice: appearance of, 25, 34; as beatifying female power, 7, 17; as Christ-figure, 3–4, 17, 59, 80; departure of, 9; as goal, 26, 27, 29, 30, 31; as guide, 7–10, 59, 74, 78, 88, 99, 115, 118, 136; identity of, 11–17; as justice, 29, 30, 31; as Lady Nine, 8, 13–14, 15, 16; Lucia compared with, 8, 15–16, 17; as Muse, 7; as myth, 8–10, 17; in objective process of salvation, 7–8, 11–12, 15–17; as "physician," 10; praise song for, 156–57; prophecy of, 18; as representation of grace, 4–5, 16, 29–30, 31, 80; as supernatural light, 4–5, 16, 29–30; as trope, 7
Belacqua, 48–49
Bernard, Saint: appearance of, 9; as guide, 11, 85; as personification of love, 11; preaching of, 31
Bernardus Silvestris, 86, 91–92
Blake, William, 3
Boccaccio, Giovanni, 12–13, 58, 59, 137
Boethius, 155, 156
Bolognese, Franco, 45
Bonaventure, Saint, 147
Borges, Jorge Luis, 6
Brigata, 124
*Brothers Karamazov, The* (Dostoyevski), 121

Cacciaguida, 46, 51, 100
Caesar, Julius, 44, 46, 47
Caiaphas, 67
Carlyle, Thomas, 17
Casale, Ubertino da, 146
Casella, 48, 116–17, 151–58

Catholic Church, 18, 122–23, 147
Cato, 47, 72, 151, 155
Cavalcanti, Guido, 36, 98–99, 138, 143–45
Ceix, 148
Chalcidius, 86
"Changing Light at Sandover, The" (Merrill), 3
Charles Martel of Anjou, 36, 152
Chaucer, Geoffrey, 2
Cherubim, 146
Church Fathers, 137
Ciacco, 48
Cicero, Marcus Tullius, 138
Cimabue, 45
*Confessions* (St. Augustine): apologetic intent of, 97; as autobiography, 101–2; body vs. soul in, 81–84; commentary on, 89–90; conversion scene in, 79–80, 81, 85–86, 89; *Divine Comedy* compared with, 58, 60, 77–90, 93–94, 98, 99, 101–2; Eucharist explained in, 131–32, 133; exegetical language of, 80; exemplums in, 79, 80; faith as theme in, 146; natural vs. spiritual existence in, 106; neoplatonic influence on, 82, 83, 84–86, 89, 93, 94–95, 97, 98; Platonic influence on, 80–81, 84; "prodigal son" example in, 93–94; seventh book of, 84, 85; theory of knowledge in, 103; will as concept in, 93–94
*Congedo*, 156
Consistency principle, 1
*Convivio* (Dante): autobiography in, 15–16, 78–79; *Divine Comedy* compared with, 137–39, 155, 156–57; eros vs. ethos in, 153; Lady Philosophy of, 15, 154, 155–57, 158; "perfect age" in, 8, 16; philosophical system of, 138–39; *Vita nuova* compared with, 154, 155–56, 157, 158; writing of, 153
"Cosí nel mio parlar voglio esser aspro" (Dante), 141
Courcelle, Pierre, 82, 84, 89, 91, 94, 95
Covenant of Jehovah, 84
Curtius, Ernst Robert, 7–8, 9

Daedalus, 91–92, 94
Daniel, Arnaut, 151
Dante Alighieri: Aristotle's influence on, 1–2, 21, 139, 140; audacity of, 7–8; biography of, 78–79, 80, 99–100, 101, 152, 154; as Catholic poet, 8, 53; directness of, 43; eye problems of, 15–16; as Florentine, 17–18, 36–37; influence of, 17, 46–47, 53–54; literary career of, 36; literary influences on, 3, 6–7, 10, 40, 49–50; as master of mimesis, 1; medallion of, 17; mysticism of, 4, 13–15; numerology of, 13–15; originality of, 5, 6; orthodoxy of, 8–9; personality of, 1, 17, 18; poetic maturation of, 7; as poet of secular world, 3; politics of, 17–18, 121–22; as prophet, 5, 8, 16; Shakespeare compared with, 1, 2, 5–6, 19; in transition from Middle Ages to Renaissance, 17–19, 58, 99; Virgil compared with, 6–7, 10, 35, 47, 49, 53; as visionary, 9, 18; world view of, 53
Davidsohn, Robert, 15
Day of Judgment, 40
*De beata vita* (St. Augustine), 95–97
*Decameron* (Boccaccio), 58, 59
*De praescriptione haereticorum* (Tertullian), 139
De Sanctis, Francesco, 126
Deuteronomy, 89
*De vulgari eloquentia* (Dante), 17, 149
Diomedes, 123
*Divine Comedy* (Dante): abstraction in, 38–39, 49, 116; Adam's transgression in, 25–26, 87–88; Advent represented in, 59; *Aeneid* compared with, 73, 91, 128, 144;

aesthetics of, 7; as allegory, 4, 5, 6, 7, 15, 17, 24, 58, 59, 71, 77, 80, 92, 97, 101, 104, 129, 133, 155, 156; allusions in, 140; ambiguity in, 5, 99, 100, 104, 128–29; analogies in, 3–5; apocalyptic mission of, 8, 16; apparatus of salvation in, 7–8, 11–12, 15–17; as arrow's flight, 61–62, 63, 69–70, 71, 73, 76; *askesis* of, 83, 93; astrology in, 13, 52; Athens vs. Jerusalem in, 138, 139; Attic comedy compared with, 43; authority in, 136, 138; autobiography in, 78–79, 80, 99–100, 101, 152, 154; autocitations in, 151–52; biblical references in, 2, 88, 89, 101, 125–26, 132, 135–36, 137, 145, 146, 148, 154; binary opposition in, 128, 130; biographical mode in, 150; blindness as theme in, 142–44, 145; body vs. soul in, 40, 50, 52–53, 81–84; Catholic Church represented in, 18, 122–23, 147; changeless nature of, 2, 5–6, 40, 50; characterizations in, 2, 33–35, 99–100, 124; charity as theme in, 128; Christ as figure in, 2, 3–4; Christ's Crucifixion as event in, 65–72, 73, 75–76, 128; as Christian poem, 2, 4, 7–9, 24, 40, 58–59; Christian readers of, 24, 58–59, 67, 71, 74, 75; as Christocentric, 59; chronological indications in, 52, 66–68, 70–72, 73, 75; church vs. state in, 17–18, 28, 122–23, 136; classical theory and, 1, 43–44; coherence of, 47, 48, 60–62, 69–70, 100, 101, 102, 106–7; commentaries on, 59–60, 62, 68–69, 71, 89–90, 92, 137, 140, 142; compatriot motif in, 36–37; *Confessions* of St. Augustine compared with, 58, 60, 77–90, 93–94, 98, 99, 101–2; confessions in, 79, 80; contemporary interpretation of, 5, 12–14, 43, 53, 86–87, 89–90, 92, 137, 140; content vs. form in, 69; conventions in, 78–79; conversions in, 29–30, 58, 79–80, 81, 83, 89, 90, 93–99; *Convivio* compared with, 137–39, 155, 156–57; cosmos of, 8, 16, 17, 18–19, 104–6; *daemon* vs. *ethos* in, 5; Dante's personality expressed in, 1, 17, 18; death as theme in, 80, 100, 142; *Decameron* compared with, 58, 59; detached viewpoint in, 99–100; diachronic vs. synchronic views in, 100; as didactic treatise, 54–55; difficult communication in, 38; drama of, 81, 85, 135, 148; earthly existence in, 37–38, 40, 51, 52; editors of, 145; ellipsis in, 130; emotions expressed in, 33, 34, 39, 51, 55; encounters with souls in, 2, 33, 35–48, 152, 155; as epic vs. tragedy, 1–2, 39–40, 43; epistemological function of, 11; eros in, 153, 154; eschatology of, 100, 122; essence vs. particularity in, 33–34, 39–40, 41; eternity in, 39, 101; etymology in, 140–41, 149; exegesis of, 8, 17, 80, 89, 137; *exemplum* in, 79, 80, 119; exodus as theme in, 89; experience of, 58–59; faith as theme in, 11, 135–50; fame as theme in, 43–46; fantasy in, 55, 105; fate in, 1, 2, 5, 39, 41, 42, 43, 48, 50, 51, 79, 101; *figura* in, 2, 3, 5, 88–89; figural interpretation in, 2–3; "flight of soul" in, 90–99; Florence as subject of, 17–18, 143, 145; form vs. matter in, 21–22, 29; general structure of, 60–61, 68, 76, 99–100, 107–8; gestures in, 48, 49, 51, 128; Gnosticism in, 8, 9, 16–17; God's judgment in, 39, 40; God's unifying vision in, 47, 105–7; grace as theme in, 4–5, 16, 29–30, 31, 80; Greek tragedy compared with, 39–40; heresy as theme in, 36, 136–40; hier-

*Divine Comedy* (Dante) *(continued)* archical structure of, 8, 16, 104–5, 107; historical background of, 3, 17–19, 40, 46, 53, 77, 100, 135, 147; historical figures in, 33–46, 48; *homo claudus* in, 83; homology in, 99; humility as theme in, 73–76, 80, 85, 97, 99; *hysteron proteron* in, 61–62, 73; idealization in, 5; idolatry in, 136; as image of earthly world, 33; imagination in, 40, 142–43; "imaginative maze" of, 135; *impedimentia* in, 27, 84, 88; insanity as theme in, 140–42, 145; intellectual knowledge in, 81, 89, 93–99, 135, 142–46; *intelletti sani* in, 137–38; "intense perception" in, 49; "interior feet" as concept in, 83; inversion of values of, 80–81; irony in, 45, 122, 124, 129, 142, 144; Italian lyrics vs., 7, 11–12, 49–50, 140–42, 151–58; Jewish legend in, 125–26; as journey, 24–25, 27, 30, 61, 71, 75, 77, 78, 79, 84, 85, 90, 97, 102; justification as theme in, 21–31, 52, 58, 59, 76, 114; knowledge vs. nature in, 85, 93; landscapes of, 52, 80–81, 85; language of, 1, 17, 18, 19, 36–37, 54, 110–11, 123–24, 125, 130–31, 133, 137, 140–41, 144, 145, 146, 147, 149, 155–56, 157–58; layers of meaning in, 18; legendary figures in, 44, 46–48; Limbo in, 29, 65; linear time in, 100; as "literary object," 101; literary tradition of, 1, 3, 6–7, 10, 39–40, 43–44, 154; locales of, 35, 38, 52, "lost dimension" of, 62; lyricism of, 11–12, 55; magic as theme in, 141–42; as masterpiece, 53–54; mediation in, 108; as medieval work, 5, 17–19, 46–47, 53–54, 57–59, 78, 85, 89–90, 105–6, 131, 132, 145; meetings with old friends in, 35–37, 152, 155; memory in, 40, 41, 51, 60, 63, 67, 68, 69, 70, 73–74, 75, 108–10; "meritorious state" in, 40; messengers in, 135–50; metamorphosis in, 5, 50–51, 148; metaphors in, 24–25, 49, 50, 51, 80, 91, 105, 113, 136, 138, 140, 142, 149; metaphysics of, 15, 90, 101; milieu of, 43; mimesis in, 1–3; misinterpretation of, 51–52, 126–27, 132, 133–34, 135, 136–40, 146, 149; modern criticism of, 1, 5, 6, 7, 8, 19, 51–52, 53, 57–59, 60, 77, 79, 101, 121, 122, 126–27, 132, 133–34, 135, 152, 154, 155, 157; morality in, 25, 59, 77, 135, 145; movement in, 21, 24–25, 49, 51, 62; Muses invoked in, 50; mystery in, 71, 105, 114, 133; *mystificatio* in, 122; mythology of, 8–10, 17, 43, 52, 140–42, 148; narcissism as theme in, 153–54; narrative structure of, 59–76, 88, 99; naturalism in, 43, 48–49, 52; as "natura sympathetica," 52; necessity in, 5, 53; neoplatonic imagery in, 82, 83, 84–86, 89, 90–99; "New Thebes" in, 123, 124, 126, 127; *nonchalance du salut* and, 57–59; "nutriment" of, 51–52, 53; omission of device in, 40, 42; opthalmological explanations of, 8, 17; organic unity of, 101; Orosius as catchword in, 17; Other World of, 41, 42, 43; oxymorons in, 131; paradigms of, 29–30, 60–62, 68, 158; paradox in, 104, 128; patterns of meaning in, 29–30, 31, 57–76, 88, 100; philosophic system of, 1–2, 11, 52, 54, 81–90, 94, 95–102, 138, philosophy vs. theology in, 22–23, 31, 65, 82, 98, 138–40, 146; physical appearances in, 48–49; pilgrim vs. poet in, 99–100, 101, 107, 111, 114–15, 117, 118, 154–55; pivotal points of, 59, 61, 62; plan of, 1, 8; "plastic manifesta-

tions" in, 48; poetics of, 18, 76, 81–82, 87–88, 94, 104, 122; polemic in, 93; political themes in, 17–18, 28, 121–24, 132, 136, 137, 143, 145; "polysemous ways" of, 58; power as theme in, 17, 18; preparation and reception in, 29–30; pride as sin in, 24, 27, 45, 84–85, 98; prologue to, 69, 77–102; prophecy contained in, 8, 16, 18, 136, 149; publication of, 13; rationalism in, 47, 51, 54–55; reader's response to, 5, 24, 25, 34, 39, 43, 44, 46, 49, 51–52, 53, 57, 58–59, 63, 67, 68, 69, 71, 74–77, 107, 108–10, 118–19, 121, 136–40, 143, 146, 149; reality in, 41, 43, 46, 50, 52, 53, 54, 101, 105; reason as theme in, 139; as record of events, 54, 55; redemption in, 7–8, 11–12, 15–17, 35, 66, 75, 131–32, 133, 158; references to author in, 78–79; regeneration in, 26–27; "region of unlikeness" in, 77–90, 102; reinterpretation in, 46–47; Renaissance criticism of, 121; representation in, 5–6; *reticentia* in, 130; retrospective understanding of, 57–76, 80; rhyme scheme of, 144, 156; Romantic criticism of, 51, 121; "ruina" in, 63–70, 73, 75; as sacred vs. secular literature, 3; self-knowledge in, 41–42, 50; self-revelation in, 2, 38–48; sensuous aspect of, 51–52, 53; as "sentence," 60–63, 68, 69, 70, 75; shadows in, 33–34; shift of poetic tone in, 81–82; signification in, 146, 149, 156; sinful acts in, 24, 26, 27, 45, 82, 83, 84–85, 87, 88, 98, 139–40, 143; spheres of light in, 4–5, 6, 18, 29–30, 51, 84, 111–12; spiritual states in, 22, 37–38, 39, 40, 50–51, 52, 68, 71, 90–99, 144, 157–58; symbolism in, 58, 73, 75, 79, 103, 146; sympathetic reading of, 57, 58–59; synoptic method in, 38–39; terminology of, 30; terza rima of, 18, 144, 156; as "testament," 78–79; text of, 152, 154, 155, 156; theology of, 4, 7–9, 16, 17, 21, 22–24, 25, 26, 29, 31, 40, 105–6, 139–40, 142, 145; Thomistic system of, 21, 22–24, 25, 26, 29, 105–6, 139–40, 142, 145, 147; time in, 2, 5, 39, 40, 41, 52, 53, 66–68, 70–72, 73, 75, 100, 101; title of, 43; tropes in, 2, 4–5, 7, 9; unfolding of, 59–76; "unquiet heart" of, 57–58; as vision, 9, 18, 54–55, 61, 77, 81, 103–19; wayfarer's state in, 40, 41, 73, 88, 99, 135; will as concept in, 30, 83–84, 93–94. *See also* *Inferno; Paradiso; Purgatorio*
Dominic, Saint, 136, 146–50
Donati, Forese, 36, 151, 152
Donatus, 149
"Donna ch'avete intelletto d'amore" (Dante), 152, 156, 157
"Donne me prega" (Cavalcanti), 144, 145
Dostoyevski, Feodor, 121

Easter Sunday, 72, 75
Ecclesiastes, 145
Eckermann, Johann Peter, 17
Eden, 25–26, 27, 87
Elijah, 94
"E' m' incresce de me" (Dante), 15
Empedocles, 65
*Enneads* (Plotinus), 82
Epicureanism, 36, 138
Epicurus, 138, 142
*Epistle to Can Grande* (Dante), 11, 68
Erichtho, 141
*Essais* (Montaigne), 57
Eucharist, 131–32, 133

Farinata degli Uberti, 36, 138, 143
*Faust* (Goethe), 11
Foucault, Michel, 5

France, Anatole, 53
Francesca, 99, 130
Francis of Assisi, Saint, 5, 136, 146–47, 150
Freccero, John, 1, 3, 6, 9, 141, 154
Frederick II, king of Prussia, 138
Freud, Sigmund, 5, 6, 10, 132
Fulgentius, 140

Ghibellines, 17–18
Giotto di Bondone, 45
Gnosticism, 8, 9, 16–17
Goethe, Johann Wolfgang von, 11, 17
Good Friday, 70, 75
Gorgons, 140
Grace, as theme in *Divine Comedy*, 4–5, 16, 29–30, 31, 80
*Gratia justificans*, 30–31
Greek tragedy, 39–40
Gregory I, Saint, 83, 145
Guelfs, 122
Guinizelli, Guido, 7, 11–12, 49–50, 151

Hagiographies, 146–48, 150
*Hairesis*, 139
Halcyon, 148
*Hamlet* (Shakespeare), 2, 5–6
Harpies, 50
Hecate, 141–42
Heresy, 36, 136–40
Hippolytus, 39
Hollander, Robert, 154
Homer, 46, 97
Hugh of St. Cher, 108–9, 110, 115–16, 117

Imola, Benvenuto da, 140
*Inferno* (Dante): abortive spiritual journey described in, 81–82; alienation in, 123–24; allegory in, 129, 133; ascent vs. descent in, 74–76, 80–81, 87; bestiality in, 129–34, 139; biblical typology in, 125–26, 132; canto 1 of, 8, 16, 69; canto 2 of, 8, 16; canto 5 of, 46, 69, 153–54; canto 8 of, 86; canto 9 of, 138, 140, 141, 142–43, 144, 145, 146; canto 10 of, 98, 138, 139, 140, 142, 145; canto 11 of, 68; canto 21 of, 66, 70, 71; children's suffering in, 121, 124–34; Christological pattern in, 124–34; communion vs. cannibalism in, 121–34; damnation in, 127, 128; death as theme in, 127–29, 130, 133; as descent, 90, 98–99; desire as theme in, 153–54; destruction of bridges in, 66–67; *digiuno* vs. *dolore* in, 130–31; ending of, 59–70; escort of devils in, 66, 67, 136; Harpies depicted in, 50; heretics, circle of, in, 136–37, 138; hunger as theme in, 128, 129–31, 132; hypocrites, circle of, in, 67; incontinence in, 139; irony in, 124, 129; language of, 123–24, 125, 130–31, 133; literal interpretation in, 126–34; Malacoda's reckoning of time in, 66–68, 70, 73, 75; modern criticism of, 121, 122, 126–27, 132, 133–34; moral structure of, 139; *Paradiso* compared with, 108; physical proximity in, 123; P's inscribed on Dante's forehead in, 27; political aspect of, 121–24, 132; *regressus* of soul in, 92–93; reification in, 130–31; "remigium alarum" in, 91, 92; Satan depicted in, 72, 103; *selva oscura* phrase in, 86–90, 100, 102; series of oppositions in, 86; sign of grief in, 128, 129–31, 133, 134; state of souls in, 37; structure of Hell in, 63–70, 139; suicides, circle of, in, 40, 50; tautology in, 133; thieves, circle of, in, 50, 123; three beasts of, 69; treachery, circle of, in, 122; Ugolino episode in, 99, 121–34; Ulysses

depicted in, 44, 47–48, 90–99, 123, 135; vengeance in, 123, 124, 125
Isidore of Seville, 139, 142, 145
*Iustificatio impii*, 27, 29, 30

Jerome, Saint, 139, 145
Jesus Christ: Beatrice as representation of, 3–4, 17, 59, 80; Crucifixion of, 65–72, 73, 75–76, 128; as figure in *Divine Comedy*, 2, 3–4; harrowing of Hell by, 65–67, 71, 72, 75–76; "mystical body" of, 131–32, 133; resurrection of, 72, 74, 75; symbols of, 103
Joachim, 149
John, Saint, Gospel According to, 80, 98, 132
John of Garland, 140
Juno, 140, 148
Justice, 21–31; as alteration, 21, 26; Aristotle's views on, 21, 22–23, 28, 31; definition of, 21–23, 28; final, 25; as form vs. matter, 21–22; *generatio* of, 21, 22, 26, 31; as given to Adam, 25–26; grace and, 29, 30–31; individual, 52; injustice vs., 23; moment of preparation vs. moment of completion in, 21; as movement, 21, 24–25, 26; as right order in soul, 22, 24, 26, 27–28, 30; St. Thomas's views on, 21, 22–24, 25, 26, 29; by "simple generation," 25–26; as summit of mountain, 25, 26–27; "sun" of, 25; of ungodly, 27, 29, 30; Virgil's views of, 27–28, 29, 30, 31

Kafka, Franz, 8

Landino, Cristoforo, 86
Latini, Brunetto, 34–35
Limbo, 29, 65
Lubac, Henri de, 132
Lucan, 50, 141, 142
Lucca, Bonagiunti da, 151
Lucia, 8, 15–16, 17

Machiavelli, Niccolò, 58
Malacoda, 66–68, 70, 73, 75
Manichean heresy, 87
Marcia, 151, 155
Mardoli, Margherita dei, 12
*Marienbader Elegie* (Goethe), 11
Massèra, A. F., 13
Matelda, 15, 88
Matthew, Saint, Gospel According to, 65
Medusa, 136–37, 140–41
Menalippus, 123
Mendicant orders, 18
Mercury, 142
Merrill, James, 3
*Metamorphosis* (Ovid), 148–49
Michelangelo Buonarroti, 19
*Milton* (Blake), 3
Milton, John, 3, 4, 8
Minerva, 140
Montaigne, Michel Eyquem, Seigneur de, 57
Montano, Rocco, 91
Montefeltro, Guido de, 38, 42
Morpheus, 148, 149
Moses, 89
*Mythologicon* (Fulgentius), 140

*Nabi*, 149
Neoplatonism, 81, 82, 83, 84–86, 89, 93, 94–95, 97, 98
Neptune, 140
Newman, Francis X., 103–4
*Nicomachean Ethics* (Aristotle), 22
Nietzsche, Friedrich, 4, 7

Odysseus, 44, 47–48, 90–99, 123, 125
Oedipus, 126
*On Monarchy* (Dante), 121–22

*Opera Omnia in Universum Vetus et Novum Testamentum* (Hugh of St. Cher), 110, 116
*Orlando Furioso* (Ariosto), 61
*Ottimo commento*, 12
Ovid, 50, 117, 140, 148–49

Padoan, Giorgio, 90, 91, 95
Pagliaro, A., 144
*Paradiso* (Dante): abstract metaphors of, 49, 116; angelic orders in, 146; "anti-images" of, 114–17; artificial structure of, 107–8; canto 8 of, 152; canto 11 of, 147, 150; canto 12 of, 146–50; canto 31 of, 9; cross as pattern in, 51, 113, 114; cross of Mars in, 51; depersonalization in, 51; Empyrean vs. heavenly vision in, 104–6, 114–15; ending of, 8, 17; as failure of poetic power, 51, 104, 106–7, 108–10; feminine souls of moon in, 51, 115, 117, 118; heaven of Mars in, 113; hierarchical structure of, 104–5, 107; as imageless, 104, 111–19; imagination in, 116; incorporeality vs. substantiality in, 111, 118; *Inferno* compared with, 108; as intellectual vision, 103–19; language of, 110–11; metaphors in, 105–13; middle cantos of, 114; mirror of Narcissus in, 112, 116–17, 118; modes of vision in, 103–4, 116–18; as paradox, 104; poetics of, 104; *Purgatorio* compared with, 103; reader's response to, 107, 108–10, 118–19; reflecting light in, 111–12; sequential form of, 107–8; sign of eagle in, 113–14; sphere of Mercury in, 51; spiritual states in, 37, 50–51; "spiritual vision" in, 103, 116–18; transcendence in, 107; as *ultimo lavoro*, 51; vision of God in, 103, 105, 116; visual experience of, 112–15, 118–19
Pascal, Blaise, 57, 58
*Pater Noster*, 158
Paul, Saint, 103, 116, 119, 139
Peripatetics, 138
Perseus, 140, 141
Phantasos, 149
*Pharsalia* (Lucan), 141, 142, 145
Pia de' Tolomei, 42–43
Plato, 22, 28, 29, 80–81, 84, 86, 87
Plotinus, 82, 83, 84–86, 97
Portinari, Folco, 12–13, 15, 17
Prometheus, 39
Proust, Marcel, 60
Psalms, 154
Ptolemy, 14
*Purgatorio* (Dante): Ante-Purgatory in, 42; artistic endeavor in, 151–58; as ascent, 72–73, 74–76, 80, 83, 93; beginning of, 59–70; butterfly metaphor in, 24–25; canto 1 of, 25; canto 2 of, 151–58; canto 6 of, 123; canto 11 of, 44–46; canto 24 of, 152; *consolare* as used in, 155–56; dialectics of, 154; ending of, 8, 17, 78; moral landscape of, 25; mountain in, 25, 41, 48, 72–73, 75, 80, 83, 96, 158; musicology in, 152; numerology in, 14; *Paradiso* compared with, 103; poetry as theme in, 151–58; rush as symbol in, 73, 75, 97; state of souls in, 37; terraces in, 27, 36; upward movement of, 151, 154; "verbal sweetness" of, 157–58; women invoked in, 151
Pygmalion, 141

Rabelais, François, 39
Reade, W. H. V., 139
*Republic* (Plato), 22, 28
Richard of St. Victor, 89–90
*Rime petrose* (Dante), 17, 140–41, 142, 145
Rimini, Francesca Malatesta da, 46, 153
Ruggieri, Archbishop, 122, 123, 124, 133

Sartre, Jean-Paul, 101
Scholastic philosophy, 11
Seraphim, 146
Shakespeare, William, 1, 2, 5–6, 19
Shelley, Percy Bysshe, 121
Singleton, Charles S., 1, 3–4, 6, 81, 88
Socrates, 85
Sordello, 37, 123, 151
*Statesman* (Plato), 80–81
Statius, Publius Papinius, 35, 142, 145, 151
*Status recipientis pro meritis*, 40
*Status viatoris*, 40, 41
Stevens, Wallace, 3, 5
"Stil nuovo" poets, 45
*Stilo de la loda*, 156–57
Stoics, 138

Tertullian, 2, 3, 139
*Thebaid* (Statius), 142, 145
Thomas Aquinas, Saint, 105–6, 139–40, 142, 145, 147; justice as viewed by, 21, 22–24, 25, 26, 29
Thurber, James, 7
*Timaeus* (Plato), 86
Tisiphone, 140
*Totem and Taboo* (Freud), 132
Tydeus, 123

Ugolino, Count, 99, 121–34
Uguiccione, 124
Ulysses, 44, 47–48, 90–99, 123, 125

Venus, 141
Vico, Giambattista, 43
Vigna, Pier della, 50
Virgil: appearance of, 34; Dante compared with, 6–7, 10, 35, 47, 49, 53; departure of, 25; as guide, 3, 27–28, 29, 30, 34, 35, 36, 37, 59, 63–67, 71, 72, 99, 136–37; justice as viewed by, 27–28, 29, 30, 31; as Mantuan, 37, 123; as natural light, 4, 6, 29; as personification of reason, 6, 11; as poet, 6–7, 10, 35, 47, 49, 53, 73, 91, 128, 144, 155; as "poetic father," 6–7, 10; prophecy of, 18
*Visio intellectualis*, 103–19
*Vita nuova* (Dante): *Convivio* compared with, 154, 155–56, 157, 158; *donna gentile* of, 13–14, 15, 155–56, 157, 158; legendary style of, 15
"Voglio del ver la mia donna laudare" (Guinizelli), 49–50

Weber, Alfred, 17
Whitman, Walt, 4
Wordsworth, William, 6

Yeats, William Butler, 7

Zingarelli, Nicola, 12, 13

# VIVA Modern Critical Interpretations

## Available Titles in the Series

Viva

**Alice's Adventures in Wonderland**

9788130906362 Rs. 145

**Animal Farm**

9788130906355 In Print

**As You Like It**

9788130918723 Rs. 195

**The Adventures of Huckleberry Finn**

9788130907390 Rs. 165

**Beowulf**

9788130907406 In Print

**Beloved**

9788130918884 Rs. 195

**Black Boy**

9788130906737 Rs. 125

**Brave New World**

9788130906348 In Print

**Cat on a Hot Tin Roof**

9788130906393 Rs. 99

## VIVA Modern Critical Interpretations

### Available Titles in the Series

Viva

**Crime and Punishment**

9788130906409 Rs. 175

**The Chronicles of Narnia**

9788130907468 Rs. 145

**The Crucible**

9788130906416 Rs. 125

**Darkness at Noon**

9788130906423 Rs. 145

**David Copperfield**

9788130918730 Rs. 145

**The Death of Artemio Cruz**

9788130907475 Rs. 145

**Death of a Salesman**

9788130906744 Rs. 125

**The Divine Comedy**

9788130918846 Rs. 175

**Don Quixote**

9788130904658 Rs. 125

# VIVA Modern Critical Interpretations

## Available Titles in the Series

Viva

**Dracula**

9788130906430 Rs. 195

**Emerson's Essays**

9788130906577 Rs. 175

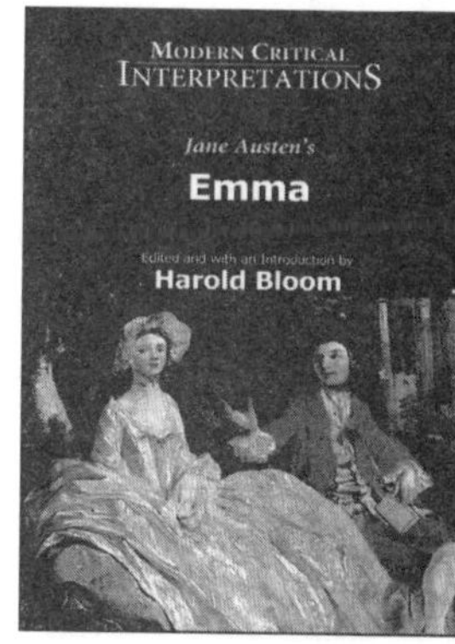


**Emma**

9788130918839 Rs. 165

**A Farewell to Arms**

9788130918754 Rs. 175

**Frankenstein**

9788130907413 Rs. 145

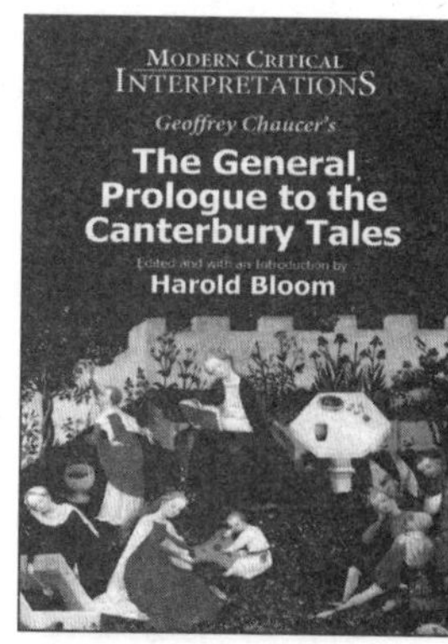


**The General Prologue to the Canterbury Tales**

9788130918747 Rs. 175

**The Glass Menagerie**

9788130907482 In Print

**The Grapes of Wrath**

9788130906751 Rs. 145

**Great Expectations**

9788130904597 Rs. 175

## VIVA Modern Critical Interpretations

### Available Titles in the Series

**The Great Gatsby**

9788130906454 Rs. 145

**Gulliver's Travels**

9788130906461 Rs. 195

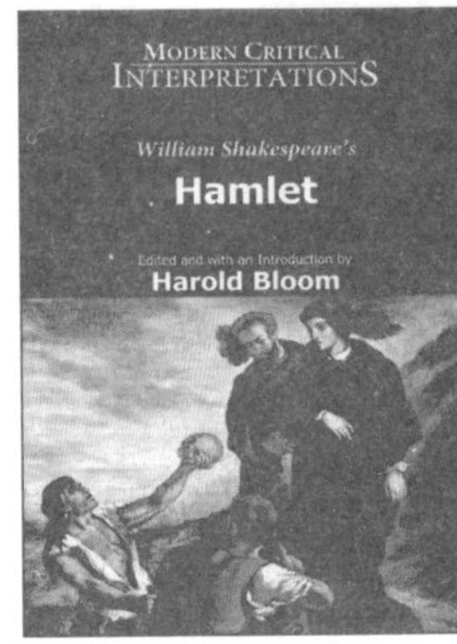


**Hamlet**

9788130918877 Rs. 165

**The Iliad**

9788130907895 Rs. 145

**Invisible Man**

9788130906485 In Print

**Heart of Darkness**

9788130918815 Rs. 165

**Jane Eyre**

9788130918860 Rs. 195

**Julius Caesar**

9788130906492 Rs. 125

**King Lear**

9788130918853 Rs. 165

## VIVA Modern Critical Interpretations

### Available Titles in the Series

Viva

**Long Day's Journey into Night**

9788130904634 Rs. 99

**Lord of the Flies**

9788130904603 Rs. 145

**The Lord of the Rings**

9788130907956 Rs. 145

**The Man without Qualities**

9788130907499 Rs. 145

**The Merchand of Venice**

9788130906522 In Print

**Macbeth**

9788130906515 Rs. 125

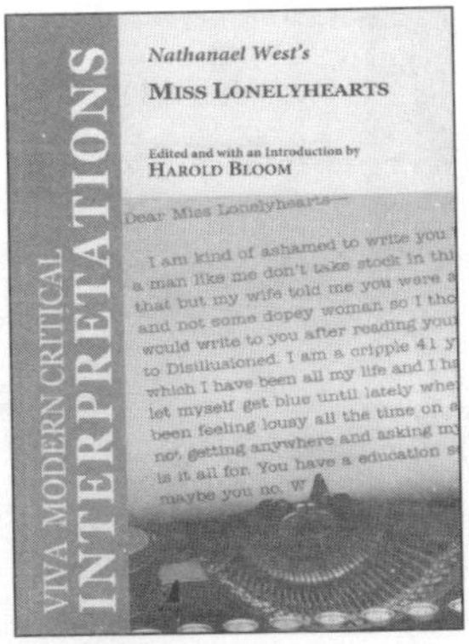


**Miss Lonelyhearts**

9788130907437 Rs. 125

**A Midsummer Night's Dream**

9788130918914 Rs. 165

**The Metamorphosis**

9788130904573 Rs. 99

# VIVA Modern Critical Interpretations

## Available Titles in the Series

Viva

**Moby-Dick**

9788130906546 Rs. 165

**Oedipus**

9788130906768 Rs. 165

**One Flew Over the Cuckoo's Nest**

9788130907444 Rs. 125

**One Hundred Years of Solitude**

9788130907451 In Print

**The Old Man and the Sea**

9788130906553 Rs. 125

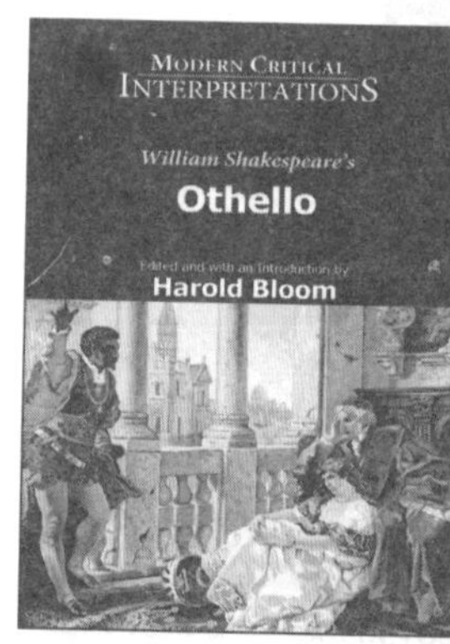


**Othello**

9788130918891 Rs. 165

**Paradise Lost**

9788130906560 In Print

**The Pardoner's Tale**

9788130904665 Rs. 125

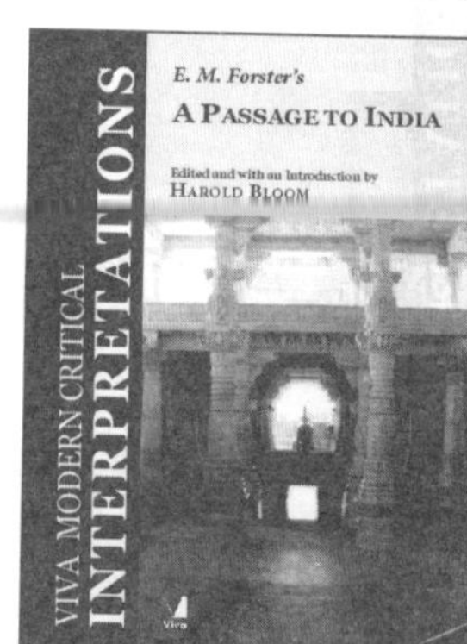


**A Passage to India**

9788130906584 Rs. 145

# VIVA Modern Critical Interpretations

## Available Titles in the Series

Viva

**Persuasion**

9788130906591 Rs. 175

**Pride and Prejudice**

9788130906607 Rs. 195

**The Red Badge of Courage**

9788130906614 Rs. 145

**Romeo and Juliet**

9788130906621 In Print

**The Rubaiyat of Omar Khayyam**

9788130904641 Rs. 145

**The Scarlet Letter**

9788130907505 Rs. 175

**Silas Marner**

9788130906638 Rs. 125

**Song of Solomon**

9788130906645 Rs. 145

**Sophie's Choice**

9788130906652 Rs. 175

## VIVA Modern Critical Interpretations

### Available Titles in the Series

Viva

**The Sound and The Fury**

9788130906676 Rs. 195

**A Streetcar Named Desire**

9788130918716 Rs. 145

**Sonnets**

9788130918907 Rs. 165

**A Tale of Two Cities**

9788130906683 Rs. 145

**The Tempest**

9788130918822 Rs. 175

**To Kill a Mockingbird**

9788130906775 Rs. 125

**Waiting for Godot**

9788130906706 Rs. 99

**Ulysses**

9788130906690 Rs. 145

**The Waste Land**

9788130904689 Rs. 175

**Wuthering Heights**

9788130906713 Rs. 175

**Young Goodman Brown**

9788130906720 Rs. 125